Gender and Popular Culture

Gender
and
Popular Culture

Katie Milestone
and
Anneke Meyer

polity

First published in 2012 by Polity Press

Polity Press
65 Bridge Street
Cambridge CB2 1UR, UK

Polity Press
350 Main Street
Malden, MA 02148, USA

ISBN-13: 978-0-7456-4393-9
ISBN-13: 978-0-7456-4394-6(pb)

A catalogue record for this book is available from the British Library.

Typeset in 10.5 on 12 pt Plantin
by Servis Filmsetting Ltd, Stockport, Cheshire
Printed and bound in Great Britain by the MPG Books Group

For further information on Polity, visit our website: www.politybooks.com

Contents

Acknowledgements

We would like to acknowledge colleagues (past and present) from the Department of Sociology, Manchester Metropolitan University, for their encouragement and support. Immense gratitude in particular to those involved in work on popular culture and/or gender for providing a stimulating, welcoming and good-humoured academic environment.

From Katie to Mike, Esme, Freddie and Miles – thanks for putting up with my sporadic withdrawal from family life whilst writing this book and for your love and support. Thanks also to my mum, sisters and in-laws for the same. Thanks to former colleagues from the Manchester Institute for Popular Culture for motivation and good times. I'd like to dedicate my contribution to this book to my late father, Chris Milestone.

From Annie – a big thank you to all my family and friends for all the support and good times together. A few people deserve a special mention. Tony for getting me through the ups and downs of life and always remaining positive – I couldn't have done it on my own. Hannah for simply being the best friend anyone could wish for. Meine Mutter Carmen, auf die ich mich immer verlassen kann.

We would like to thank Andrea Drugan from Polity for her great patience and support in this project and to the reviewers for their helpful comments. Thanks also to Lauren Mulholland for dealing with the nitty gritty and to Justin Dyer for his excellent copy-editing.

1
Introduction

Gender and popular culture are connected in inextricable, pervasive and complex ways. Popular culture is an amorphous concept which encompasses an enormous range of cultural texts and practices, from cinema films to newspaper articles, from designing computer games to playing music. Much of popular culture is media culture; popular culture includes mass media such as radio, the press, film and television, as well as new media such as the internet or email. In this book we concern ourselves with the ways in which gender, i.e. masculinity and femininity, connects to popular culture. We do not aim to provide a general overview of the field of gender in popular culture, recounting and reviewing all the existing academic literature; this would be virtually impossible in the space of one book and only produce simplistic generalizations. Instead, we aim to offer in-depth and analytical insights into how gender relates to the three cultural processes of production, consumption and representation by analysing and illustrating each process through exemplary case studies. Some of these studies constitute primary research conducted by the authors, while others are drawn from wider academic literature.

We aim to show how gender is produced, represented and consumed in popular culture, and how the three processes interact to construct what we commonly identify as gender identities. We do this by looking at a range of literature, case studies and examples drawn from modern Western culture. The first part of the book is devoted to the process of production. In this part we look at who produces popular culture, including visible producers such as artists and performers and less visible, behind-the-scenes ones such as producers and managers. We also investigate patterns of gender regarding employment and careers, and examine how this links to genres and types of popular culture, and attempt to explain them by looking at a range of factors such as gender discourses, individual aspiration and economic structures.

The second part of the book focuses on the process of representation. Popular-cultural products, or texts, are symbolic because they carry meanings. These meanings are produced through linguistic and visual representations. We concern ourselves with the ways in which women and men are represented in popular culture, drawing out similarities and differences, and examine how normative notions of femininity and masculinity are constructed and sustained. Moreover, we investigate the implications of representations and gender norms in terms of status, power relations and gender (in)equality.

The third part of the book deals with the process of consumption. Consumption is a gendered practice. There are, for example, differences between men's and women's consumption patterns and different subject positions set up for men and women in popular-cultural texts. We investigate the reasons behind these gendered patterns, looking at a range of factors from space to gender norms. Moreover, we examine how popular culture can be used by individuals to construct gender identities by performing masculinity and femininity. The book is clearly structured into these three parts and each part consists of two distinct chapters. For the remainder of this first chapter we outline in detail the key concepts which are used throughout the book.

Popular Culture and the Media

Popular culture is a contested concept. It is vague and diffuse and can therefore be filled with many different meanings. In order to investigate these meanings, we will start by looking at the more general concept of culture.

Raymond Williams (1983) put forward three meanings of the word 'culture', arguing that it can refer to (a) intellectual, spiritual and aesthetic development, (b) a particular way of life of a group or historical period, or (c) texts and practices which produce meanings. The concept of popular culture is of course different from that of culture. Williams' first definition refers to culture with a capital C, i.e. those aspects of culture commonly called high culture, for example literature or opera. We usually do not associate popular culture with this definition. According to John Storey (1993), the notion of popular culture mobilizes Williams' second and third meanings. On the one hand, popular culture refers to the cultural practices or lived culture that people engage in, for example going on holiday or religious festivals. And on the other hand, popular culture also refers to cultural texts which are symbolic and whose main function is the production of meaning, for example a newspaper article, a television programme or a pop song. The word 'text' has a wider meaning in the discipline of cultural studies than it has in everyday life: it refers not only to written or spoken words but to any aspect of culture whose predominant purpose it is to signify, i.e. to produce meanings. The terminology reveals the linguistic-humanist roots of the discipline of cultural studies and its concern with textual analysis. In contemporary culture most meanings are produced through language and images, which are our most pervasive communicative systems; but the word 'text' also includes deeply symbolic practices such as getting married or having some tattoos done. At this point it becomes obvious that Williams' second and third meanings of culture intersect and overlap – cultural practices are both lived culture and cultural texts. This is inevitable; most cultural practices are habitual, in the sense of being part of a way of life, and symbolic, in the sense of signifying certain meanings. Indeed these two aspects are often inextricably linked. In this book we use the term 'cultural text' in its wider, academic sense to include culture which signifies through language, images and (lived) practices. So we concern ourselves, for example, with newspaper articles, television images and the practices of people who work in the industries that produce popular culture. At its simplest, popular culture consists of a wide range of cultural texts.

The concept of popular culture has a quantitative dimension (Storey 1993). The word 'popular' suggests that it is liked and/or practised by many people. And indeed many aspects of culture which we would commonly class as popular culture are widely appreciated and consumed, such as pop music or television. However, the connections are not always straightforward. There are certain aspects of culture which we would commonly class as 'high' culture but which are still popular in the sense of being liked or practised by many people. We could think here of certain performers of classical music such as Pavarotti. Conversely, certain aspects of popular culture, for example niche television channels, may not have wide audiences at all. Popular and high culture also often mix, for example when classical literature is turned into television serials which are watched by millions of viewers. Is this high or popular culture? While popular culture has a quantitative dimension, this alone is not necessary or sufficient to define it. The other factor to emerge as important here is that popular culture in all its definitions is compared, explicitly or implicitly, to some 'other' culture. Most commonly this other culture is so-called 'high' culture, which is usually taken to include serious and classical forms of culture such as works of old literature, paintings, poetry or classical music. The juxtaposition of popular and high culture is a normative one in that high culture is seen as superior (Strinati 2004). High culture is deemed intrinsically worthy, serious, quality art, while popular culture is judged superficial, simplistic and driven by profits rather than skill or quality. Often these judgements are linked to the commercialization of culture and the creation of a culture industry. Popular culture is seen as the epitome of commercialization, a mass culture which only arose with capitalism and is produced by big businesses for the purpose of profit. Popular culture is considered to be of intrinsically low artistic quality because the pursuit of profits necessitates meeting the lowest common denominator. In contrast, high culture is associated with a bygone golden age free of commercialization, where art thrived for art's sake. Contemporary high culture is seen as true art relatively untouched by profit logic. The juxtaposition of high and popular culture is flawed in various ways. Firstly, this categorization is elitist and fails to recognize that the standards by which the quality of culture is measured are not universal or neutral but themselves a product of culture (Eagleton 2000). Secondly, in contemporary Western culture the economic system of capitalism shapes the production of all forms of culture and art – there is no space totally free of commerce.

The media are central to popular culture in many ways. The media are symbolic institutions because their products signify. Media texts construct meanings through the use of language and images. Whether we think of a pop song, a television drama or a newspaper column, all these texts construct certain meanings, for example conveying a particular message or creating a narrative. Much of what we think of as popular culture is media culture: television, computer games, pop music, film, and so on. The mass media, notably radio, film, television and newspapers, have been central to making culture available to the masses, hence the association of popular culture with mass culture (Strinati 2004). Much of this book is concerned with the mass media, but we also discuss new media. The term 'new media' refers to media such as the internet, email, digital radio and television, podcasts and video podcasts, blogs, wikis and websites, MP3 players and iPods, to name but a few. The new media can be defined as information and communication technologies (ICTs) which have evolved since the mid-1990s and deliver content to audiences (Breen 2007). In contrast to the mass media, new media blur the lines between producers and consumers and allow users much more flexibility. The advent of the new media has intensified the connection between media and popular culture. New and additional forms of popular culture have been created, for example websites, interaction through social networking sites or the growth of niche television channels. Moreover, already existing forms of mass culture are now also accessible through an increasing number of new media formats. For example, music can be downloaded through the internet, books are available in electronic versions, newspapers have online websites which allow you to read current editions and sift through archives of past editions. Popular culture is increasingly mediated. There are of course aspects of popular culture which are not media culture. Everyday practices which have cultural meanings, whether we call them cultural texts or lived experience, are not necessarily linked to the media. Celebrating a wedding or getting a tattoo done are cultural practices but not media practices. However, these examples illustrate that while popular culture and the media are not identical, they are increasingly intertwined. No wedding is complete without an enormous number of photographs and often a video recording too. Individuals' ideas and tastes regarding tattoos are to some extent shaped by media coverage of tattoos.

In this book we use the term 'popular culture' to refer to a range of cultural texts which signify meaning through words, images or practices. Reflecting the mediatization of contemporary culture, all the case studies we use, from newspapers to video games and pop music, are media culture. There have been long-standing debates around the political positioning and ideological effects of popular culture. Some commentators, such as John Fiske (1989a) or Paul Willis (1990), see it as potentially radical and subversive because it gives power to the masses and consumers and undermines elites. However, others, such as Theodor Adorno and Max Horkheimer (1993), have identified popular culture as necessarily conservative, working in the interests of those in power and helping to maintain the status quo by pacifying the masses and justifying capitalism. Following Gramsci's work, Stuart Hall (1982) and others have conceptualized popular culture as a site of political contestation where sets of ideas, such as ideologies and discourses, are struggled over. In the process, dominant ideologies and powerful interests can be challenged and resisted, adapted and reproduced. This conceptualization marks popular culture as fundamentally political and allows us to analyse particular aspects in terms of their resistance to or reproduction of dominant gender norms and ideologies. This is particularly important when studying a phenomenon like gender, which is a deeply political, contentious and complex subject.

Production, Representation and Consumption

Production

Production is a fundamental, but often overlooked, element of the sphere of popular culture. Theorists have dedicated a good deal of research into looking at how culture is represented and consumed, and a large portion of this research has analysed cultural representation and consumption from a gender perspective. However, apart from the occasional ethnographies of cultural industries (e.g. Nixon 2003; Powdermaker 1951) which emerge every now and then, it is only in the last decade that a substantial body of work on cultural production has started to flourish. A lot of this work began with the arrival of new cultural and media industries connected with new media. Technological and cultural shifts led to new forms of working and new avenues of cultural production. Initially, in terms of gender, there was some optimism that these new industries might be welcoming to women. However, as we discuss later in this book, there are still significant issues of gender and power affecting who stakes a claim in the frontline of cultural production.

In the context of this book we are using the notion of cultural production in terms of the process of making media and culture. We look at the groups and individuals who make popular-cultural texts such as films, computer games and adverts, for example. Often these people have job titles that explicitly refer to their production roles – such as film producers or record producers. A theatre director might say 'I'm working on a production of. . .'.

Arguably the production of culture is very different to other forms of production. Culture is not made on a production line (although Adorno argues that there is a 'production line' ethos to cultural products in capitalist societies). Generally it is widely held that cultural and artistic production is connected with the realms of the symbolic, identity and aesthetics.

In this book we are interested in taking a close look at who produces popular culture in terms of gender. We examine the extent to which the production of popular culture is male-dominated and whether this is becoming less so as time (and attitudes to gender equality) progresses.

Closely linked to issues of production are issues of ownership and control. Who owns the newspapers, the film companies, the commercial television channels and the internet? Do the apparatuses of media and cultural production continue to be owned and controlled by men?

Representation

Representation as a process of communication means to depict or describe something or someone (Webb 2009). In the media, language (both written and spoken) and images are the key symbolic systems through which representations are made. In the process of representation, language and images stand in for something or someone and thereby render it present (Webb 2009). Representation is so important because it is an active process of creating meanings: for example, the words we choose to describe a group of people or the images we use to depict an event, i.e. the ways in which we represent them, shape the meanings of these people and events (Hall 1997a). At the time of writing this book, the G20 summit took place in London to produce an international agreement on how to solve the current financial crisis. This summit attracted large and diverse groups of protesters campaigning for the installation of a new world order, rather than 'more of the same'. The media variously described these protesters as 'anarchists', 'anti-capitalists' or 'climate-change campaigners', and they showed images of peaceful street marches as well as the violent destruction of a branch of Royal Bank of Scotland. The choice of words and images obviously shapes the meanings of the protests as peaceful or violent, as legitimate or illegitimate, as grounded in good reasons (e.g. 'climate-change campaigners') or simply a desire to cause chaos and destruction (e.g. 'anarchists').

Meaning is produced through representation across different cultural sites; the media are of particular importance in late modernity, but others include art, customs and habits (Hall 1997b). In contrast to art, the mass media maintain that their material accurately represents reality, showing and telling things as they really are to their audiences (Webb 2009). Among the mass media, factual media such as newspapers or factual genres such as television news, investigative programmes or documentaries have a claim to truthfulness and objectivity. This arguably gives them particular persuasive and ideological power. Both print and broadcast media represent through images and language. Language is the most fundamental and privileged system of representation, but visual representations also possess distinct strengths, such as the ability to communicate instantaneously (Hall 1997b).

Gender is one of the key social structures in contemporary culture and marked by power struggles and inequalities. Gender hierarchies and inequalities are maintained, among other factors, by meanings and belief systems, and these are in turn generated through representation. Representations are constructed through language, images and social practices, and possess a material as well as symbolic dimension. In this book our analyses tend to focus on the symbolic aspect of representation but continually make links to other areas of gender(ed) practice such as the law or social policy.

Consumption

In the discipline of sociology the term 'consumption' refers to the process of purchasing and using (up) a commodity. Commodities are products which can be sold and bought in the marketplace, and popular culture produces a wide range of them. But there is a difference between, say, commodities such as a washing machine and a film. The difference is that the latter is a symbolic text containing meanings. The mass media and popular culture are therefore producers of commodities and their meanings; they generate certain meaningful representations and messages and communicate them to an audience. Hence, consumers are also audiences who consume these meanings as they listen, view or read the media. In this instance consumption is not limited to using (up) a product but involves consumers in the active role of making sense of what they listen to, view or read. This is why in the discipline of cultural studies, consumption is understood as a process of making sense of cultural texts.

Much academic theorizing and research on consumption has revolved around the notion of media audiences. Different theoretical models have been developed which conceptualize how audiences respond to meanings produced by the media. While early, simplistic models such as the direct-effects theory suggest that audiences simply believe whatever the media tell them, soaking up meanings like a sponge, the more sophisticated theories, such as Stuart Hall's (1980) encoding/decoding model, allow audiences some degree of activity and intelligence, suggesting that individuals can reject or negotiate media messages as well as take them on board. However, in all theories, audiences remain rather passive; ultimately they can only respond and react to the media who set the terms of engagement in the first place. This encouraged the ethnographic turn in academia: that is, the empirical investigation of how actual media audiences use and interact with the media. Ethnographic studies have showed that media consumption is a much more complex process than commonly thought. Social context, for example who we are with, greatly impacts on how we consume and what we make of media representations. There are also different modes of consumption, varying from deep engagement to casual dipping in and out.

Understanding consumption has become even more difficult in the age of the new media. In case of the mass media, it is relatively straightforward to identify the communicators of meaning (the media) and the receivers of meaning (the consumers). The flow of communication is one-way: consumers cannot communicate back to producers in any meaningful fashion. In contrast, new media communication is no longer one-way and the lines between producers and consumers have become blurred. For instance, individuals can leave comments, feedback and reviews on large websites, such as online retailer Amazon, or in the comments facilities which exist on many newspapers' websites. They can also set up their own blogs and wikis or create personal profiles on networking sites, such as Facebook or Myspace, to produce their own contents. The technological properties of new media allow for genuine dialogue, interaction and debate with others and for individuals to consume and produce meaning in the media. This change towards the active, multiply involved person is reflected in the change of terminology. In the case of new media, academics no longer talk about 'consumers' or 'audiences' but 'users'. The term 'user-generated content' has emerged to describe new media content which is produced by ordinary users as opposed to big corporations or institutions.

In this book we want to look at the role which gender plays in connection with consumption. Examining mass media and new media, we address the ways in which gender may shape consumer choices as well as responses to media representations. Moreover, we will look at theories on the production of gender identity to see how individuals can use the media to construct masculine and feminine selves.

Feminism, Post-Feminism and Patriarchy

Second-wave feminist theories and research emerged from the 1960s onwards. Feminists noted that gender inequalities continued to exist in all spheres of life, whether education, the labour market or crime, and committed themselves to both explaining and combating these inequalities. In this sense, feminism has always been a movement as well as a theoretical perspective, including activists and academics who aim to understand and change the social world. Feminist academics also noted that sociological theorizing and research had been conducted from a very male-centred perspective which either ignored or marginalized women's situations and experiences. This they set out to change.

There are numerous strands within feminism, including radical feminism, liberal feminism, Marxist or socialist feminism, black feminism and postmodern or post-structuralist feminism. All strands agree that gender inequality and oppression of women are real problems which need to be remedied, but they differ in their explanations and solutions to these patterns. One key concept developed by feminists is patriarchy. Patriarchy literally means the rule of the father and refers to an overarching system of male dominance. This system oppresses and exploits women, works in men's interests and legitimizes male domination. Dominance can take the form of individual control: sexual violence, for example, can be seen not just as a criminal act but as an instance of a man asserting his power and dominance over a woman. This is a form of private patriarchy. But there is also a system of public patriarchy which refers to dominance being realized in impersonal ways through certain institutions or structures (Walby 1990). For example, rape conviction rates in the UK currently stand at a very low 6 per cent, and many other European countries, ranging from Germany to Greece, display similar rates (Lovett and Kelly 2009). The UK figure means that out of 100 reported rapes, 6 cases end in a conviction and 94 cases are either dropped by the police or Crown Prosecution Service or end in acquittal at trial. Research estimates that the rate of false allegations for rape is around 2 per cent, the same percentage as for all other crimes (Benedict 1992). This means that most rapists are not punished; rapists have little to fear from the law, while victims have little chance of getting justice. The criminal justice system fails to deal adequately with rape. This is an example of an institution exercising patriarchal control. The law allows men to rape women with few consequences, which keeps women in a state of fear and often leads to self-restrictions in order to protect themselves (Daly and Chasteen 1997).

Sylvia Walby (1990) argues that in advanced capitalist democracies of Europe and North America, public patriarchy is largely indirect. Women are not directly excluded from the public sphere; they do have formal access to important institutions such as the labour market, politics or education and they are not legally prohibited from doing things which men do. There is formal equality. Instead, in a system of public patriarchy women are controlled indirectly and collectively. This control works through six key structures: household production, the organization of paid work, the state (including the law), male violence, heterosexuality and cultural institutions. Popular culture, including the media, plays a crucial role in contributing to the maintenance of patriarchy by perpetuating gender ideologies.

Post-feminism is critical of second-wave feminism and challenges many of its fundamental propositions. It is based on a belief that gender equality has largely been achieved in developed nations. Post-feminists point to equal opportunities for men and women and suggest that women face little discrimination today. In one scenario this means feminism has become redundant because it has won its major battles. In a second scenario, feminism is blamed for women's less-than-perfect situation. It is claimed that feminism holds women back by continually framing them as victims of largely non-existing gender inequalities. Feminism is blamed for making women unhappy, driving them to pursue careers and lifestyles they do not actually want in order to 'win' the battle of gender equality. The conservative media in particular have adopted these aspects of post-feminism for their own agenda. In the UK, the newspaper market is highly partisan and divided into liberal newspapers, such as the *Guardian* or the *Independent*, and conservative ones, such as the *Daily Mail*, the *Daily Express* or the *Daily Telegraph*. These conservative voices, which vastly exceed the liberal newspaper voices in terms of number of publication titles and amount of copies sold, suggest that what women really want is to be stay-at-home mothers and wives and blame feminism for 'de-valuing' these roles. From the conservative perspective, the problems of contemporary women, for example the exhaustion of working mothers, prove their point. The problem is not that men are not equally sharing the burdens of housework and childrearing, but that feminists have told women they can 'have it all'. Hence feminism is blamed for causing a range of social problems which are the product of gender inequality. This movement and line of argumentation are what Susan Faludi (1991) terms a backlash reaction against feminism.

Gender: Social Construction and Performance

Early feminists coined the concept of gender in order to emphasize that maleness and femaleness are not simply about physical biology or 'nature' but also social constructs. While 'sex' refers to biological, bodily differences between men and women, 'gender' refers to the socially constructed categories of masculine and feminine and the socially imposed attributes and behaviours which are assigned to these categories. The fact that certain attributes and behaviours are linked to men or women is not 'natural' but a matter of convention. For instance, there is no 'natural' reason why women are associated with housework – men are equally capable of it. Which characteristics and practices are seen as typically and appropriately feminine and masculine is a matter of social construction.

Social constructionism is opposed to essentialist understandings of gender. Essentialism stipulates that men and women are inherently different beings who belong to separate categories. All category members, for example all women, are seen to share a set of essential characteristics, or an essence, which defines them and sets them apart from other categories and their members, for example men. In contrast, social constructionism suggests that phenomena, objects, events and identities are the product of society rather than nature. Social (inter)actions and structures shape the world we live in and the meanings which it has for us. Differences between men and women, masculinity and femininity exist but they are the outcome of social processes. The socially constructed nature of femininity and masculinity is clearly illustrated in the changes of meaning which we find across different cultures and different historical periods. For example, in Northern American and European countries, work used to be seen as unfeminine a century ago, yet today the majority of women are in some form of paid work. If gender was 'natural', then it would be universal, i.e. identical and unchangeable, across cultures and time.

Initially the concept of gender was radical because it demonstrated that being a man or woman was not simply a natural state but to a large extent a product of society. Simone de Beauvoir (1972), writing originally in 1949, suggested that we are not born but become men and women, which means that gender is not something that we are but something that we do. This idea was picked up and developed by several writers, including Erving Goffman (1959) and, much later, Judith Butler (1990). They theorized that gender is a performance or performative construct. That means gender is not a fixed, inherent identity but the product of a sequence of practices and characteristics which have over time become labelled as masculine or feminine. These practices, which individuals forever repeat, congeal or solidify into what is then recognized as a gender. There are, however, some major differences between Goffman's and Butler's thinking around gender.

For Goffman (1959), masculinity and femininity are gender roles which individual men and women perform. They are actors who perform their gender act by constantly engaging in practices which are deemed typical and appropriate for men or women. For example, women perform femininity by wearing skirts and dresses, sitting with their legs crossed and doing housework and childcare, while men perform masculinity by wearing suits and trousers, sitting with their legs wide apart and pursuing careers outside the home. Goffman calls these performances gender displays: that is, conventionalized portrayals of culture's idealization of femininity and masculinity. Symbolic interactionsts, like Goffman, have pointed out that rules become most evident when they are broken. This certainly applies to gender and illustrates the theory of performance. Women who do not perform femininity correctly but engage in practices that are deemed masculine, for example playing football, having short hair or wearing no make-up, are often labelled 'tomboys', 'butch' or 'lesbians'. They are denied femininity. Similarly, transgender individuals who undergo sex changes have to learn the rules of how to be and pass as feminine or masculine, for example how to sit, dress or interact with the opposite sex (West and Zimmerman 1987). Both examples help us recognize that gender is a performance which entails adhering to a great number of behavioural rules. One of the problems with Goffman's idea of gender as a role being performed by individuals is that it makes gender appear as a conscious, optional identity which we only perform when we decide to do so, at certain points in time. This, according to Candace West and Don Zimmerman (1987), underestimates the extent to which social structures require us to do gender continually. They emphasize that doing gender is an ongoing, routine, everyday activity which is deeply embedded in the social and largely requires no thought.

Some of these criticisms are addressed in Butler's theory of performativity. In contrast to Goffman, Butler (1990) talks about performative constructs rather than performance. Individuals habitually do gender through a series of practices or performances, but, as a post-structuralist, Butler does not believe that there is a performer behind the performance. Performance pre-exists the performer in the sense that culture has already determined which acts and characteristics count as masculine or feminine. Our individual actions are not conscious but simply habitual, repetitive re-enactments which congeal into gender. Gender is a category that appears natural and permanent, and, as such, independent of individual action, because it is constantly repeated. Or, to put it differently, gender identity is the effect, the outcome of performativity rather than its cause. Differences between women and men that we may find in our culture, i.e. notions of masculinity and femininity, do not exist because of essential differences that cause men and women to behave in different ways, but are the result of the structural category of gender which produces the scripts of femininity and masculinity that men and women continually re-enact. The performative nature of gender is not something we usually notice because the performativity of femininity and masculinity is so routine and naturalized that it remains invisible. Drag, however, lifts the curtain and makes visible the performative nature of gender. Here, men present themselves as women by copying femininity, for example using make-up, wearing feminine clothes such as skirts and high heels and adopting feminine demeanours and gestures. They emphasize the performative and playful nature of this by not trying to eradicate their masculinity and by exaggerating femininity through excessive make-up or ridiculously high heels. For Butler, drag is subversive because it reveals to us that all gender is a perfomative construct and as such not linked in any necessary way to sex: men can do femininity, women can do masculinity.

The distinction between sex and gender was made by second-wave feminists. In some sense it was radical, for the first time putting forward the idea that there is a social dimension to being a man or woman. But in other ways the distinction was conservative and limiting. It reinforced the notion that there are only two sexes or genders, men and women, who are binary opposites. Moreover, it identified two dimensions of being a man or woman, one social and one physical. The physical or 'natural' side, i.e. sex, was seen as purely biological and not in any way socially constructed. And many conservative or essentialist thinkers held that gender was determined by sex: that is, that it was simply the social or cultural expression of 'natural' physiological realities.

Subsequently, many feminists, including Butler, have taken issue with the sex–gender distinction. Butler deconstructs this dichotomy of sex and gender and the relationship between the two. The common assumption is that sex and gender are inevitably related, as respective biological and social components. But Butler suggests that the two concepts are not at all related but radically independent or contingent. You do not have to be a biological female to display feminine behaviour. Gender dissonances, such as intersex people, show that gender is a fictive production. It is not determined by sex, not a fixed thing we possess, but something people do. Moreover, for Butler, as for many other feminists, nothing, not even the body, is purely 'natural' or outside the social. Sex may have a biological dimension but it is also socially shaped. Bodies are always deeply gendered and never purely 'natural'. For example, women's and men's bodies are more similar than they are different – but what society focuses on and deems important are the differences. Or, to use another example, while genital differences are used to categorize humans into men and women, who appear as entirely different species, no one suggests that blue-eyed and brown-eyed individuals are different types of persons. The body as such has no inherent meanings, but it gains its meanings from us. In that sense it is just as socially constructed as gender. However, as far as public discourse and 'common sense' goes, these ideas have not penetrated very widely or deeply; in the 1960s Garfinkel (cited in West and Zimmerman 1987) commented that in everyday life we still live in a world of only two sexes. We were very much reminded of this by the furore surrounding the South African athlete Caster Semenya at the 2008 Beijing Olympics. Caster was accused of not 'really' being a woman because of a lack of obviously visual markers of femininity as well as her outstanding sporting performance which left competitors far behind. Caster had to subject herself to lengthy 'gender-testing' and was cleared to compete again in 2010. No details of this testing were released, yet this only fuelled speculation that she suffered from an intersex condition and may need 'treatment' before being allowed to return to athletics. This controversy shows not only that contemporary culture continues to enforce gender and sex binaries, but also that these binaries are not as stable as they might at first appear. Butler suggests that the categories of sex and gender are powerful but unstable, which is why they have to be continuously reaffirmed through repetitive performative acts. The controversy surrounding the Semenya case very much supports her point.

Ideology

Ideologies are sets of ideas or systematic frameworks of social understanding (Macdonald 2003). The term 'ideology' often has negative
connotations: for example, ideologies are assumed to be interested
or even false and they are associated with manipulation and indoctri-
nation. This is because of the strong Marxist influence on common
understandings of ideology. Marxist conceptions of ideology revolve
around the two key elements of dominance and distortion.

For Marx, ideology was always dominant ideology. Ideologies are
sets of ideas which are dominant in three ways (Macdonald 2003).
Firstly, they are produced by the dominant groups in society. Marx
was primarily concerned with social class and envisaged the ruling
class as the dominant group, but we could also relate his theory to
other dominant groups such as men or white people. Secondly, ideologies work in the interest of the dominant social group, yet they
pretend to be neutral, which is why Marxists often say that ideology hides behind itself. Thirdly, ideologies are the dominant ways
of thinking in society: all social groups, including the subordinate
groups, believe in dominant ideologies, because they are imposed on
them by those in power (Abercrombie et al. 1980). Hence, power
is material, almost an 'object' which can be possessed. It is concentrated in the hands of a few people at the top who directly control the
powerless masses at the bottom of society. Power takes the form of
imposing rules on what individuals are required to do and believe.

For Marx, ideologies are marked not only by dominance but also
by distortion. Ideologies are sets of ideas which are false; they misrepresent reality and distort the truth. As a consequence, ideologies
deceive people about the way things really are, they conceal the truth
and pull the wool over people's eyes. In Marxist terms, ideology
induces 'false consciousness' among the people. For Marx, the key
truth which ideology hides is the truth about capitalism. Capitalism
is a fundamentally exploitative system which benefits a few people
at the top and capitalist societies are marked by inequality and the
passing on of privilege. One good example of Marxist conceptions
of ideology is the American Dream. This suggests that anyone can
be whoever they want to be, can rise from poor circumstances to
become famous, successful and rich. For Marx, the ideology of the
American Dream conceals the fact that capitalist societies are marked
by a fundamental inequality in life chances which makes it difficult
for those who are structurally disadvantaged by their social class,
gender or ethnicity to rise to the top (Abercrombie et al. 1980).

For Marxists, the media, and popular culture more generally, are key ideological forces. The media are owned and controlled by the dominant social groups who hold leading positions in government and big corporate businesses. As institutions concerned with the production of symbolic material, the media necessarily generate meanings and messages through which we as consumers understand the world. The meanings and messages which the media produce encapsulate the dominant view of the world, even though the media may at times recognize, if not endorse, some alternative ideas. The dominant ideology is actively disseminated and imposed through the media as well as other institutions, such as politics, the education system or the Church. Althusser, a neo-Marxist, called these institutions Ideological State Apparatuses. The nature of ideology's dominance is such that it is widely reinforced across society. The ideologies which the media promote serve the interests of the dominant group, which owns the media. This group uses its economic power to cement its position and power through ideological means. The dominant ideologies disseminated by the media conceal and misrepresent reality; they hide inequalities inherent in capitalism and thereby legitimize existing patterns of domination as fair and right. For example, rags-to-riches stories so popular with Hollywood cinema (e.g. *The Pursuit of Happyness*, 2006) promote the ideology of the American Dream, suggesting that everyone in capitalist societies is free and equal and that those who rule and succeed do so thanks to their efforts and talents, not to structural advantages such as connections or personal wealth (Abercrombie et al. 1990).

Influential as Marx's ideas have been, there have also been major critiques. One of the key problems identified is that 'dominance' is too fixed a notion for understanding how power and ideology work. It suggests that power, both economic and ideological, is concentrated in the hands of a few, the ruling elite, and that once established it cannot be changed. A certain number of ideologies are dominant within a given culture, circulated by the dominant group and imposed on and accepted by all people. These ideologies simply continue forever as there are no alternative ideologies to challenge or replace them. This is a very fixed and static picture which we do not necessarily recognize in contemporary society or media. While some ideologies seem widely accepted, others are less so, and there is certainly always scope for resistance, challenge and change. The media are not one monolithic whole, and different elements of the media may well support opposing ideologies. For example, in the US, news channel Fox has become notorious for its openly conservative bias, while other outlets such as the *New York Times* are at the more liberal end of the spectrum. For these reasons, it is more helpful to adopt a Gramscian notion of ideology and talk about hegemonic rather than dominant ideologies.

Gramsci was a neo-Marxist who coined the term 'hegemony' to refer to a form of power which is characterized by leadership and the manufacturing of consent rather than imposition and control. Hegemony is exercised by the ruling classes, but it is fragile and has to be constantly struggled for and maintained against challenges from the subordinate group. The ruling group cannot simply rule against the people's will but needs to form alliances with other groups and achieve agreement with its ideas and position of power. This is where ideology comes in: it is a tool to achieve hegemony because it is central to the manufacturing of consent. Ideology convinces the subordinate classes to agree to the power structures of the society they live in by granting superficial concessions and compromise. Certain ideologies are hegemonic: that is, they are widely accepted and work in the interests of those in power. In that sense they are dominant, but hegemonic ideologies constantly have to struggle to maintain this dominance. There are alternative ideologies challenging them and competing for authority. Hence, hegemony is a position of fragile dominance and ideologies themselves are flexible and changeable. This allows for social change; hegemonic ideologies can be replaced by alternative ideologies or they can adapt to maintain their hegemonic position in changed social climates. This latter process is known as co-option or incorporation (Macdonald 2003). It refers to ideologies maintaining their hegemonic status by including aspects of opposing or new ideologies into their own frameworks, thus broadening their appeal and avoiding resistance in new social climates. We can often see this at work in the media. For example, the worldwide Dove advertising campaign 'Campaign for Real Beauty' uses models who are relatively old and big by the standards of the advertising industry. This campaign arguably co-opts feminism, adopting its critique of society's narrow and unrealistic definitions of feminine beauty which are impossible for most women to meet. However, the campaign does not adopt the feminist critique that society's definition and judging of women by their physical appearance is sexist, derogatory and infantilizing. In fact, the campaign reinforces the notion of physical beauty as central to femininity by focusing yet again on women's looks and little else.

There is a second fundamental aspect which distinguishes Gramsci's theory from Marx's. While the dominant ideology thesis suggests that subordinate groups experience a state of false consciousness induced by deception, the theory of hegemony proposes that people knowingly compromise and consent. There is certainly an element of persuasion present and many compromises are superficial and largely work in the interests of the dominant group, but nevertheless subordinate groups have some stake in hegemonic ideologies and have not been duped. In this book we adopt a Gramscian take on Marxism and conceptualize ideologies as hegemonic rather than dominant. This allows us to retain the critical edge of analysing gender in terms of ideologies and power relations while being open to the possibility of change, flexibility and awareness. This is particularly important when analysing late modern societies characterized by rapid social change, the spread of feminist critiques of gender inequality and media-savvy consumers.

All Marxist conceptualizations of ideology as outlined here are based on what can be called the representational view of media and reality (Macdonald 2003). This view is based on a realist notion of reality which assumes that a fixed, physical reality exists independent of the media. The media represent this reality through symbolic codes of language and images. This means that the media may represent reality more or less accurately. The media can represent the same event, object or person in different ways, which allows not just for accurate and inaccurate representations but also for many 'inbetween' forms of representation which are neither totally right or wrong but biased and self-interested, such as stereotyping, demonization or one-sidedness. Generally speaking, from a representational perspective, coming as close to reality as possible is the desired goal of representations and the standard by which they are measured. Representations which fail in this task are criticized as false representations, misrepresentations or ideologies. As ideologies are false, they are always necessarily misrepresentations.

Gender Ideologies: Hegemonic Masculinity and Emphasized Femininity

Gender ideologies are ideologies of masculinity and femininity. According to Connell (1987), there are multiple and diverse masculinities and femininities in contemporary culture. But gender ideology reinforces only one type of masculinity and femininity, the traditional type, which is hegemonic. Hegemonic masculinity represents men as 'naturally' rational, efficient and intelligent. Men are associated

with strength and power (physical, mental and social), being active
and ambitious, tough and competitive, assertive and aggressive. The
'natural' sphere of the man is the public, the place where he works,
socializes and makes a difference to the world. Men are represented
as going to extremes, seeking success, enjoying excess and experiencing pleasure. They work hard and play hard. They are rational but
not necessarily sensible. Masculine sexuality is characterized by a
natural, strong sex drive which needs constant satisfaction. Connell
suggests that this traditional type of masculinity is hegemonic in two
senses. Firstly, it is dominant over other masculinities, for instance
gay or metrosexual masculinities, which are subordinate to it.
Secondly, hegemonic masculinity is culturally idealized: it incorpo-
rates the behaviours, attitudes and practices which are seen as good
and right for a man to have and do. The normative dimension of
gender ideologies emerges here: the characteristics and practices outlined as typical of men are also positively sanctioned as appropriate.
This double function is captured in the words 'normal' and 'norm',
which value something as both common and good (Pickering 2001).
Hence, gender ideologies such as hegemonic masculinity prescribe
certain characteristics and practices as appropriate for men and on
the same basis devalue and rule others out as inappropriate. For
example, men who are perceived to show weakness or softness are
deprecated through derogatory terms such as 'sissy', 'wuss' or 'being
wet'. In a nutshell, hegemonic masculinity is the most powerful, culturally endorsed type of masculinity which subordinates other forms
of masculinity as well as women and has succeeded in positioning
itself as superior. Being hegemonic, however, means that dominance
has to be achieved and constantly struggled for against the challenges
from femininities and subordinate masculinities.

The female equivalent of hegemonic masculinity is emphasized
femininity (Connell 1987). There are several types of femininity, but
the traditional kind is hegemonic in the sense of being the commonly
endorsed one. Emphasized femininity centres on women's compliance with subordination and the accommodation of men's interests
and desires. Women are presented as being 'naturally' kind and
caring, predisposed to looking after men and children. The private
domain is a woman's 'natural' sphere and her family is her life.
Women are said to be fragile and weak (both in a social and physical sense), find it difficult to assert themselves, are peaceful and shy
away from confrontations. They are irrational, driven by emotions
rather than reason, and not as cognitive or technically competent as
men. Women are also associated with moderation and self-denial;

they are the sensible gender responsible for curbing men's excesses. Female sexuality is deeply bound up with emotions, relationships and commitment rather than purely bodily pleasure; women are said to want love and commitment while men seek sexual gratifications. Generally speaking, emphasized femininity frames women as compatible with men by accepting domination and moulding themselves to men. Emphasized femininity is the most hegemonic of all femininities because it is widely endorsed, for example across the media, the law or politics. However, Connell labels it 'emphasized' rather than 'hegemonic' because this femininity is not hegemonic in the way that hegemonic masculinity is. Firstly, emphasized femininity does not exercise institutional or structural power in the way that hegemonic masculinity does, partly because positions of power are usually occupied by men. Secondly, emphasized femininity does not actively negate other types of femininity in the same way as hegemonic masculinity. We can see this negation at work in hegemonic masculinity constantly ridiculing gay or 'effeminate' masculinities.

Gender ideologies such as hegemonic masculinity and emphasized femininity construct certain characteristics and practices as 'natural' and 'typical' of men and women. But of course they are not 'natural'; like all other ideologies, gender ideologies are social constructions which pretend to be natural. Gender ideologies are suffused by power and contribute to the maintenance of patriarchy. Connell's theories propose a multi-layered model of gender power relations, which means that not all types of masculinity are equally oppressive or equally contribute to patriarchy. Hegemonic masculinity subordinates other masculinities as well as femininities, and femininities do not have to be related to all masculinities through subordination. For example, gay masculinities may join femininities in their battle against the heterosexuality of hegemonic masculinity, thereby helping to challenge patriarchy. But it is also the case that not only masculinities are patriarchal. Emphasized femininity, for example, helps maintain patriarchy by encouraging women to take on social roles, such as the stay-at-home mother, which are undervalued, involve large amounts of unpaid labour, are detrimental to women's careers and encourage financial dependence on men.

The juxtaposition of masculinity and femininity is important to understanding patriarchy. 'Men vs women' is one of the key binary opposites in contemporary culture. Men and women, masculinity and femininity are presented as polar opposites; whatever men are, women are not. Yet their meanings depend on each other as men are defined by their difference from women. This juxtaposition itself is not value-neutral but takes the form of violent hierarchies (Hall 1997c). The characteristics associated with men are more valued than their opposites which are associated with women. For example, being rational and cognitive has a higher currency than being irrational and emotional (with its connotations of being hysterical), strength is better than weakness, and so on. This is not to say that all the characteristics of emphasized femininity are negative, for example being caring has positive meanings, but in comparison, women's characteristics tend to be less valued than men's. Moreover, women's positive attributes usually have value in terms of 'nice-ness', e.g. being caring and kind, while men's positive traits are valued in terms of ability and success, e.g. rationality, competitiveness, strength. As a consequence of these violent hierarchies, women appear as inferior to men in the things that matter: they are positioned as weaker, less intelligent and cognitive, less rational, less competitive. This maintains patriarchy by legitimizing male power and advantage as grounded in men's 'nature' and 'natural' superiority rather than exploitation and oppression.

Discourse

The concepts of discourse and ideology share a concern with power relations and inequalities and they both recognize the importance of symbolic systems of representation, such as media language or images. But there are also major differences which we will discuss throughout this section.

Femininity and masculinity can be conceptualized as discourses. But what exactly is a discourse? Stuart Hall's definition of discourse provides a useful starting point: 'Discourses are ways of referring to or constructing knowledge about a particular topic of practice: a cluster (or formation) of ideas, images and practices, which provide ways of talking about, forms of knowledge and conduct associated with, a particular topic, social activity or institutional site in society' (Hall 1997a: 6). This means that discourses are systems of representations which exist in the form of language, images and social practices. Foucault's conceptualization of discourses aims to overcome the traditional distinction between saying and thinking (language) and doing (practice), by stipulating that discourses necessarily involve both. The definition also illustrates that discourses are processes through which meaning and knowledge are produced (Macdonald 2003). It is through discourses that we make sense of the world because discourses give us meaningful ways of talking and thinking about and acting in relation to a particular issue. These meaningful ways count as knowledge. From this perspective, masculinity and femininity are discourses: they consist of series of statements on what is masculine and feminine as well as men's and women's practices which are in line with these statements. For example, the discourse of masculinity revolves around strength, competitiveness, a high sex drive, rationality and authority, while the discourse of femininity associates being female with weakness, a caring and gentle nature, shyness, emotionality, asexuality and chastity and the quest for a committed relationship. These discourses allow us to talk about men and women in gender terms and to make sense of their practices in terms of gender. For example, a man's success at work can be explained through his competitive and rational nature, i.e. his masculinity, while a woman who uses internet dating agencies can be understood as looking for love, commitment and a family, i.e. the very things that femininity desires. And by acting in these ways, individual men and women reproduce the discourses of masculinity and femininity, respectively.

Foucault's discourse theory adopts a structuralist perspective, which means that there is no agency in the traditional sense. We cannot identify individuals who create discourses; all we know are the different sites across which discourses appear and we can enquire into the structural conditions which make certain discourses possible and rule out others. Individuals are not free, undetermined agents but subjects whose agency is strongly shaped by social structures. Foucault sums this up in his proposition that subjects do not produce discourses, but discourses produce subjects. This works in two ways. Firstly, a discourse produces a subject which personifies it; here the subject becomes the bearer of discourse. For example, a 'feminine' woman personifies the discourse of femininity. Secondly, a discourse produces several subject positions from which the discourse makes sense. For example, the discourse of femininity produces subject positions such as the 'normal' woman (i.e. the feminine woman), the girly girl (the hyper-feminine woman), the tomboy (the unfeminine but heterosexual woman), the butch lesbian (the unfeminine lesbian woman). Women can agree or disagree with discourses, but they have to adopt a subject position offered by the discourse in order to make sense of the world, and in doing so they subject themselves to the rules of discourse. Individuals may argue against it, for example by adopting a feminist view, but they are not radically deconstructing or subverting the discourse structure itself (Hall 2001).

The example illustrates that certain subject positions are

considered more 'normal' than others. According to Foucault, this
is an effect of power. Or, to put it differently, the exercise of power
takes the form of normalizing strategies. Power works through discourses. Discourses produce knowledge. Knowledge is never neutral:
it classifies certain behaviours and characteristics as abnormal and
deviant and thereby produces the norm. Psychological discourses are
a good example. They constitute scientific knowledge and thereby
seem objective and value-free, but they are concerned with the
identification, labelling and treatment of 'abnormal' psychological
conditions (e.g. diseases, 'strange' behaviours, mental health issues)
and thereby also produce a picture of which psychological states
are 'normal' (Rose 1989). Normalization is important in relation
to gender because discourses of femininity and masculinity render
certain characteristics and practices as normal and abnormal for men
and women (Charles 2002). As a consequence, individuals orient
themselves around the same standards of normalized gender behaviour in order to be, and be identified as, a man or woman. Going
along with discourses of femininity and masculinity is rewarded by
being seen as normal, while resisting them results in being criticized
as abnormal and deviant (Haug 1983, cited in Charles 2002).

Social construction, reality and truth

One of the key differences between the concepts of discourse and
ideology concerns their positions on media and reality (Macdonald
2003). Marxist conceptualizations of ideology are based on a representational view which assumes the existence of a fixed, physical
reality which is independent of the media. From this perspective, the
media reflect reality; they may deliberately manipulate representations (e.g. bias, spin, demonization), but this does not change reality
itself. Media representations can be criticized for lacking accuracy or
being misrepresentations. One of the problems with this approach
is that it assumes the existence of one, uncontested reality which we
would want the media to represent. But different groups of people
have different realities: for example, feminists and conservatives will
have very different interpretations of the fact that women tend to do
the majority of housework and childcare, as an indicator of gender
oppression or as grounded in the natural predisposition of women,
respectively. And whose reality is the right one and should be represented in the media? Another problem concerns the assumption that
the 'real' world and representations of it are separate, which is too
neat and simplistic. For example, the media construct ideas which

real people have in their heads and influence their practices; in this sense representations become reality (Macdonald 2003).

Discourse theory is part of a school of thought called social constructionism. This sees the media, and other symbolic institutions and practices, as not simply representing but as socially constructing reality. This means they do not only stand in for or document reality but they are reality and help constitute it. The boundaries between what is reality and what is representation can no longer be drawn because the two are inextricably intertwined. From a constructionist perspective we can still use the term 'media representations', but see representations as constitutive rather than reflective of reality. Some writers prefer the term 'constructions' to 'representations' in order to emphasize the constitutive element and avoid association with the representational perspective (Macdonald 2003).

From a constructionist perspective, reality – such as physical objects, events, persons – does exist, but it has no fixed or inherent meaning. Meanings are always produced and attributed by humans and it is only through these meanings that we can access or know about reality. Things that have no meaning we cannot know; it is in this sense that our reality (the one we know) is always socially constructed through our meanings and not 'pure' or independent of representations about it (Hall 1997b). From a Foucauldian point of view, reality becomes meaningful through discourses; discourses provide us with meaningful ways of talking and knowing about the world and nothing can meaningfully exist outside discourse.

While the representational view allows for a realist critique of the media along the lines of inaccuracy and misrepresentation, the position of social constructionist approaches like discourse theory is more complex. No idea, ideology, knowledge or position can simply be true because they are all produced by discourses and therefore enmeshed with power relations. All forms of knowledge and ideas are socially constructed and there is no independent reality which could function as a universal standard according to which we measure their accuracy. There is no ultimate truth but only what Foucault calls 'regimes of truth ideas', namely ideas which have become accepted as true and which have real consequences because they are sustained by powerful discourses. Knowledge and discourses are not simply true or false but only become true when they become real: that is, when they are accepted and have real consequences (Hall 1997b). The advantage of this relativist conception of truth is that it acknowledges that the standards by which we measure truth are themselves socially constructed: for example, what counts as 'true' in one culture is not necessarily 'true' in another. Truth is not universal but relative, not neutral but interested. There is not one reality, but many. The downside is that this relativism makes it difficult, if not impossible, to engage in critical analysis. For example, we cannot critically evaluate media representations because there is no independent reality to measure them by, only versions of reality which we know through discourses. But some contemporary thinkers, such as Macdonald (2003), have argued that it is still possible and desirable to assess at least the relative truth and accuracy of a discourse. By comparing discourses on a sliding scale, we can attempt to assess which ones are more or less accurate, taking into account all the existing evidence and discourses.

Power, knowledge and discourse

While both theories of discourse and ideology are very concerned with power, their understanding of how power works is very different. For Foucault, power is not simply possessed by a few people at the top and imposed on those at the bottom. Instead, he sees power as a relation or strategy which circulates through society like a dispersed network. Power is everywhere because it resides in and works through discourses. Discourses are forms of meaning and knowledge and as such they enable the exercise of power. For instance, medical knowledge about pregnancy allows the medical profession not only to increase the health of women and foetuses, but also to exercise power in the form of regulating women's behaviour (Lupton 1999); the furore surrounding women's drinking of alcohol during pregnancy is a case in point. That means no discourse or knowledge is ever neutral, purely objective or value-free, but they are always suffused by power. Discourses are also linked to power in the sense of having the capacity to make certain forms of knowledge count as true and others as false. There is no independent truth, but discourses which society widely accepts as true can be called regimes of truth.

The fact that power resides in discourses means that everyone has access to power. Discourses are (re)produced not only in a few institutions such as the government or the law, but across all social sites and practices, including everyday conversations, settings and actions. Access is differential – for instance, some people have better access because of their formal education or social position – but widely spread and not limited to an elite few. Everyone is to some extent involved in the (re)production of discourses and the exercise of power, and as a consequence not all discourses work in the interests of those in power. At certain points in time, certain discourses may be particularly powerful or hegemonic, but this hegemonic position has to be constantly asserted. Every discourse contains the potential for the exercise of power as well as resistance, so that the struggle for hegemony is not simply about discourses but works through them. This also means that all of us wield some power and are simultaneously restricted by the power of others. In this context, ideas of dominance and co-option are far too simplistic: women, for example, are actively involved in (re)producing the power relations which subordinate them, but they can also resist by refusing to behave in socially sanctioned ways (Charles 2002).

While Marxism conceives of power as a repressive force which is used to impose rules on the masses against their will and prevent people from carrying out certain practices or having certain beliefs, Foucault conceives of power as simultaneously productive and repressive. Power both suppresses and enables certain practices and beliefs. For example, the discourse of femininity restricts what women can do, by, say, proscribing aggressiveness or the drinking of alcohol to excess. But it also instructs women on how to behave to present themselves as feminine, for example by being caring or having children. It is in this sense that power works through discourses and is always both repressive and productive. Moreover, this example illustrates another important point of Foucault's thinking: power works not simply at an institutional but an everyday level; it is constantly (re)produced and challenged through individual practices (Connell 1987).

Power for Foucault is not repressive or restrictive in any direct sense. While Marxists see power as taking the form of direct control of the people, Foucault believes power works as indirect regulation or 'government'. Government does not refer to state power; instead, Foucault defines it much more broadly as the 'conduct of conduct': that is, the more or less calculated means which are used to shape people's behaviour and actions (Gordon 1991). Government, which works through discourses, does not directly prohibit certain behaviours or impose rules on society, but always seeks to shape people's conduct indirectly through the individual and his or her desires, interests and beliefs (Dean 1999). In this sense, the exercise of power and government is always to some extent self-regulation; individuals regulate themselves in order to achieve certain goals, but the goals which they have internalized and think of as their own are shaped by structural forces such as culture, politics or education. For example, no one directly tells women that they have to diet, yet a lot of women do so in order to achieve the slimness which is central to feminine beauty ideals in contemporary society. For our purposes it is important that the media are one of the sites where government is effected as behaviour is regulated through media representations.

The example of dieting illustrates another key aspect of Foucault's work, namely that government and power often work on and through the body (Mills 2003). The regulation of the conduct of the population is effected through the disciplining of people's bodies. The aim is to produce 'docile bodies': that is, compliant individuals who regulate their bodies in the ways intended. Contemporary examples of this disciplinary regime range from campaigns for healthy eating to campaigns against binge drinking. Foucault's ideas are embedded in a theory about the nature of modern society. He argues that it is marked by a proliferation of power and extension of discipline, enabled by an increase in knowledge. However, this tightening of the disciplinary regime is not fully recognized because power in modernity operates in very subtle ways, through knowledge and discourses. The explosion of scientific knowledge on health is a good example. While it has made for a healthier population, it also means that there is no aspect of life, from food and leisure to sport and work, where we are not encouraged to discipline our practices in order to increase our health. However, Foucault did not recognize the gendered nature of the disciplinary regime. Many feminists, such as Bartky (1990), have pointed to the ways in which women are subject(ed) to more constant and rigorous disciplinary strategies than men, because femininity is achieved through physical compliance with conventional beauty ideals. This involves dieting and exercising to be thin, putting on cosmetics to 'enhance' their features, dressing up, nurturing long hair, depilation of unwanted body hair, and so on. Hence women's bodies are rendered even more docile than men's and women themselves become complicit in the perpetuation of patriarchy and their own subordination by regulating their bodies through these practices.

Space

In the last few decades the social sciences have increasingly become fascinated with issues connected to space and place. This has been most explicit in the emergence of 'cultural geography', although all areas of the social sciences have shown a 'spatial turn'. Theorists are interested in power and space, how space is produced (Lefebvre 1991), consumed (Shields 1990; Urry 1995), regulated (Jessop 1990) and imagined (Anderson 1983). The fascination with space and place emerged concurrently with emergence of debates about post-modernity and the processes of globalization (Castells 1996; Harvey 1989; Lefebvre 1991). However, whilst people were interested in global shifts, this also provoked a focus on the local and indeed the ways in which the local and global interact. There has also been a dramatic surge of interest in virtual space, or cyberspace, because of the arrival of new information and communication technologies that have allowed for intense 'space-time compression' (Harvey 1989). The arrival of the virtual world has provided a new dimension of space (Turkle 1995) which has stimulated new processes of identity formation and performance.

Theorists continue to be interested in how people use 'real', physical spaces particularly in terms of cultural uses of space. There has also been a massive interest in place image and identity. This has in part been provoked by increased migration patterns, diasporic movement (Cohen 2008) and cultural hybridity (Young 1995).

Feminist geographers such as Doreen Massey (1994) were quick to point out that space and place have a gendered dimension. As most architects, builders and town planners are male, the physical manifestations of space have a masculine origin. Whether legally prohibited or through the dictation of self-regulation, there are spaces that women, and occasionally men, cannot enter. As Juliana Mansvelt notes: '[P]laces are not simply areas on maps but shifting bundles of social-spatial relations which are maintained by the exercise of power relations' (2005: 56). Power is a gendered concept, and we are centrally interested in examining these power relations in this book. Quite simply, how do men and women's bodies exist and interact in space and place? How do men and women perform gender in space? As we are also concerned with popular culture, we are specifically concerned with spaces that involve the production and/or consumption of popular culture.

In this chapter we have provided a broad overview of some key themes and terms. We will now analyse the production of popular culture, cultural representations and the consumption of popular culture in more detail.

PART I

Production, Gender and Popular Culture

Introduction to Part I

This part deals with men's and women's participation in cultural work and cultural production. Because there are significantly fewer frontline female cultural producers than men, it is not effective to divide the chapters along gender lines. The structure of this part of the book is organized by looking at two time periods in order to assess the extent to which issues around gender and cultural production have altered from the 1950s to the twenty-first century.

The first chapter (chapter 2) looks at gender and cultural production in the mid-twentieth century and focuses on case studies from the 1950s through to the 1970s. In Western democracies, this was an era of enormous social and cultural change in terms of both popular culture and gender relations. In the 1950s, gender relations were organized along patriarchal lines. Women were still predominantly connected with the domestic sphere and men with the world of work. Production often followed the Fordist model of organization, and cultural industries were still in their infancy. However, there was an abundance of new consumer goods and a dazzling array of new popular-cultural products.

In the 1960s, many social and political changes threatened the permanency of hitherto accepted gender roles and divisions. The impact of highly active and politicized 'second-wave' feminists, and political action by other oppressed groups, paved the way for enormous changes across every facet of society and the world began to change dramatically.

Chapter 3 considers the legacy of these socio-cultural changes and the impact they have had on contemporary gender relations in the world of cultural work. For example, what impact have equality laws and cultural changes had on gender and cultural production? Are more women now at the forefront of the design and conception of cultural products that circulate in the mainstream? Some claim that feminism is now irrelevant because equality between the sexes has been achieved. Yet others argue that women are being 'retraditional-ized' (Adkins 1999) and that there is a vast disjuncture between the rhetoric of 'equality' and the reality of women's lived experience. We look at a range of contemporary case studies on cultural production to discuss these conflicting claims.

2
Gender and Cultural Work

Post-War to the Late 1970s

In this chapter we seek to encourage a discussion of cultural work in terms of gender. Cultural production is an area that has been frequently overlooked by media and cultural studies researchers but provides much in the way of food for thought in terms of discussions about gender. We begin this chapter by highlighting the dominant concerns in media and cultural studies research since the 1940s, when this type of research began to gain momentum. We will demonstrate that the area of cultural work/ers is one which seems to have evaded the concerns of media scholars. In the vast body of work on media and popular culture there are remarkably few qualitative studies of creative businesses and the experiences of workers within these organizations. However, the area of cultural work is fantastically interesting in terms of discussing gender politics in the workplace and the gendering of creativity and cultural production. There is a large body of theoretical work on media audiences, genres, media texts and representation, but markedly less research on the individuals and groups who actually make the media and culture.

In its fledgeling years, studies on popular culture tended to concentrate on examining 'what the media do to people' rather than 'what people do with the media' (Halloran 1970). A range of perspectives, from the ideas of the Frankfurt School through to the 'media effects' approach, assumed that consumers/audiences were passive dupes willingly accepting the ideologies encoded in cultural products. The Frankfurt School saw the 'culture industry' as an agent of capitalism – destroying radical possibilities by distracting the masses with mindlessly benign popular culture. The 'culture industry' played a vital role in the new system of monopoly capitalism and its exploitation of the working class. Adorno and Horkheimer (1993) argued that popular culture, especially that emerging from America, was being used to control modern workers both at work and during their leisure time. Culture, like other goods, was being produced along Fordist-type mass production techniques, rendering it bland and standardized. Adorno and Horkheimer looked at a range of examples from the newly emerging popular culture of the period – film, radio and popular music – to illustrate their arguments. Crucially for them and for other Marxist thinkers, not only were these cultural products dull and unchallenging, they were also laden with ideological messages all aimed at securing a compliant workforce of willing consumers.

Furthermore, as Marxist feminists argue, there are ideologies about gender that are engrained in popular culture that also contribute to the success of capitalism. Marxist feminists argue that for capitalism to work efficiently there needs to be a gendered division of labour – women need to produce the workforce and nurture them so they are fit to work, and men need to work. It is therefore in the interest of capitalism to reinforce ideologies about the 'naturalness' of gender roles and to imply that there are universal qualities of masculinity and femininity that neatly assign men and women to their rightful place in the world. The opposing argument is that there is nothing natural about gender roles: we have been brainwashed to believe that they are so, dutifully accepting our roles and contribution to the capitalist system, whereas in fact these roles are cultural constructs. These theories about the media were developed by analysing structural patterns of inequality. In this early work on ideology and media/popular culture there was an absence of in-depth research on both cultural producers and cultural consumers, although many assumptions were made about producers as agents of capitalist ideologies and consumers as willing believers. As Mark Banks notes, views about the ideological force of the culture industry were not informed by empirical research: '[W]hile Marcuse often wrote about the alienating effects of labour, his observations that work "cripples all human faculties and enjoins satisfaction" . . . and that industrial production instils a "drugging rhythm" . . . were not backed by substantive empirical observations' (2007: 25). Of course, we must consider the context in which the arguments of the Frankfurt School were located, which was in an era of the rise of fascism and its highly effective mobilization of popular culture as a powerful ideological tool.

As with the work of the Frankfurt School, the 'media effects' theories of the 1950s and 1960s were also based on the premise that the relationship between cultural products and consumers was a 'one-way street'. It was not until the 1970s that an emphasis on exploring active, as opposed to passive, consumption began to emerge. Inspired by Antonio Gramsci's work on hegemony, cultural theorists including Stuart Hall (1980), David Morley (1986) and Janice Radway (1984) championed an analysis of cultural consumption that acknowledged the agency of the audience. This kind of emphasis on consumption was in response to an absence of audience-focused research in earlier media and cultural studies work. New work on cultural consumption challenged standard assumptions, and in-depth qualitative research was undertaken with audiences in order to demonstrate the multifarious ways that consumers interpreted and resisted the messages they were receiving. Stuart Hall's (1980) encoding/decoding model, and subsequent work by Charlotte Brunsdon and David Morley (1978) paved the way for a new body of work that emphasized the fact that consumption needs to be located in the context of the consumer's identity, gender, race, social class, and so on. In particular, the emphasis on consumption came from a number of feminist academics, and their important work is highlighted in chapter 6 of this book. The possibility of pleasurable readings of 'low' popular culture also became increasingly acknowledged (e.g. Fiske 1989a; Radway 1984). Rather than dismissing women's cultural consumption as unworthy and assuming the effects of the media upon them, researchers gave women the space to articulate their negotiations with popular culture. The type of material studied within the paradigm of women's genres – soap opera, romance fiction, lifestyle magazines – was labelled as 'low' culture. Highlighting Celia Lury's work (1993), Sue Thornham notes:

> The high culture/low culture divide . . . is a thoroughly gendered one, corresponding to a division between mainstream cultural activity and public professionalism on the one hand, and a critically marginalised, privatised and less 'original' form of production on the other. . . . Thus the 'feminisation' of 'mass' cultural forms (the romance novel, the woman's magazine), in opposition to 'authored' writing, does not simply reflect gendered social divisions. It also helps construct notions of the feminine which align it with commodification, standardisation and passivity, and which maintain it within the sphere of the private, understood as subordinate, emotional and domestic. (2007: 13)

It is not surprising that feminist academics focused on women's consumption, as this was the principal – indeed pretty much the only – way that women were linked to popular culture. As we shall see below, women were not present in the realm of cultural production.

Whilst not wishing to undermine the importance of audience ethnographies and the active consumer approach, we also want to encourage an analysis of gender and popular culture that looks at cultural production. We seek to examine cultural work – cultural jobs in the creative (Hartley 2005) or cultural industries (see Hesmondhalgh 2007; O'Connor 2000).

Cultural products do not emerge from a value-free vacuum; they are the result of the ideas and imagination of individuals and institutions – each with differing agendas, perspectives, resources, freedoms and constraints. Detailed research into the area of cultural production is a field that has frequently been overlooked, but one which we argue is vital to consider in terms of the entire complex cultural circuit of production, representation and consumption. Cultural work is a field that reveals massive inequalities in terms of gender and power, yet, as Banks recently argued, 'cultural workplace studies remain rare' (2007: 26). In this chapter we will look at a series of case studies of cultural industries and cultural producers and consider what role gender has to play in the dynamics of cultural production. Quite simply, who is responsible for producing popular culture? Whose ideas, dreams, agendas, are being prioritized? What impact does gender have on the type of cultural products that are circulating in the public domain? What can we make of the anomaly that although women are often described as being more creative than men (apparently using the creative left side of the brain more frequently), the majority of frontline cultural producers are male?

We deal with these questions in two ways. In this chapter we focus on cultural production that has emanated from large, well-established media and cultural industries – from the pre-digital age (namely from the post-war period to the late 1970s). Part of the reason for this is to focus on long-standing case studies that have been extensively debated by theoreticians, which will be widely familiar. The post-war era is a fascinating one to examine as this was such a boom period in terms of popular culture, particularly in terms of youth culture and popular music. It is also an era which underwent huge challenges and transformations in terms of gender roles, rules and rights. In chapter 3, the second chapter on cultural production, we will focus on examples from the late twentieth and twenty-first century, the digital age, in which, some claim, gender inequalities are a relic from the past and opportunities for previously excluded groups have been laid wide open.

Some Definitions: Cultural Producers, Cultural Work

What is a cultural producer?

What do we mean by the term 'cultural producer'? Quite simply we are referring to teams and individual people who create cultural products. We need to acknowledge that it may not always be that easy to distinguish what the cultural producer has created by his or her individual will and what has been determined by the constraints and demands of the larger organization within which the individual cultural producer operates. With the case of music, for example, there are a number of cultural producers involved in the creation of a piece of music – songwriters, musicians, performers, sound engineers, producers, managers, and so on. Conversely, a painting is often the production of a lone individual. From a Frankfurt School perspective, creative workers are implied as being agents of capitalism. As Banks identifies,

> [A] focus on cultural workers, as 'creative' agents or subjects, is viewed with acute suspicion because of sociological inclinations to view creativity as a phenomenon that ought not to be theorized at the romantic level of the 'individual genius' . . . thus a focus on workplace creativity in itself, and the 'creative' worker runs the risk of appearing to idealize, naturalize or label as voluntary that which is substantially generated in the context of social and political structures. (2007: 28)

David Hesmondhalgh uses the term 'symbol creator' to describe frontline cultural producers, and identifies these as including 'those who make up, interpret or rework stories, songs, images and so on' (2007: 5). He also includes technicians in his category of those who are involved in primary cultural production roles 'such as sound mixers who, as record producers, have become increasingly important in the music industry' (2007: 64). Walt Disney was a producer of cartoons, Alfred Hitchcock a producer (or more accurately a director) of films and Phil Spector a producer of music. These are examples of individual men who became famous because of their 'creative genius' (see Battersby 1989), and who indeed produced cultural products of immense power and influence. Their ideas, imagination and ability to create fantastic works have had a huge impact on society and culture and their legacy is still important today. A significant point in the context of this book is that these cultural producers whom we have cited are all male and it is not easy to think of female counterparts who have achieved similar levels of fame, status and respect. In fact, shocking as it may seem, it was only very recently, in 2010, that a woman, Kathryn Bigelow, won an Oscar for the role of best director. This is a staggering statistic, yet the fact that year on year only male directors have won this award has made this state of affairs seem normal and natural. Beyond some of the world's most best-known cultural producers, we need to think about whether or not these distinct cases are also indicative of the gendered power relations of more 'mundane' cultural production. We could argue that for much of the twentieth century women were not granted the same access to and status within the labour market as men, which partly accounts for the absence of female cultural producers. However, there are a range of other complex factors at play, as we highlight and explore below. Sometimes feminist writers are criticized for being crude and simplistic in playing the 'numbers game' when highlighting the absence of women in positions of power. But how else do we 'measure' social relations and power if not by highlighting that there are more or fewer black people, women, disabled people, and so on, clustered in particular roles or areas of the labour market? Commentators are happy to talk about ownership and control along class lines, so why not look at ownership and control using other social variables such as gender? Women are distanced and excluded from the means of (cultural) production, as Coote and Campbell point out: 'Men control the means of expression – from the press and broadcasting, to advertising, film, publishing and even criticism – by occupying dominant positions within them and by using the power this gives them to convey the ideas and values of a patriarchal order' (1982: 189).

The post-war explosion of cultural work

Periodization is notoriously problematic. Although cultural industries have a long history – for example, newspapers have a history dating back several centuries, photography emerged in the early nineteenth century and cinema later that century – we are going to focus on the twentieth century as the basis of discussion on modern cultural industries – and more specifically the post-war period. Hesmondhalgh deals with the issue of periodization in his work. Drawing on the work of Raymond Williams, he describes the 'complex professional era' of cultural production as 'starting from the early twentieth century, but increasing from the mid twentieth century', and as a period in which 'commissioning of works became professionalised and more organised, new media technologies appeared, advertising became increasingly important and larger numbers of people worked for cultural businesses than in the past' (2007: 309). This 'complex professional era' is the focus of our interests.

The period we are dealing with in this chapter – from after World War II to the late 1970s – is one which saw an explosion of opportunities for cultural work. Whilst there had been cultural industries in each of the case studies used in this chapter – advertising, cinema and popular music – in the pre-war period they were in their infancy and their development was somewhat interrupted by the war. After World War II there were a number of factors that led to each of these industries becoming larger, more sophisticated and more wide-reaching. Firstly there were immense technological advancements in terms of the production and distribution of popular culture. Sophisticated factory production techniques and the emergence of new types of popular-culture 'hardware' in the form of televisions, transistor radios and juke-boxes opened up access to popular culture to more audiences than had previously been thought possible. This was also the era of the consumer society and conspicuous consumption (Veblen 1912) when people began to use 'positional' goods to signify to their peers (and those whom they aspire to have as their peers) what they were about. In the West, workers had more disposable incomes and more leisure time to spend on popular culture, notably in the newly emerging youth market (Abrams 1959). An increased demand for products such as recorded music, films, televisions and consumer goods meant that there was more work in the sphere of cultural work or cultural production. It was in the USA that these burgeoning cultural industries were at their most advanced, but in other industrialized nations cultural industries were starting to be established. This was a type of work that was a world apart from the earlier creative work undertaken by artists and craftspeople. As Hesmondhalgh observes, '[C]reativity has been a more or less permanent presence in human history but its management and circulation have taken radically different forms in different societies. In Europe, for example, systems of patronage gave way in the nineteenth century to the organisation of symbolic creativity around the market. It was at this point that cultural industries began to emerge' (2007: 5). However, there were clear distinctions made in terms of men's cultural production compared to that of women. Women's creative work was positioned as inferior to that of men, as Mary Celeste Kearney argues: 'Largely utilitarian in nature, the domestic arts of girls and women have long been disparaged as "handicrafts", products of manual household chores that allegedly do not require much intellect, reflection, or creativity to produce, and thus do not hold the same cultural status as the nonutilitarian artistic objects created by wealthy individuals' (2006: 25).

The plethora of jobs in cultural production that grew exponentially throughout the twentieth century were markedly different to the roles in creativity that had been possible in earlier centuries. One could now become a cultural producer in a wider range of contexts in what was emerging as a very alluring and exciting sphere. We had entered an age where there was a boom in 'symbolic goods' which were linked to a greater awareness of self-identity. The emergence of these new forms of work called into question some aspects of Marxist labour theory and the notion of the 'alienated' worker. On this point Hesmondhalgh concurs that creative workers sacrifice

> financial reward and security for creative autonomy. But a model of power as coercion is insufficient to explain this. There is rarely an authority figure present to tell symbol creators to work so hard for so little reward. In fact, all cultural workers . . . seem to accept poor working conditions (for example, long, difficult hours) for the benefits of being involved in creative projects and the glamour surrounding these worlds. (2007: 207)

These new jobs offered more opportunities for 'meaningful labour' in ways that had been previously largely impossible. Mike Featherstone's work on this period is important in defining this cultural shift. Featherstone, drawing on Bourdieu (1984), refers to groups of workers as 'new cultural intermediaries': 'those in media, design, fashion, and "para" intellectual information occupations whose jobs entail performing services and the production, marketing and dissemination of symbolic goods' (2007: 19). Hesmondhalgh is wary of the term 'new cultural intermediary', because it is woolly and uncritically over-used. It is vague because it seems to forget about the cultural producers – without whom there would be no culture to mediate. However, it is a useful term because the expansion of cultural goods and cultural producers did bring about a whole new stratum of occupations precisely in the mediation of culture – A & R, artist management, marketing, and so on. Of course in the 1950s no one would have described themselves as a new cultural intermediary – these occupations were marked by their novelty and offered careers that were largely free from the rules and constraints of more well-established sectors.

Featherstone argues that a distinctive feature of the new groups of cultural intermediaries is the mixing of new class fractions. Take, for example, the mid-1960s London pop scene and the explosion of cultural work in music, fashion, photography and media – this scene's much-fetishized novelty was seen as deriving from the fact that its cultural producers came from a range of diverse class backgrounds. Unfortunately, although these industries became more egalitarian in terms of class, the opportunities for women and black minority ethnic groups were not immediate. However, it would be scurrilous not to acknowledge that by the 1960s some dramatic and highly significant changes took place in terms of power and control in cultural industries. The case of Motown Records is a major example of a new black-owned and -controlled cultural industry. Likewise there were some enclaves of cultural production work where women were able to gain an entry. In the UK context the new breed of cultural producers flourished in part due to the innovations taking place in British art schools (see Frith and Horne 1987). However, as Angela McRobbie's research reveals, there were strong biases towards the male students within these institutions. Drawing on an interview with Barbara Hulanicki (founder of Biba) and a report by Madge and Weinberger (1973), McRobbie concludes that the 1960s/1970s art school was institutionally sexist: '[T]wo very different accounts both point to the same thing, namely the exclusion or marginalisation of girls from the fine art culture which still prevailed' (1998: 34). Women's cultural production was devalued and seen as inferior to men's. Women were shunted away from fine art towards fashion design, but even there it was the male designers who achieved fame and notoriety. Although women and those from black and minority ethnic backgrounds have made some inroads into the realm of cultural production, this has been sporadic, and institutional sexism and racism prevail.

We will now examine some specific cultural production case studies in order to discuss gender and power in cultural work.

Sterling Cooper: A Fictional Representation of Cultural Work

We begin our examination of gender and cultural work by focusing on a piece of popular culture, the multi-award-winning US television drama series *Mad Men*, as a way of introducing some of these issues about gender and popular culture in the post-war period and getting a feel for the spirit of the times. *Mad Men* centres on Sterling Cooper (latterly Sterling Cooper Draper Pryce), a fictional Madison Avenue advertising agency in 1960s New York. This is a fantastically useful tool because *Mad Men* is squarely about a cultural industry, the advertising industry, and explorations about gender roles are foregrounded throughout. *Mad Men* is also an interesting case because it focuses on creative processes within a cultural industry. We see the workers 'being creative', trying to come up with ideas and tapping into contemporary intellectual currents, from Freudian psychoanalysis through to semiotics. As Cynthia B. Meyers notes, in the 1950s consumers were treated as a monolithic group, but by the 1960s there was a 'Creative Revolution' in the advertising industry with the advent of niche marketing and extensive consumer research: 'Advertising agencies outdid each other in their efforts to tap into the cultural zeitgeist, adopting countercultural dress and engaging in behaviours such as using marijuana, taking LSD, and having encounter group therapy. With these strategies, advertising executives hoped to generate advertising that communicated more effectively with their audiences' (2009: 76). This is communicated very clearly in Matthew Weiner's depictions of 1960s ad men.

Firstly, though, we must make clear that *Mad Men* is a piece of fiction, using artistic licence to conflate, play down and exaggerate the structure of feeling of early to mid-1960s US culture and the socio-political changes occurring at the time. Praised for its exquisite period detail and subtle, yet powerful allusions to the bubbling undercurrents in terms of the women's movement, black power and gay rights, *Mad Men* skilfully presents us with a vehicle through which to gain a deeper insight into men's and women's roles at work and at home in this most radically changing decade. The representation of the marriage of Don and Betty Draper reveals the mobility of men and the domestic confinement of women.

Interestingly, the 1960s TV series *Bewitched* also focuses on a couple where the man is an ad man and the wife is a stay-at-home mum. So dull is the domestic drudgery, and so unattainable the perfect home, that Samantha uses her witchcraft powers to deal with the housework (see also Metz 2007).

Women's enslavement to unhappy marriages and a life of domestic drudgery is shored up by patriarchal legal structures which deny them entitlement to their children, property and financial resources if they seek to divorce their husbands. This is highlighted in *Mad Men* in discussions between Betty and her divorce lawyer. Don Draper is presented as a new cultural intermediary, with his finger hot on the pulse of psychology of selling things by tapping into people's dreams, aspirations and desires. He is a dark and complex character who is sexually promiscuous whilst expecting his trophy wife to wait patiently at home. He is depicted as a *flâneur* taking full advantage of the metropolitan delicacies of the Lower East Side.

Katherine Shonfield, in her analysis of popular culture and the city in the mid-twentieth century, makes some observations that are highly pertinent to the Madison Avenue ad execs depicted in *Mad Men* and the dual lifestyle that they manage to operate between home and the bright lights of the big city: 'Manhattan, at the centre of the archetypal 20th-century city, has anonymity in stacks. But the split between work and home has reached such a pitch that the majority of senior executives in the office population, who would be best placed to take advantage of Manhattan's drifting opportunities, live well away from the centre . . .' (2000: 91). The split between the suburban home and the urban cultural worker lifestyle facilitates Don Draper's ability to lead a double life. He commutes and often stays over in town. Freed from tiresome domestic commitments, he is able to blur work and leisure, entertaining clients in Manhattan's cocktail bars and restaurants and indulging in sexually promiscuous behaviour. In contrast, Betty, who knows of her husband's serial adultery, is squarely entwined in the domestic milieu, waiting and waiting for her husband to return. A significant barrier to many women's ability to penetrate those frontline cultural production jobs such as those in advertising comes because of their caring roles. Many women, particularly if they were married with dependants, would have found it impossible to engage in the post-work, but heavily work-related, social scene. The lifestyle and habitus of the cultural producers was far removed from the reach of most women. This was in addition to the social mores of the time, which presented powerful behavioural expectations of the 'happy housewife heroine'. There is a lifestyle attached to cultural work which men are much more able to take up and participate in than women. Sean Nixon's (2003) work on the advertising world in the 1980s reveals this to have continued to be an intrinsic part of this job. Women were still largely absent from frontline creativity in the advertising industry of the late 1980s, so this would seem to confirm the authenticity of the depiction of gender relations in *Mad Men* and their continued pervasiveness.

In spite of his many flaws, Don Draper is a man of insight and intuition who gives a female employee, Peggy Olson, a break by recognizing her skill as an ad woman and rapidly promoting her from clerical worker to creative with her own office and ultimately to be a partner in a new advertising venture. This administrator-to-creative route is a career path rarely, if ever, taken by men. The relaxation of some societal rules in the 1960s did open up some possibility for Peggy Olsons to emerge and grow. As the only female creative in the company, Peggy is an exception to the rule; she has no other female contemporaries in terms of cultural work, no female counterparts. She is different, she is novel and she has a quirky self-determination. She observes the power structures dominated by her male colleagues closely. She asks for (often refused) pay rises, she drinks and smokes marijuana with 'the fellas' and seeks out no-strings sexual encounters. After her concealed pregnancy and subsequent breakdown, Peggy gives away her baby, aware that she will lose her precious and rare success at work if she disappears to raise a child. She knows full well that, unlike her male colleagues, she cannot 'have it all'.

The Sterling Cooper office layout is vividly zoned along gender lines – the men, the creatives, sit in their glass-fronted offices, which encircle the typing pool and their female gatekeepers, who fix everything, acting as personal assistants or 'girl Fridays'. When looking at cultural work, it is illuminating to analyse the physical layout of the cultural workplace – at how space is designed and whether there are power issues at play. What are the semiotics of the workplace itself? The workplace in *Mad Men* is organized to maintain relations of gender and power. When Peggy finally gets her own office, this is a highly symbolic moment. Her male colleagues are clearly put out that she is given this space.

When *Mad Men*'s Joan Holloway gets married, she removes herself from the workplace. It is expected of her. As Shonfield notes, by the mid-1960s, secretaries were no longer stereotyped by the frumpy spinster image. Instead, '[m]iniskirted and made-up, they embodied a portable interior phantasmagoria, a new design furnishing that was commonly referred to as "brightening the place up"' (2000: 94) – this was the arrival of the 'dolly bird'. The dowdy middle-aged woman was replaced by the sexy female office worker whose main role is to undertake undervalued or menial tasks in a short skirt. Women are largely invisible in terms of frontline cultural production – they are support staff, wives, lovers, mistresses, secretaries and personal assistants. They are depicted as being expected to be patient and tolerant of the bad behaviour of the male creative genius and their delicate egos.

Invoking the Jack Jones song 'Wives and Lovers', Shonfield observes that women in the workplace are young and single whilst married women are consigned to the home: 'Jones' authoritatively male voice assumes that the same woman cannot be in the office and be within the home. If so, how could she perform the impossible act of running to her husband's arms the moment he comes home? The wife is in the home, the lover is at work' (2000: 95).

Given women's roles as consumers, and given that women were performing the majority of the 'keeping up with the Joneses' consumption at home, it seems strange that they were so underrepresented at the creative end of advertising work. Surely if there was one area that women should have been respected for it was knowing what other women might want to buy. However, the notion of 'creative genius' as a masculine preserve was powerfully entrenched at this time.

By recalling these popular-cultural representations of gender roles and the creative workplace in the mid-1960s, we hope you are able to gain an insight into the expectations of male and female behaviour in advanced Western economies at that time. *Mad Men* is particularly useful because it skilfully depicts society and culture on the brink of huge changes. The world represented in the first series is about to be disrupted by the actions and protests of the oppressed and their supporters. The mid- to late 1960s saw rising power and influence wielded by the women's movement, black political activism, lesbian and gay men and anti-war protesters. *Mad Men* deftly evolves and engages in the 'reality' of the time.

With the help of *Mad Men*, our historical imagination has been awakened and it is hopefully a little easier for us to think vividly about mid-twentieth-century cultural production. This prop, whilst first and foremost a piece of fiction, tells us something about the look and feel of the mid-1960s New York-based advertising industry, gender relations in the workplace and the gendering of creative labour. We will now consider some aspects of the production of popular music with issues of gender at the forefront of our minds.

Gender and the Production of Pop Music

Music is a highly productive cultural industry to look at in terms of mapping gender. Very crudely, we might note that women are largely absent from areas such as music production and technical aspects of the industry such as sound engineering. They rarely feature as manipulators of the finished cultural product – as producers. Of course, women do feature more often as performers, songwriters, singers, musicians. However, even at the level of performance there are strong gender divisions – bands in the 1950s and 1960s almost never featured a woman guitarist or drummer. For much of the period that this chapter focuses on – the 1950s to the late 1970s – women were experiencing a period of intense refeminization and retraditionalization in the aftermath of the gender role disruptions provoked by World War II, which had seen them undertake highly 'masculine' work. Certain instruments and performance style became masculinized, as authors such as Mavis Bayton (1997) and Simon Frith and Angela McRobbie (1990) have argued. Bayton, a pioneering writer on women in rock music, claims that women in rock bands are at odds with normative notions of acceptable femininity because femininity is a social construct: 'It is difficult to stay "feminine" in a rock band precisely because "femininity" is an artifice: . . . it is assumed that their hair stays in place . . .'(1997: 40). Emma Mayhew (2005) describes the way in which women's marginalization in the popular music industry is profoundly connected with gendered ideas about creativity and skill and notes that these ideologies have a long history dating back to the medieval period, if not earlier, where binary oppositions were established with women connected with craft and low culture and men with (fine) arts and high culture. Mayhew highlights the work of Christine Battersby on 'gender and genius'. Battersby argues that '[t]he genius's instinct, emotion, sensibility, intuition, imagination – even his madness – were different from those of ordinary mortals. . . . The genius was a male – full of "virile" energy' (1989: 3). Battersby bases her arguments on Romanticism, but as Mayhew argues, there are many echoes of these gender distinctions within twentieth-century (and now twenty-first-century) popular music.

The rise of rock and roll music and the advancements of the music industry had a profoundly indelible impact on twentieth-century culture. Popular music, particularly that emerging from the USA in the early 1950s, caused shockwaves as it began to enter the mainstream. It was wild, sexy, youthful, rebellious and incredibly exciting. Rock and roll became inextricably linked with youth culture and the burgeoning post-war consumer society. In the USA in the early 1950s the music industry became increasingly sophisticated and wide-reaching with the dominance of increasingly professionalized record companies, publishers, radio stations, live venues and charts/hit parades. Its progress was helped by its contemporaneous emergence with key technological advancements – the 45 rpm vinyl disc, juke-box, transistor radio and television. There was a coming together of manufacturing technology and music technology.

Defining features of early rock and roll were sexuality and youthful rebelliousness. Key performers such as Elvis, Eddie Cochran and Gene Vincent were perceived as threatening by the conservative mainstream. Contemporaneous with the mainstreaming of rock and roll was the explosion in cinema of films aimed at young people which featured rock and roll music and/ or themes of rebellion and teenage angst. Some films of the period did involve female rebels such as Natalie Wood's role in *Rebel without a Cause* (1955). However, in rock and roll music women were absent from all aspects of the industry landscape. There was no female equivalent to Elvis or Sam Phillips. Rock and roll in the 1950s was masculinized from the outset. Rebelliousness and overt sexiness were at odds with the categories defining the femininity of the time, which were connected with domesticity and demureness. Female pop role models in women such as Rosemary Clooney were distinctly wholesome. In an interview with the music journalist and writer Gillian Gaar, singer and songwriter Holly Near explains the way in which the powerful ideologies of the mid-twentieth century led women unwittingly to exclude themselves from certain areas of music and performance. In her own case, even though she was an accomplished acoustic guitarist, when the electric guitar was introduced, she didn't make the transfer over to it in the way that her male contemporaries did: 'I played the guitar, probably knew more chords and more about music than any of the guys who were diving in and plugging in their guitars. And it never even occurred to me to plug it in. It's not even that I was told not to, it just didn't even cross my mind' (Gaar 1993: 56).

Bayton's (1997) extensive research into women and the electric guitar provides further detail about the exclusionary practices that inhibit women's relation to the electric guitar and rock culture. This has many echoes with the separation of women from technology that can be seen in numerous areas of popular-cultural production, such as DJing and computer gaming. There is a comprehensive body of literature on the gendering of technology (see Spender 1995; Wajcman 1991).

At a defining moment in pop history the stage was set for men to figure as key performers, producers, managers, music journalists, record company executives, songwriters, and so on, and for women to be positioned as fans/consumers or performers whose greatness was positioned as being largely defined by the exceptional talents of a male producer. As Mayhew argues,

> Although the recording process has been important in popular music since the 1940s, women have on the whole been able to access this space only as singers, or to a lesser extent as instrumentalists. Women who have dominated the position of pop singer have often been devalued through a construction of femininity as an unskilled, and/or a 'natural' musical position. (2004: 150)

She goes on to argue that this positioning has a history dating back to the Renaissance period and highlights the work of Citron (1993). 'The eighteenth and nineteenth century saw the solidification of the creative subject as male' (Mayhew 2004: 150). At the level of producer and creative performer, women were invisible.

Girl's and women's relationship to rock and roll was restricted to the level of fandom. Barbara Bradby, a key scholar in examining women's roles in popular music, highlights the 'associations of girls being involved in popular music as members of the audience, rather than being the performers' (1993: 159). Kearney argues that the dual pressure of women to be consumers and housewives (and therefore not producers and creators) meant that their leisure interests became increasingly focused on domestic/private activities:

> With the retrenchment of traditional gender norms, female youth were encouraged not only to idolize young male celebrities, like Elvis Presley and the Beatles, but to identify with the housewife as the ideal form of feminine subjectivity and to understand the domestic sphere as the space in which their presence was most valued. As a result, older girls, especially those of the middle class, began to focus less on hobbies that could be developed into professions, such as writing and photography, and more on those that would attract a male partner and produce a good homemaker, such as dieting and shopping. (2006: 39)

The fandom was intense and itself seen as rebellious and threatening. So potent and strong was it that a relationship between gender and popular music based on extreme binary oppositions became established. This was exploited by the music industry, which saw the benefits of the gendered fan/consumer relationship. Issues connected with gender and sexuality were at the heart of popular music – lyrics were, more often than not, focused on heterosexual sexual courtship, pop stars were produced to be idolized – typically, male pop stars were produced to be idolized by their adoring female fans. Gendered stereotypes about behaviour of male and female fans abound – screaming female fans (see Garratt 1990) and nerdish male record collectors (see Straw 1997).

Although musicians could have 'produced' their own music, the role of the record producer became a crucial mediator in the chain of musical production. The professionalism of the music industry led to new hierarchies of management. Managers such as Colonel Tom Parker and Brian Epstein, and record producers such as Phil Spector and George Martin, became as famous as, sometimes more famous than, the musicians and performers they represented. It was the role of record producer that garners the most attention in terms of cultural creativity/production, and the case that we will now focus on.

In looking at music producers, there are many crossovers with film directors – both perform very similar functions. Both have often had the 'genius' tag applied to them. The notion of the auteur, most commonly used in discussions of cinema, also becomes highly pertinent here.

As Mayhew observes, most record producers are male: 'At one extreme they may be taken to task for their interference in the artist's work. At another they may be lauded as artistic geniuses in their own right, controlling and creating the music sound of an album. . . . However, feminists studying popular culture would point out that the producer's role has remained a male domain' (2004: 149). She goes on to argue that the reason for women's absence in the role of producer is partly explained by their lack of economic independence and the prevailing discourses in music criticism that creative genius is a 'naturally' male preserve. In the 1950s and 1960s there were some notable female songwriters and performers, such as Carole King and Ellie Greenwich. What is particularly relevant here, however, is that these female songwriters wrote in partnership with their husbands, which raises questions about credibility and authorship. As Gaar argues: 'In spite of the contributions to the girl group genre made by Florence Greenberg, Carole King and Ellie Greenwich . . . when rock historians write about the "male Svengalis" who called the shots behind the girl group scene they are usually referring to one man in particular: Phil Spector' (1993: 43). It is to the case of Phil Spector, arguably the most influential (and now, following his 2009 conviction for murder, infamous) record producer of all times, that we will now turn.

Spector rose to fame in the 1950s and was notorious because of his obsessive, all-consuming quest for his trademark 'wall of sound'. He began as a performer and songwriter but it is his music production work for which he is most famous. Spector was a pioneer in the formation of 'girl groups' such as The Chiffons and The Ronettes and their powerful harmonies. Spector cannot be accused of working within a major label over which he had little control. He formed his own label, funded by his successes as a singer and a songwriter, and secured artistic control and freedom for himself. His wall of sound was created by bringing large orchestras into the studio, getting numerous musicians to perform the same thing at the same time, recording in an echo chamber and using a variety of other techniques to produce a sound so dense and multi-layered that it would be impossible to achieve in a live performance context. The girl groups were harmonious not only aurally but also visually – matching outfits, matching hairstyles, and so on. They were 'manufactured' insofar as Spector dictated their entire image, sound and aura.

As Jacqueline Warwick's work on Spector identifies: 'His production style is so distinctive that we often tend to think of records that he produced as "Phil Spector records", forgetting the names of the groups who sang them and the songwriters who wrote them . . .' (2004: 196). Spector made the singers anonymous and interchangeable and it was Spector only who was the genius; everyone else was dispensable. Warwick notes that with the case of the girl groups this was a 'rare instance of girls at the forefront of mainstream culture' and that this was also a multicultural musical moment. However, she is highly critical of the misogynistic way that women vocalists have been dismissed, undermined and devalued:

> Music centred around female voices is often dismissed as derivative and 'fake'. This kind of assessment assumes that songwriting and playing instruments constitute more creative and important work than mere singing, and disallows the possibility of understanding the girl singer as an auteur of her music. But when songs exist in most listeners' ears only because of the highly individual vocal performances that brought them to life, should we attach too much importance to the roles of producers, songwriters, and recording engineers? (2004: 192)

She goes on to note that a performer such as Elvis was not chastised for repeatedly using music that had been written by others.

In terms of the debate about the genius record producer, film auteur, and so on, Hesmondhalgh makes the following observation: 'Because high value has been attached to products that are created by gifted individuals (especially supposed "geniuses"), putting a known name on a text suggests some distinctive personal vision' (2007: 201). Hesmondhalgh goes on to argue that this obliterates the presence of other creative producers who must have been involved and makes the superstar wages of so-called 'geniuses' all the more unpalatable.

By looking at the case of girl groups in the 1960s we have highlighted the gender/power relationships at play. Women in the girl group era were chosen, managed, produced, married, divorced, designed and dictated to. With the arrival of heavy rock in the late 1960s and punk in the mid-1970s, gender inequalities still continued to be a powerful force. With the case of heavy metal, for example,

Robert Walser (1993) highlights that this was actively constructed as a male domain.

Frith and McRobbie (1990) have focused on the 'cock rock' attitudes of rock culture and numerous others have noted how these gender strategies continue to imbue the popular music world (see Bayton 1997; Cohen 1997; M. Leonard 2007; Richards and Milestone 2000; Straw 1997).

At the start of our case study time period – the 1950s – women are invisible in numerous aspects of the music industry. In the late 1970s punk happens and some argue that this disrupted elements of the established gender relations of the music industry. For example, Kearney claims that,

> [d]uring the late 1970s, . . . a new habitus of gender relations began to emerge in Western societies, altering girls' relationships to masculinity and male-dominated forms of cultural production in ways unprecedented for any previous generation. In turn, the broad diffusion of inexpensive media technologies and entrepreneurial youth cultures during this period allowed more girls to gain access to the tools and infrastructures of cultural production than ever before. (2006: 48)

Kearney cites punk and hip hop as arenas where girls were able to become more productive. We shall explore whether or not punk marked a turning point for women's involvement in cultural production in the next chapter.

Gender and Cultural Work: Film

We will now look at the case of the cinema industry. It is clear that Hollywood is one of the most vivid examples where producers of popular culture – film-makers – are involved in transmitting ideas about gender roles. If we briefly bring to mind Walt Disney's film adaptations of folk tales and fairy stories, our heads will be swimming with images of princes and princesses, heroes and villains, beautiful innocents and wicked stepmothers. Emblazoned in glorious technicolour are images and ideologies of ideal masculinity and femininity often juxtaposed with antithetical caricatures of those who fail to live up to the expectations of their gender – the ugly sisters and lazy villains. Disney cartoons aside, the Hollywood dream factory has worked tirelessly, both on screen and off, to paint and reinforce cultural ideas about gender norms. Although some of the examples we are about to look at concern Hollywood in the mid-twentieth century,

Hollywood still operates as the most powerful force in global cinema. Moreover, gender continues to be an important dynamic in the motion picture industry. Men have not relinquished their dominance in terms of producing and directing. Very traditional gender rules seem to operate within the film industry landscape with the majority of technical roles being undertaken by men and hyper-feminine roles such as costume and make-up artistry being undertaken by women. The notion of 'creativity' has different connotations between the sexes. Whilst men only have to turn up in a tuxedo on the red carpet, female stars have every inch of their bodies and attire scrutinized by the paparazzi and celebrity press. Whole genres are marketed at gender-specific markets – 'chick flicks', action hero films, for example. Adorno and Horkheimer's (1993) theories on the culture industry are relevant here. The cinema industry keeps reproducing these films marketed at gender groups and audiences keep flocking to them even though they are ostensibly consuming 'more of the same'. Adorno and Horkheimer argued that the culture industry supports the capitalist system in two highly significant ways. Firstly, popular culture such as cinema provides an uncomplicated means of escape from the drudgery that the unfair capitalist system offers us and thereby stops the masses from revolting. We work in alienating, badly paid jobs, and things like blockbuster films or pop music or glossy magazines distract us from meaningfully reflecting on the unjustness of a world where the many work hard in exploitative jobs for the profit of a few.

The second element to Adorno's highly influential argument is the way that we willingly accept unchallenging, unworthy popular culture and keep buying it. Popular culture is standardized, made into easily digestible pieces. Adorno's arguments were made a lifetime ago yet there is much to be said for his theories when applied to popular culture today. Films continue to be marketed along gender lines, stock gender ideologies continue to come to the fore and the films are formulaic.

Women have made notable inroads into the previously male-dominated cinema industry, but women in positions of power and control are still the exception rather than the rule. As with the figure of the music producer, the film industry promotes the individual (male) genius notion of the film director with unstoppable enthusiasm. As Kearney observes:

> Patriarchal ideology, whose hegemony has long relied on a sexual division of labor, has sustained the male domination of, and female

marginalization within, commercial filmmaking for decades. Indeed, as has been the case since the first motion picture camera was invented, men far outnumber women in virtually all sectors of contemporary film production. Such male dominance puts interested females at a severe disadvantage, as the primary roles involved in film production, especially director and cinematographer, have been naturalized as male. (2006: 192)

The auteur

In the 1950s a group of writers and film-makers contributed to the journal *Cahiers du Cinéma* and developed the notion of the auteur. An auteur is an author, but in this context applied to cinema. The idea was that, as with a novelist, you could take the work of a particular film director and recognize the style, approach, methods, trademarks, and so on, of a particular auteur. The work of directors such as Alfred Hitchcock, Jean-Luc Godard and François Truffaut was picked out for celebration along these lines. To be an auteur requires an assertion of masculinity and power. The idea of the auteur presupposes that it's the vision of one person – the director – that gives a film its charm, brilliance and ideas:

> The dominant critical paradigm regarding film authorship is of course the auteur theory, which posits the director as a film's principal (if not sole) author. This approach was developed in the 1950s by a group of young French critics to assess classical Hollywood directors like John Ford, Howard Hawks, Vincente Minnelli, and Alfred Hitchcock, whose body of work manifested a distinctive personal style – that is, consistent patterns of narrative, thematic, and formal-aesthetic expression – despite the constraints and commercial requirements of the system. (Schatz 2009: 49)

When we think of the huge crew of people involved in the making of a film, it is a confident assertion indeed to give so much credit to the director. What of the contribution of the writer of the novel or play that has been adapted for screen, producers, cinematographers, actors, and so on?

The film director Alfred Hitchcock has frequently been discussed in the context of auteur theory. Hitchcock was a prolific film director who made more than fifty films during his career. The majority of his well-known films were made in the 1950s and early 1960s – the period we are concerned with in this chapter. His visually compelling thrillers were innovative, exciting and subject to wide critical acclaim.

Hitchcock's films have been widely scrutinized by academics – many using psychoanalysis and/or feminist theory. One of the most famous pieces of writing about gender and popular culture is Laura Mulvey's article 'Visual Pleasure and Narrative Cinema', which was first published in 1975. Here Mulvey uses the case of Alfred Hitchcock to illustrate her theory that women are positioned as merely 'to be looked at' in Hollywood cinema. Mulvey focuses on two of Hitchcock's most famous films, *Rear Window* (1954) and *Vertigo* (1958), to explain that these films (like all other Hollywood films) are constructed with prioritization of men's voyeuristic pleasure. The power and pleasure of looking is described as scopophilia, and Mulvey argues that it is men who have this power and that Hitchcock's films are framed in such a way that there are three levels of looking at women – through the camera, the (male) character and the spectator (who is interpellated as male). The woman is both consuming and consumed. As Kearney argues: 'Though Mulvey does not elaborate on it, the idea that men control the cinematic apparatus . . . is the keystone to her theory of the male gaze. . . . Mulvey relates the masculinizing of the camera's perspective to the gender dynamics involved in the practice of looking, thus contextualizing the male gaze as an effect of patriarchy' (2006: 200). Like Mulvey, John Berger (1972) concurs that 'men act and women appear'. Not only is the figure of the genius masculinized, but according to Mulvey the world constructed in these auteurs' films reflects masculine fantasies and a masculine way of framing the world.

Conclusion

In this chapter we have sought to highlight some significant examples from the mid-twentieth century in order to discuss and account for the massive gender inequalities at the level of cultural production. We have demonstrated women's absence as frontline 'symbol creators' and attempted to provide socio-cultural explanations for this.

Some explanations are more straightforward than others. Women's absence as cultural producers can be explained via the post-war project to return women to the home, to domesticate them and refeminize them and make them into what Betty Friedan (1963) described as the 'happy housewife heroine'. There were not as a many women in the labour market as there were men. This is a straightforward social explanation. Other reasons for the absence of women as cultural producers are more subtle and potentially more damaging. These other explanations are linked to ideologies which have naturalized the subordination of women.

In our three examples of *Mad Men*, pop music and film we saw how the figure of the creative genius was masculinized. In the cases used in this chapter we see a recurring discourse centred on the genius as awkward, bloody-minded, excessive perfectionists, a male puppet master shaping his women – such as Spector and his Ronettes and Hitchcock and his blondes. As writers such as Mayhew (2004), Citron (1993) and Battersby (1989) have noted, this gendering of the genius has a long history and its ideology has seeped far and wide into culture and individual consciousness. The lack of role models inhibits women and encourages men only to 'appoint in their own image'.

In addition to notions of genius being a masculine quality, there is also an ideology about men and women's adeptness with technology. Judy Wajcman (1991) describes how multiple cultural stereotypes serve to construct women as being technically incompetent. Given that film directing and music production require some technological intervention, this might also explain women's difficulty in gaining credibility and acceptance. But technology is only a small facet of these roles.

Until women are more powerfully linked to the means of cultural production in our media- and popular-culture-saturated world, the vision we are given is a view of the world from the privileged eyes of the white heterosexual male. We ask a provocative question – does it matter if most of the culture that men and women consume is produced by men? We argue that it matters a great deal, not least because it maintains a particular, mainly white, mainly heterosexual, male view of the world. It is not representative of a diversity of viewpoints. A set of values emerging from a particular group are being promoted as universal and normal. This constant reproduction of these values constructs ideologies that suggest that women are not naturally 'cut out' for frontline cultural production. Those in power 'appoint in their own image' and so the cycle continues. The notion of 'ideal types' (see Acker 1990; Tams 2002) of cultural workers claims a hegemonic dominance. Patriarchal values are continually imposed on society and individuals. Angela McRobbie's work is of central importance here and we discuss her work at many points throughout this book. From her early work on women's magazines through to more recent work on cultural production, she convincingly highlights the numerous ways in which damaging patriarchal ideologies are being promoted which trap women in traditional 'women's' roles.

In the next chapter we look at women and cultural production in more recent times and examine the extent to which the rhetoric of greater equality in the workplace in the late twentieth century (and beyond) is backed up by statistical evidence of significantly greater representation of women working in primary cultural production roles. When compared with the mid-twentieth century.

3

Gender and Cultural Work

Punk and Beyond

In the last chapter we focused on some high-profile case studies in order to examine the gendered dynamics of cultural work from the mid-twentieth century to the late 1970s. We saw how a combination of disparate influences resulted in a severe underrepresentation of women in frontline cultural production work. Ideologies about the 'naturalness' of men and women's roles, the notion of 'creative genius' as a masculinized force and cultural myths and stereotypes about women's abilities with technology all conspired to make it very difficult for women to make inroads into areas such as film directing, record producing and the role of advertising creative. We saw how women's cultural production was rendered as less impressive than that of men, how it was dismissed as domestic, craft-based or only really satisfactory under the guiding direction of men. In this chapter we move forward in time to analyse gender and cultural work from the late 1970s to the present in order to examine the extent to which women have come closer to the centre of the field of cultural production.

There have been a number of dramatic socio-cultural changes since the late 1970s which ought to have reconfigured the gender dynamics of cultural industries. Most notable of these, in terms of this book, is the impact of feminism and the women's rights movement on women's experience in the workplace. In the West, many policies and laws which are designed to promote equal pay between men and women and end gender discrimination in the workplace have been implemented (see Rees 1998, 2006) as a result of campaigns for equality. There have also been progressive developments in terms of other marginalized and oppressed groups. The rights of gay men and lesbian women have increased and positive examples of antiracism have contributed towards greater numbers of black and minority ethnic men and women gaining entry into roles from which they were excluded by discrimination in earlier decades. There are improved conditions for some disabled people. A broader range of sexual and lifestyle preferences is accepted and legally protected. There is certainly rhetoric, if not always a reality, of greater social 'diversity', tolerance of 'difference' and the redrawing of older hierarchies of power. Of course, the terms that are used, such as 'diversity' and 'difference', still imply the hegemonic dominance of that which certain groups are defined as being 'different' or 'diverse' from.

The late 1970s, the era when punk became prominent, provides a useful turning point between our time frame in the previous chapter and the period with which we start this chapter. Punk provided the impetus for new forms of cultural production which, on the face of it, were more accessible and less hierarchical than earlier modes of cultural production. The punk movement heralded the arrival of massive disruptions to established standards of cultural production. Unlike some music-inspired youth cultures, punk was not manufactured by the music industry; its origins were underground. Helen Reddington notes that punks were highly productive and inhabited a new type of dole-inspired bohemian lifestyle: 'It was a busy subculture . . . punks "worked at" the subculture twenty-four-hours a day creating a space for themselves' (2007: 20). Making music, making clothes and fanzines and a range of other productive activities were central to the emergence of punk. Dick Hebdige's analysis of punk in his landmark book *Subculture: The Meaning of Style* (1979) provides a dazzling analysis of the stylistic elements of punk creativity. Angela McRobbie describes subcultures as 'job creation schemes' for the cultural industries. The creative activities sustaining subcultures (DJing, producing fanzines, buying and selling clothes) 'provide the opportunity for learning and sharing skills, practising them, for making a small amount of money; more importantly they provide pathways for future "life skills" in the form of work and self-employment' (McRobbie 1994: 161). However, given that boys and girls are shepherded into very different leisure interests as children, there is a strong gender dimension to the way in which youthful hobbies become mapped onto later career choices. McRobbie argues that girls' leisure was constructed within an overarching ideology of patriarchal romance that instantly set limitations on career and leisure aspirations. Finding 'Mr Right' was the pivotal raison d'être of heterosexual female existence. McRobbie argues that this ideology of patriarchal romance dampened and limited female career aspirations.

Comics and magazines aimed at boys, by contrast, had no space for romance but instead focused on male engagement with a range of hobbies and leisure activities.

The anarchic DIY zeitgeist of punk cancelled out the need for the 'genius' record producer and sometimes circumvented the established cultural industries infrastructure and powerbase (see Laing 1985; Savage 1991; Straw 1991). Punk stimulated subcultural entrepreneurial activities outside the established cultural capitals of New York, LA, London and Paris and saw the flourishing of cultural production in peripheral towns and cities. However, in terms of the experience of girls and young women, their proximity to the centre of the action was sporadic. Whilst women were involved as both producers and consumers of punk, they were often marginalized, and there are many who point out that punk did not open up as many cultural production opportunities for women as might have been hoped (Bayton 1998; M. Leonard 2007). McRobbie (1980) concedes that although girls were more visible in punk, like earlier subcultures punk tended to be street-based, and this meant that male dominance prevailed.

McRobbie also makes the point, however, that punk lyrics were not love-oriented and that this provided a new space of expression for women, as exemplified by performers such as Poly Styrene and Siouxsie. Women singers had never constructed themselves in such wild, nihilistic and rebellious ways before. As Barbara Bradby and David Laing observe, punk had an enormous impact on the way that women could express themselves in popular music: 'If punk in Britain is best known for its parody of the anger of class warfare, it also opened up an important space for women to express anger, a space that has subsequently be occupied by a variety of women musicians to express a range of concerns, often centring on the self and abuse' (2001: 229). This is an important legacy of punk and its impact on the gender dynamics of cultural production.

In spite of reservations about the gender equality of punk, it would indeed be unfair not to acknowledge the various ways in which punk offered women new spaces of expression. Helen Reddington's recent research, where she carried out a series of interviews with women involved in punk and post-punk, looked at the longer-term impact of punk on women's lives and found that punk had provided some women with a new expressive paradigm. Reddington argues that the high unemployment of the late 1970s created a space for women to delay growing up and therefore avoid the expectations of their gender (2007: 20), and that '[a]lthough there had been no specific mention of girls and young women in any of punk's "manifestos", this and the atmosphere of enablement that was formally created for women by the Equal Opportunities Act provided an additional force to their feeling that they were entitled to their position on stage' (2007: 24). This is significant because it provided a greatly expanded repertoire of identities for young women.

The cultural production aspect to punk paved the way for a new form of pop-cultural entrepreneurialism that was rooted in a hand-made, small-scale, ad hoc approach. The possibilities for young people to set up seed-bed businesses connected with their cultural interests began to become a reality.

In the immediate post-punk era, the early 1980s, new types of cultural industries began to emerge which were often micro-businesses or small- to medium-sized enterprises (SMEs) in fanzine and magazine production, fashion design, trading in second-hand clothes (see McRobbie 1988) and graphic design of flyers and record covers. In the early 1980s in the UK the Thatcher government's drive to eliminate 'welfare dependency' and encourage entrepreneurialism saw the establishment of the Enterprise Allowance Scheme, which ran from 1983 through to the early 1990s. The scheme worked by paying people a weekly allowance in addition to their basic welfare benefits if they set up a business. There were few restrictions on the type of businesses that could be set up and this led to an explosion of lifestyle/hobby-based enterprises. For several years this provided the impetus for some young people to establish businesses based on their cultural interests. Manchester's Northern Quarter is a case, albeit somewhat exceptional, where a significant number of small popular-cultural businesses began to congregate (Milestone 2002; Wynne and O'Connor 1996). In other places similar creative or bohemian areas emerged, such as New York's SoHo (see Zukin 1982[1]), Milan's Tichinese (Bovone 2005) and Chicago's Wicker Park (Lloyd 2006). Alongside the existing global record companies, Hollywood, and so on, new, independent, regionally embedded cultural industry districts began to establish. Regeneration of decaying downtown areas saw the congregation of creatives who revitalized areas through creating a new buzz of animation (see Zukin 1982). Popular culture became an increasingly more important facet of urban life. The bohemian, avant-garde, grass-roots nature of this gave voices to some previously disenfranchised groups and provided new oppositional spaces for creativity. The increased visibility of creativity on the street

[1] See Zukin's warnings about the danger of gentrification of artists' quarters.

encouraged more people to become involved. However, if we take the case of 'Madchester', for example, we can see clear gender patterns in the formation of these new bohemias – men dominate in terms of the demographics of the bands, the DJs, the promoters, the record company directors, club owners and the music journalists. Women feature as small-scale fashion designers or occasionally as backing vocalists. Punk had not significantly disrupted conventions of gender and cultural production as much as might have been expected.

These micro-changes were taking place against a backdrop of wider social, cultural and economic shifts. Critics began to talk about a sea change toward postmodernity and an era in which established hierarchies were being destabilized. Commentators such as David Harvey provided convincing accounts of these huge cultural shifts. Harvey argued that

> the experience of time and space has changed, the confidence in the association between scientific and moral judgements has collapsed, aesthetics has triumphed over ethics as a prime focus of social and intellectual concern, images dominate narratives, ephemerality and fragmentation take precedence over eternal truths and unified politics, and explanations have shifted from the realm of material and political-economic groundings towards a consideration of autonomous cultural and political practices. (1989: 328)

All the old rules were being discarded or recast and numerous cultural critics described huge socio-cultural shifts: Bauman's (2000) 'liquid modernity', Baudrillard's (1988) 'hyperreality' and Castells' (1996) 'network society' are cases in point. In terms of culture there was a collapse of distinctions between high and popular culture, the end of 'grand narratives' (Lyotard 1986) and the aestheticization of everyday life (Featherstone 2007).

The mode of cultural production altered and markets became more fragmented and specialized. As Justin O'Connor notes:

> In the later 1980s political economists and economic geographers began to talk of a shift from mass production to 'flexible specialisation' and 'Post-fordism'. . . . Predictable patterns of mass consumption had given way to smaller niche markets and the proliferation of goods and services which had a higher 'symbolic' content and could appeal to new ways of constructing social identity away from the 'mainstream'. (2007: 28)

This shift provided a ripe context for emergence of new cultural industries.

This era also saw the process of globalization take on a dramatic momentum. Large companies, notably media industries in the context of this book, expanded their international markets through vertical and horizontal integration. The possibility for global media flows was extended through the arrival of satellite television, MTV culture and, a little later, the internet, leading to sporadic new networked global communities (bearing in mind the differential patterns of access to technology and the 'information rich' and 'information poor'). George Ritzer (1998) talked of the McDonaldization of culture: a standardized, sanitized, global mono culture – Adorno writ large. At the same time, others wrote of differentiation and flexible specialization. Both processes were happening. The process of global outsourcing galloped on, and in the West, capitalist-inspired de-industrialization led to talk of a crisis of masculinity as traditional heavy industry (the source of male employment) was shifted to cheaper labour markets.

By the late 1980s, there was a growth of debates that pointed to the increased significance of creative or cultural industries to Western economies and these industries began to be taken more seriously; The slippery nature of the term 'culture' (see Williams 1958) has contributed to confusion and debates about what can legitimately be classed as a cultural industry. Film, television and the music industry are obvious contenders, whilst printing and architecture might be deemed less so. In the UK context, O'Connor (2007) cites the 1980s and the Greater London Council's cultural industries policies as highly significant because there was a development of a notion that culture could be a legitimate and rewarding source of employment. Culture was now considered as a viable focus for economic development but also seen as a sphere that could harness the passions and interests of previously marginalized groups and provide space for new voices in terms of defining cultural value. A decade later, cultural confidence was inspired when the 'New Labour' government of 1997 promoted the notion of 'the creative industries' against a backdrop of 'cool Britannia' and 'creative Britain' (see Smith 1998). O'Connor argues that the name change from cultural to creative was highly significant. It was about expanding the definition of the sector so that it could justifiably bring in new media and other ICT businesses as well as broadening its connotations to include the arts.

Cities that had previously not been valued for their cultural assets were beginning to establish themselves as viable tourist destinations – often because of their cultural production and pop-cultural leisure opportunities. In the UK many deindustrializing cities were linked with popular culture, and in Manchester popular-cultural industries became a central plank in the city's post-industrial regeneration and reanimation. In other parts of the globe, cities became linked with their popular-cultural offerings – New York, Tokyo and Sydney, but also 'second-tier' cities such as Barcelona, Seattle and Reykjavik. Writers such as Richard Florida (2002) convinced city managers about the benefits of attracting the 'creative class'. Those who were once part of the cultural underground were asked by the mainstream to advise on how to run urban culture. As Wynne and O'Connor (1996) argued, culture moved from 'the margins to the centre' of urban life.

The arrival of the internet, digital technologies and 'new' media disrupted some aspects of the powerbase of the old media giants. The internet and the numerous forms of social media it supports have precipitated radical challenges to social organization, sharing of popular culture and the undermining of old media forms such as print media. File sharing presents a huge threat to the established music industry and legal challenges to protect it abound. The issue of intellectual property rights has moved to centre stage. Some speak of the democratizing effects of new digital technologies – because they are relatively cheap and accessible they are seen as able to open up possibilities for those previously excluded from the realm of cultural production.

Responses to the cultural industries in terms of gender and other markers of 'diversity' were initially very positive. If we recall some of the changes that took place, then it would appear that new opportunities for women should have considerably expanded. There was a growth in the number of cultural industries jobs particularly at the SME and micro-business level. The sites of cultural production increased and formal rules about cultural production were eroded by punk attitudes and other cultural shifts. Cultural hierarchies were redrawn and this had huge implications for women given the earlier derogatory assumptions about the links between women and low culture. Campaigns for women's rights had seen a move towards equal pay, and greater numbers of women going into higher education and the workplace. This era saw the arrival of cultural production technologies which were cheaper, lighter and more user-friendly. With all of these changes one might have thought that increasingly more women would have become involved in cultural production. Worryingly, though, in both the 'old' cultural production industries and the more recently emerging digital sector, there is little to suggest that women are entering new roles in significant numbers. The 'new' cultural production roles such as DJing, interactive games design and web design, for example, have already been defined as masculine realms. Women in frontline cultural production roles in all of these sectors are the exception rather than the rule.

From Masculine Creative Genius to the Masculine Creative Class?

We saw in the previous chapter how normative notions of creative genius had become closely linked with masculinity, making it incredibly difficult for women to gain entry or credibility in cultural production roles. In more recent times, particularly in the wake of the expansion of new media, and the growth and importance of cultural industries, commentators began to speak of a new 'creative class' and its antecedent, self-directed identity projects. The best-known champion of the creative class is Richard Florida, particularly through his book *The Rise of the Creative Class* (2002). According to Mark Deuze: 'Florida's creative class can be seen as a vanguard of a distinctly individualized class, whose workstyle is highly dependent of information and communication technologies . . . living an immediate life where work and play are one and the same' (2007: 12). Florida speaks of phenomena such as 'creativity indexes' and 'gayness indexes' of cities. Cities that gain high scores in these terms produce the type of space that allows the creative class to thrive. Florida claims that this new class relishes being close to diversity. Florida forcibly argues that attracting the creative class can only be a good thing for any city, and he has been invited by urban managers to cities across the globe to spread his message. In similar vein, sociologists, notably Beck (1992) and Giddens (1991), wrote about the new opportunities for self-identity projects in late/postmodernity. Freed from the shackles and constraints of social structures and institutions, individuals are able to master their own biographies. However, as Beverley Skeggs argues, these individualized lifestyle projects are not available to all: 'There is no sense in Giddens that the possibility of having a self may itself be a classed, raced or gendered issue. . . . The self appears in Giddens as a neutral concept available to all, rather than an inscription, a position of personhood produced to retain the interests of a privileged few, requiring for its constitution the exclusion of others' (2004: 53). As well as condemning Giddens, Skeggs also singles out Beck and his notion of the reflexive self as displaying a similar blindness to the exclusive nature of the self-identity projects of late modernity. On interrogation the defining features of the creative class appear to be very white, very masculine and very middle class (in spite of many claims to being 'open' and 'diversity'-loving). Being able to construct a lifestyle requires high levels of cultural and economic capital and a great distance from caring roles.

Advertising, Music and Film

We will now scrutinize some recent examples of cultural work to discuss the changes in terms of gender and cultural production and consider why women do not appear to have progressed as much as might have been expected. Let us briefly review the case studies focused on in chapter 2.

Advertising

In advertising, all the evidence reveals that this is still a male-dominated sphere of cultural work. There are very few women working as 'creatives'. Recent research by Sheri Broyles and Jean Grow provides depressing statistics about women's involvement in advertising in the USA. In their survey of various reports they conclude that

> [o]verall women make up 66 percent of the workforce in advertising (Bosman, 2005). Yet, according to an informal study in *Creativity*, only one in three in creative departments are women (Cuneo and Petrecca, 1997), with even fewer in the higher executive ranks such as creative directors. *Adweek* looked at the top 33 agencies and found that only four had flagship offices with female creative directors (Bosman, 2005). More to the point, the 20th anniversary issue of *Creativity* featured the 50 most creative people of the last two decades, and none were women (*Creativity*, 2006). (Broyles and Grow 2008: 5)

Many lists, polls and recently defined cultural canons appear to be blind to the achievements of women and reflect the fact that women just are not present in key creative roles.

In research on the UK advertising sector, in a study commissioned by the IPA (Institute of Practitioners in Advertising), *Women in Advertising – 10 Years On*, Debbie Klein uses the following quote to sum up the opinions of women who have worked in the industry for over ten years and found that little had changed at the top: 'It's got worse because everyone thinks it's got better' (2000: 19). Additionally, Klein found that, whilst 88 per cent of women surveyed believe the industry needs to take action to ensure that women are better represented in senior management positions, only 48 per cent of men share this view (2000: 12). In the rampantly commercialized world of advertising, there seems to be scant attention paid to diversifying the creative workforce.

Michele Gregory's research identified strategies used by men in the advertising industry which served to exclude women. She describes this as male 'locker room' behaviour: '[T]he use of sports, humour, banter, the sexualization of women, drinking and going to strip clubs also represent the embodiment of hegemonic masculinity at work' (2009: 327). Drawing on the work of Connell (2005) and Connell and Messerschmidt (2005), Gregory highlights the importance of examining 'how men in the dominant culture use their bodies to claim and maintain their positions of power and privilege' (2009:327).

In the UK, the advertising industry has become a vital sector. Frank Mort argues that by the 1980s the UK had become the most important centre for the sector when many Madison Avenue companies were bought out by UK firms. Mort cites a 66 per cent growth of the UK advertising sector from 1976 to the 1980s (1996: 92). The 1980s were the decade that saw UK companies such as Saatchi and Saatchi and Bartle Bogle Hegarty become internationally dominant and highly praised for their creative output. Mort's research looked at changing notions of masculinity against the backdrop of social and cultural changes in the 1980s, including new masculine identities that were promoted by the advertising industry and the new male-orientated lifestyle magazines. Although to an extent masculinity has been softened via the influence of gay culture and the 'new man' figure, Mort acknowledges the extreme heterosexual male domination of the advertising sector. More recently, Sean Nixon's in-depth studies of male creatives in advertising have explored contemporary gender workplace identities. Drawing on the work of Rozsika Parker and Griselda Pollock (1981), Nixon notes that the 'creative genius as male' discourse is alive and well in the contemporary creative department:

> I explore the ways in which these departments were infused with a set of diffuse, but none the less strikingly gendered representations of the creative person. These representations drew on wider cultural repertoires in which the links between creativity and masculinity were forged. In particular, they owed much to the distinctly masculine set of attributes associated with the figure of the artist, which had deep roots within the cultural milieu of advertising and beyond. (2003: 99)

Once again we find these discourses about men's natural disposition towards creativity continuing to pervade cultural industries. Parker and Pollock (1981) trace this back to the eighteenth century. Whilst they argue that notions of artistic genius have been redrawn in some areas of cultural production, they persist in the advertising industry. Given the power that creatives have in transmitting ideologies about gender, it is worrying that the advertising industry maintains traditional, sexist ideas about women.

Music

In music, a much larger and more complex entity, we find uneven patterns of women's advancement. At a very simple level it is clear that there are some large gender divisions in terms of the music that is produced, the way performers are constructed and responded to and the roles that men and women undertake 'behind the scenes' when working in the music industry. Of course there are areas where boundaries are blurred and transgressions made – particularly away from the mainstream. As Amy Lind and Stephanie Brzuzy argue in their recent US book on gender: 'While there are now many commercially successful popular female musicians, ranging from Mary J. Blige to Melissa Etheridge, Sheryl Crow, Madonna and Christine Aguilera, most female musicians continue to face a set of institutional and cultural barriers when it comes to how they are represented in the visual media and reviewed by their peers' (2008: 230).

It is telling that although there are successful individual female performers, and female lead singers of bands, there are few all-female guitar bands, for example. In research on women in the music industry in Manchester (Richards and Milestone 2000), a female musician expressed the following:

> I did not want to be perceived as the girl in the band who just sang. You know, the pretty thing at the front. This sort of love interest. I wanted to make sure that my creative input wasn't limited to singing and writing the songs. Because I had ideas on all levels. . . . I just remember being interviewed and people automatically assuming that [male partner] produced [the band] and I was just a singer. And it is really hard to turn that around, that whole perception. You know that people come with that perception.

So engrained are the (lack of) expectations about female contributions to the creative process that a range of dominant ideologies persist.

Let us return briefly to punk. Many feminist researchers have acknowledged that punk did not reconfigure female power in music and subcultures to the extent that it might have done. Marion Leonard, who has carried out extensive research into the riot grrrl movement, writes this 'whilst embracing the spirit of punk, riot grrrls were aware of how this music genre had excluded girls and women. . . . [P]unk was problematic for female performers who are often considered incidental rather than central to the movement' (1997: 237).

A significant cultural shift in terms of music was the emergence of dance and club culture in the 1980s and beyond. Emerging from the USA but having a profound influence throughout the Western world, dance music heralded the dominance of recorded music over live performance, the rise of the superstar DJ as arbiter of taste and the emergence of new spaces of musical consumption. However, even a cursory glance at much dance and club culture reveals a world where the producers, promoters and DJs are predominantly male with just a handful of women gaining any sort of foothold. Much of women's lack of involvement in the music industry stems from the ways in which cultural consumption is understood, theorized and stratified. Sarah Thornton (1995) has pointed to the ways in which notions of subcultural 'authenticity' are linked to masculinity. In order to have their cultural consumption legitimized and recognized, women have to attempt to fit into masculine patterns. This ensures that women always have to struggle to find a positive model for their own experiences and creativity.

Maria Pini writes about the liberating effects of raving for women and the freedom and friendship that rave culture offers. Pini criticizes Thornton's work on dance culture, asserting that

> her failure to go beyond the levels of production and organization, to say more about other levels of event participation and other experiential sites, amounts to a failure to address the significance of club cultural involvement for the hundreds of thousands of women who regularly participate in dance cultures, and who claim that such participation is central to their lives, their friendships and their identities. (2001: 7)

However, the fact that a woman behind a set of decks remains an unusual sight suggests that this is an area of cultural production that has been naturalized as male. Women feature as fans and as dancers in a space defined and controlled by men.

Laura Mulvey's work on the male gaze is relevant to discussions of women in contemporary pop and dance culture. As Reddington argues, the rise of MTV and the pop video unleashed a new cycle of gender stereotyping and a demand that female performers and musicians conform to hegemonic notions of physical beauty. In the same vein, Sara Cohen argues that in music 'women have been associated with a marginal, decorative or "less creative role". . . . [W]omen's authorship and creativity have been denied, they have been judged on their appearance rather than their musicianship' (2001: 232). Evidence from a wide range of sources produces similar conclusions.

In terms of women and popular music, Madonna is a female performer who has provoked a great deal of response from cultural critics and academics. She has been heralded as a unique female figure because of the control that she exerts over her identity; she is a powerful businesswoman and entrepreneur. Is she a feminist icon? The jury is out, but her presence has sparked a wealth of academic debate ('Madonna studies', as it has come to be known). However, whilst Madonna might maintain tight control of her image, this is still within a paradigm riven with masculinized fantasies about female beauty. As Fran Lloyd argues: '[W]hile Madonna may be able to subvert or control the male gaze, she is still using it and aspects of the patriarchal stereotype to which it belongs' (1993: 40). One notable feature about Madonna and her image is her quest and ability to appear much younger than her now fifty-plus years. This taps into a discourse that demands that women must remain youthful and beautiful if they are to be successful and valued. Female performers continue to be judged primarily for their physical attractiveness rather than their musical talent. One only has to think of the global furore about the *Britain's Got Talent* contestant Susan Boyle to be graphically reminded of this. The YouTube clip of her performance has become the most watched YouTube clip in history to date. The remarkable voice emanating from a dowdy, middle-aged woman provoked a global public debate about whether Boyle should try to alter her physical appearance to conform more actively to acceptable models of femininity or whether she should be 'allowed' to remain her unadorned, natural self – make-up-free, greying hair and unplucked eyebrows. Because she is neither young, nor thin nor heavily made-up, the music industry and consuming public are confused about how to respond to her. The issue of older women in the public eye has also been the subject of controversy outside the musical sphere. In Britain in 2010, there was a scandal at the BBC about the 'putting out to grass' of female newsreaders and presenters who were considered 'too old' to be the acceptable face of the corporation. In 2011, BBC bosses were found guilty of victimizing the female TV presenter Miriam O'Reilly because of her age. Many other female TV presenters, aged forty and above, complained that they were sidelined or axed from television programmes in ways that their (ageing) male counterparts were not.

Film

In film, in spite of enclaves of independence from the studios (see Biskind 1998 on the 1970s) and a wealth of new 'world' cinema, women continue to be scarcely represented in director and production roles. Recall here from chapter 2 the startling statistic that only in 2010 did a woman, Kathryn Bigelow, win the first Oscar for best director. Susan Christopherson blames the underrepresentation of women in the US film and television industry on the culture of networking in these sectors. As she notes:

> These networks have always existed in the project-oriented media entertainment industry but arguably they have become stronger and more important given the uncertainties of industry production and job access. These networks foster and reinforce labor segmentation among women and men, and among ethnic groups, restricting access to job opportunities and careers. (2008: 75)

Christopherson observes that there is a divide in this labour market between those who earn a salary and those in more tenuous or precarious roles. Christopherson cites a report by Hunt for the Writers Guild of America which highlights that film is 'an insular industry that white males have traditionally dominated, where employment opportunities rest squarely on personal networks steeped in gender, race and age' (Hunt 2007: 14). Christopherson notes that women fare slightly better in the television industry than the film industry. However, in film the situation seems even to be deteriorating for women as '[w]omen comprised only 15 percent of all directors, executive producers, producers, writers, cinematographers and editors working on the top grossing films. This is a decline of 2 percent from the 1998 figure' (Christopherson 2008: 90). This is against a backdrop of an industry that often believes itself to be 'diverse', equal and free from the rigid hierarchies of other sectors.

John Caldwell's (2008) recent book on the US film and television industry is also littered with anecdotes and descriptions of entrenched gender divisions. Caldwell also highlights the ageism of

the sector and the burnout of young men in what he describes as
'digital sweatshops'.

This brief survey of advertising, music and film can only lead us to
conclude that women continue to remain marginalized and distanced
from core decision and production roles. We continue to see patterns where 'old boys'' networks dominate, where women are seen
somehow to lack technical and artistic competence and where hegemonic masculinity defines cultural capital and female value. We will
now look at a contemporary case study in detail to examine the subtle
yet ubiquitous ways that discrimination against women manifests
itself in the creative workplace.

The New Media Sector

As we move into the digital age, some have optimistically argued that
owing to the accessibility of new creative technologies, traditional
values and norms about male and female relationships to technology will be discarded and a new era will dawn. As Helen Kennedy
observes:

> The flexibility inherent in new media work has also been hailed for its
> potential to address gender inequalities in this sector (Women's Unit,
> 2000). What is more, the unpaid labour of the knowledge economy
> has been celebrated, for example in Barbrook's (1998) proposition that
> new media knowledge work represents a high-tech gift economy which
> offers a radical alternative to capitalist models. (2009: 179)

She goes on to note that this optimism has frequently been challenged. Not only is the sector unwelcoming for women, it is also a
sector which demands high levels of self-exploitation from the male
workers in this industry. (See Gill and Pratt 2008 for detail about
'precarious labour' in the new economy.)

In terms of technology training and education, women are often felt
to be uninterested in and incapable of developing new media skills
and better suited for caring/support/non-technical roles. The stereotypes about women's lack of aptitude in the use of technology have
been well documented (e.g. Henwood et al. 2000; Wajcman1991).
There are many factors that conspire to limit female participation
in new media, such as the underrepresentation of girls in techno-
logically focused subjects at school and then in further and higher

education and a scarcity of female role models in the 'techy' roles in new media businesses (as well as in creative and decision-making roles). The new media sector provides an example of a new cultural industry where women are likely to encounter barriers because of the male domination of the adolescent training grounds for multimedia, namely computer games and arcades. As with the music industry, childhood experiences appear to have a significant impact on cultural production careers. Computer games continue to be heavily designed and marketed to boys (and men): 'Males create male-centred products, often without realizing it. This creates a vicious circle: women do not see their needs and interests reflected in technological products, so their interests in all things technical does not grow' (Wright 2001). However, even women who do have formal education and training in terms of subjects relevant to the creative and innovative side of new media experience difficulties breaking into creative and decision-making roles. The emphasis on networking in the creative sector works against women. In terms of recruitment practices, there is a tendency for word of mouth recruitment and poaching from rival firms (see Banks and Milestone 2011). This immediately presents a problem in terms of equal opportunities because people tend to be recruited within closed social networks – and this, of course, inhibits diversity. As Rosalind Gill argues:

> The increasing prevalence of this kind of practice for hiring staff or issuing contracts raises grave concerns for equal opportunities – concerns that are extremely difficult to contest or even discuss, because of the lack of transparency in the process. It challenged new media's view of itself as both meritocratic and egalitarian because contracts are bestowed on the basis of informal connections or personal recommendations rather than on the result of open competition. (2002: 83)

Let us examine some interviews with employers and employees of small and micro-businesses involved in new media in Manchester, conducted as part of a research project under the directorship of Julia Owen.[2] These companies specialize in web design, internet marketing, graphic design and games design.

The aim of the research was to examine the extent to which factors such as recruitment strategies, new patterns of working and organizational 'cultures' within new media businesses directly or indirectly

[2] The Emerging Sector Opportunities Programme. Joint funded by the European Social Fund and the Department of Sociology, Manchester Metropolitan University (MMU). Project Director: Julia Owen, Department of Sociology, MMU.

discriminate against women. The research questions were stimulated by results from several earlier projects about Manchester's cultural industries where it became clear that, far from being diverse, many of these businesses were almost entirely populated by educated, white males who managed and determined creative production and undertook decision-making roles. This was against a background where many policy-makers and academics were promoting new cultural industries as open, diverse and inclusive, free from the direct and indirect discrimination inherent in many traditional occupations and sectors. The fact that new media and cultural industries are often anything but beacons of good practice in terms of supporting a diverse workforce is echoed in the findings of Gill (2002) and also Angela McRobbie (2002) about similar types of businesses:

> In the cultural sector, with its emphasis on the creative and expressive, it might be imagined that this could be the right place for social minorities to succeed and for women to achieve equal participation. However it seems possible that quite the opposite is happening. What we see – in as much as it is possible to track these developments – is the emergence of working practices which reproduce older patterns of marginalization (of women and people from different ethnic backgrounds), while also disallowing any space or time for such issues to reach articulation. (McRobbie 2002: 523)

This is an important observation, and nearly a decade later there seems little evidence that cultural industries are an exemplar of equality in practice.

The myth of flexibility in new media companies

One of the most dominant discourses relating to new media companies and creative industries in general is concerned with 'flexibility'. There is a perception that because new media companies do not operate within traditional working hours of '9 to 5' and because technology enables workers to be based at home, this is the key to opening up opportunities for women. However, sector business agencies and creative industries practitioners increasingly extol employee commitment to a visible (i.e. workplace-based) long hours culture and informal but relatively closed networks. Within the industry the notion of 'flexibility' is perceived in significantly different ways to the way the term is conceived of externally. For the workers in new media companies, 'flexibility' is often translated into factors such as a relaxed dress code, being able to listen to music at work, being

able to start work late and, of course, having a great degree of creative freedom. In exchange for this 'freedom', workers are expected to
put the needs of their employers before everything else, as this male
manager of a web design company expresses:

> If a job is happening very, very short term and we need to get stuff out
> of the door, people come in Saturday and Sundays unpaid and do the
> work to finish them. One of my staff a few weeks ago called me up at
> 10.30 in the morning and said like I've got an awful hangover, I can't
> come in to work today and I said fine, it's not a problem to me as long
> as it doesn't compromise the project that we're doing, and that's how
> we work.

The perceived flexibility of the sector is particularly challenging
to women with dependants – the hours are prohibitive, and working
from home is often frowned upon and is perceived to militate against
sustaining the tightly knit teams that the sector produces and so
reveres. As a male manager of a web design company explained,
he had developed a contract that 'excludes the people from the
European directive on the maximum working week'. In her research
into employment in the high-technology sector in the South East
of England (of which the workforce was 90 per cent male), Doreen
Massey (1994) found that a recurring comment by the men interviewed was that 'the boundary between work and play disappears'.
In response to this, Massey asks, 'who does the domestic labour . . .
who goes to the launderette?' Massey argues that 'flexibility' is very
often someone else's constraint; she asks who services these workers
so they are able to blur work and leisure as if there were nothing else
more mundane in between.

This version of 'flexibility' has been constructed to signify 'commitment'. Crucially, for women, this flexible/committed dualism
extends outside of the formal confines of the spaces and places of
work. Going out and networking in social spaces is defined as crucial
to the sector – an owner-manager from a graphic design and web
promotion company spoke about the importance of a club aimed at
workers in the creative sector: 'Basically it's a members-only club,
fully licensed, open to four in the morning.' In an earlier research
project about women workers in Manchester's music industry
(Richards and Milestone 2000), it was revealed that many women
distanced themselves from networking or were actively excluded
from the kinds of laddish drinking cultures identified by Nixon
(2003) and Gregory (2009) in the cultural industries.

The long hours culture and masculinity

A striking and recurrent feature of many new media companies is the 'long hours culture' that prevails. In research into Manchester's new media sector it was found that people typically start work around 10 a.m. and work late into the evening. There are many accounts of people working through the night on occasion to meet deadlines. According to Diane Perrons, there are four main reasons why people work long hours in this new media sector: 'the unpredictable nature and flow of the work; uncertainty associated with business start up; the need to continually update skills and knowledge; and the intrinsic satisfaction derived from the work itself' (2003: 77). Yet there is nothing inherent in the work that requires working these long and unhealthy hours, and the need to do so is never attributed to being the result of bad time management and planning or the taking on of insufficient staff to meet demand.

This long hours culture is promoted as a 'natural' aspect of the work and it was people's willingness to work these hours that was perceived as a valuable quality in research on new media companies in Manchester. The 'ability' to work long hours was strongly characterized as a masculine trait and there was much bravado-laden discourse about the 'stamina', 'commitment' and 'discipline' required to survive the intensity and pressure. This seems to suggest that a new form of masculinity is emerging in this new 'weightless' world of work. O'Connor identifies some key elements of cultural industries that reveal high levels of self-exploitation taking place:

> [T]he nature of creative work involves a difficult set of working conditions, long hours for little or no money, or to the de-unionised, individualised responsibility for work, pensions, unemployment and health benefits; or the unequal power relations when it comes to negotiating IP [intellectual property] rights on which they are supposed to thrive; or the constant struggle against de-skilling, usually in the face of new technologies. (2007: 52)

This produces a number of problems for the mainly male workforce of the technical enclaves of the cultural industries and reminds us that gender stereotypes can also be restrictive and dangerous for men.

Femininity at work

A strong pattern emerged in Owen's research findings of ways in which women were expected, by their male colleagues, to adopt traditionalized female roles. These expectations were particularly high in times of crisis, such as periods close to deadlines, when women would be expected to 'skivvy', 'mop up' and utilize their communication skills to deal with tense negotiations with clients (see Owen and Milestone 2005). These perceived 'naturally feminine' traits overshadowed other more highly valued creative and technical skills that the women often also had. When male managers of businesses with few or no women were questioned about why women were noticeably absent and whether strategies to recruit more women had been employed, there was a recurring discourse about the sort of positive contribution that women could bring to an organization which centred on ways in which women could potentially 'balance' an organization because of their 'softness' and 'sensitivity'. A male manager of an internet advertising company spoke of women's skills squarely in these terms: 'Certainly for the sales side I would almost definitely want a girl to do the ringing up or somebody that sounds youthful.' The possibility that a woman might be employed in the creative/innovative/technical production aspects of a new media company is not considered. Women are expected to take on supportive roles, customer-facing roles, but not the creative roles that are deemed to be highly skilled and high in status.

Recruitment practices and the 'ideal type' of new media worker

The owners and managers of many of the new media companies interviewed had very specific ideas about the types of people they liked to work with. There was a culture of managers 'recruiting in their own image' and favouring 'people who will fit in', 'people who are up for a laugh'. This ideal type was frequently defined in a much masculinized way, as clearly conveyed in the sentiments expressed by the manager of a company that designs games for mobile phones: 'I have a guy who works for us, he is as thin as a rake, never eats, appears to exist on black coffee, Red Bull and amphetamines and can survive on three or four hours' sleep a night. It is a sort of fire and energy they have which is crucial to the projects and our business.' Similarly the owner/manager of a web design company commented that 'these guys are like athletes, at the peak of their mental capabilities, driven by doing something that has not been done before and being part of something new and big.'

In Elly Tams' research on creative industries in Sheffield (UK), she analysed local creative industry policy documents and uncovered a discourse which intrinsically linked creativity to masculine entrepreneurialism, which 'conjures up images of scientists, inventors and computer "whiz kids", people who are involved in a very specific type of creativity, which can easily be translated into products and ideas of measurable, marketable value' (2002: 395). Drawing on the work of Joan Acker (1992), Tams strongly refutes the notion that the concept of the ideal worker is gender-neutral. Tams also found that the notion of commitment relies heavily on a dedication to a culture of long hours. She also argues that 'passion', an integral quality of the new creative entrepreneur, is distinctly positioned as something that men have in abundance but women do not. In Owen's research in Manchester, the ideal-type new media worker was expected to display new forms of machismo which relied on 'fire and energy', 'adrenaline', 'stamina' and 'being obsessively driven'. Women, on the other hand, were penalized for being 'too balanced' and able to 'multi-task' (see Owen and Milestone 2005). This ideal 'type' has been defined as masculine in other parts of the cultural industries too. McRobbie's research on the British fashion industry found that in both the fashion media and in art college culture '[t]he fashion star has an identity and a role more comfortably aspired to and assumed, it seems, by a boy' (1998: 70). Even in a traditionally female-dominated sector such as fashion, it is the men who are deemed to have all the rare talent.

This case study of the new media sector in a large UK city reveals a number of often subtle but pervasive attitudes and working practices that make it difficult for women to gain employment in frontline creative new media roles. Long-standing, apparently out of use, stereotypes about men and women's abilities are clearly there for all to see. A huge challenge, it appears, is that this moment also brings about a greater diversity of the employees of this industry. In the words of Gill (2002), new media is a sector that narrates itself as being 'cool, creative and egalitarian'. However, the egalitarian aspect is currently little more than lip service.

Conclusion

In this chapter, we have looked at an overview of case studies from a range of cultural industries. We briefly surveyed the contemporary state of the examples used in the previous chapter – advertising, music and film – and also looked at more recently emerging cultural industries from the new media and club culture. In all of these cases, the evidence points to a persistence of the culturally constructed ideas that inhibited women's validity as cultural producers in the 1950s through to the 1970s. Whilst there are now some women in frontline production roles, they are the exception rather than the rule. The cultural barriers that seem to persist are connected with the artistic genius as a culturally defined masculine individual. The 'ideal type'of creative worker, and indeed the whole notion of a 'creative class', is masculinized – a privileged lifestyle that is not open to all. There are prejudiced ideas about women's technological ineptitude that inhibit women from roles such as games design, DJing and film directing. Even the electric guitar has been inextricably linked to men (see Bayton 1997). There are also physical barriers where women are excluded from the 'locker room' or where they do not have the capacity to engage in the long hours work and leisure cultures of the cultural industries. We see a persistence of the male gaze where women are valued for their beauty, which is evident from a cursory survey of the music or advertising industries. This is puzzling given the apparently huge strides made in terms of women's rights in the workplace, education, and so on.

A recurring observation from both feminist researchers and women within the cultural industries is that it is a problem that dare not speak its name. There is rhetoric of meritocracy based on the idea that everyone starts off from a level playing field. However, the barriers and inequalities still persist for women.

Critics who are attempting to explain this inequality point to a discrediting or dismantling of feminism. It has long been debated and acknowledged that there is a worrying backlash (e.g. Faludi 1991) against feminism and a rise of 'new lad'-fuelled 'retro-sexism' (Whelehan 2000). More recently, writers including Gill (2007) and McRobbie (2008) have analysed popular culture and cultural work and observed a pervasive and insidious undermining and lampooning of feminism in post-feminist discourses. Women are constantly told that they have freedom and equality. Any failures of women's advancement are individualized rather than blamed on the structures and institutions of late modern society. There are few spaces for dissent and women are afraid to complain about or even acknowledge their oppression. Let us recall a comment made by a woman in the advertising industry in Debbie Klein's work: 'It's got worse because everyone thinks it's got better.' There is a strong misconception that gender equality has been achieved rather than it being 'work in progress'.

The rhetoric and myths circulating in popular culture seek to promote an ideology of gender equality. However, the hard facts contradict these claims. In addition to the lack of value and recognition of women's cultural work, women are denied status and financial reward. As Raewyn Connell reminds us: 'Men gain a dividend from patriarchy in terms of honour, prestige and the right to command. They also gain a material dividend. In the rich capitalist countries, men's average incomes are approximately double women's average incomes' (2004: 43). Women earn significantly less than men in all areas of work – including cultural work, of course. The ramifications of this are enormous.

PART II

Representation, Gender and Popular Culture

Introduction to Part II

In this part, we turn our focus onto the issue of representation in popular culture, examining how women and men are portrayed in a wide range of media, including men's and women's magazines, television programmes, cinema films and newspapers. Chapters are organized along gender lines, with chapter 4 exploring representations of women and chapter 5 focusing on representations of men. Both chapters are structured around three major themes which continue to dominate gender images, notably (a) sex(uality) and relationships, (b) the body and physical appearance. and (c) work and home. In the case of women, we have added a fourth theme of sexuality and morality, as this continues to be an important topic in the representation of femininity.

The common themes allow us to make comparisons across the two chapters to draw out similarities and differences in popular-cultural images of women and men. For instance, while the topic of sex(uality) and relationships is always bound up with commitment and romance when discussed in relation to women, media texts about and for men tend to focus on sexual pleasure and conquest. Both men and women are required to 'look good' in contemporary culture, but women are still more commonly defined through and reduced to their physical appearance.

Overall we find common historical trends of change and continuity in the representation of men and women. Both masculinities and femininities have diversified since the post-war period and are now offering several types and identities. The 'new femininity' and the 'new man' are testament to this. However, there has also been a backlash reaction as representations of men and women have, to some degree, returned to more essentialist and traditional notions of femininity and masculinity which insist on gender differences being 'natural'. These latter developments are bound up with a variety of discourses, from post-feminism to the new lad, and illustrate that historical change is neither linear nor simply a matter of progress towards more plural identities, liberal attitudes and a reduction of gender difference and inequality. Rather, a picture of contradictory and piecemeal change emerges in the representation of men and women in popular culture.

4

Representing Women

Romance, Sexuality and Relationships

Popular culture has a history of representing women as centrally concerned with and in need of love, romance and relationship. Whilst women are increasingly acknowledged to possess an active sexuality and wanting to experience sexual pleasure, often a dichotomy continues to be maintained in which men's goal in life is sex and women's aims are relationships and commitment. We can trace historical continuities and changes throughout different aspects of popular culture.

Angela McRobbie's (2000) study of popular British teenage magazine *Jackie*, published between 1964 and 1993, suggests that such magazines promote an overarching ideology of teenage femininity which is very conservative and traditional. Teenage femininity revolves around two key issues: how to get a boyfriend and how to look good. *Jackie* frames getting a boyfriend as very serious and important: romance is the essence and meaning of life for girls. While boys are shown to be doing things, e.g. playing football, and aiming for goals, e.g. being a racing driver, girls are not shown to be thinking about career success, job satisfaction or financial independence. All they want is a man. This reinforces conventional ideologies about femininity as focused on the domestic and personal and is mirrored in women's magazines, where sexual relationships and marriage are portrayed as the key goal and source of happiness (Ballaster et al. 1991). *Jackie* portrays girls' quest for romance as a response to the male quest for sex; this directly confirms the ideology of gender difference, which stipulates that men want sex and women want relationships and commitment. Getting a boyfriend is only the beginning of romance: girls' emotional lives are defined through a series of romantic moments which culminate in marriage proposal and the wedding day. This directly feeds the conventional ideology of femininity, which is necessarily heterosexual and frames marriage and a family as life-goals. In this traditional, gendered world, boys and men can only be related to as potential romantic objects, not as friends. This ideology of teenage femininity is also conservative in that it encourages girls with problems of not quite 'measuring up' to the standards set, e.g. in terms of looks or the ability to attract boys, to conform and simply make more of an effort, e.g. to beautify themselves. McRobbie (2000) argues that this ideology of teenage femininity derives its power from three factors. Firstly, it fits neatly with, and prepares girls for, the ideology of adult femininity perpetuated in women's magazines (Ballaster et al. 1991). Secondly, readers are encouraged to consent to ideologies, but because magazines are consumed in leisure time and with pleasure, their ideological nature is difficult to recognize for readers. Thirdly, the ideology of teenage femininity is promoted across many socio-cultural sites other than teenage magazines, such as the education system, the family or other genres of popular culture. Of course we cannot assume that readers simply buy into ideologies; however, their reinforcement across different cultural sites makes them difficult to resist.

Researching teenage magazines in the mid- and late 1990s, McRobbie (1997) suggests that there have been considerable changes in the representation of femininity. There has been a shift towards a 'new femininity' which is more socially and sexually assertive, confident, aspirational and fun-seeking. It encourages girls to seek success and pleasure; to have a good time with girl friends; to enjoy sex within and outside relationships; to go out and get drunk; or to go shopping. This leads girls away from the traditional femininity of being 'ladylike' and instead promotes the idea that they should know what they want and go for it. This is especially the case for sexuality, as the new femininity is above all premised on a 'new sexuality', which can be seen, for example, in the explosion of talk about sex in contemporary teenage magazines (Tincknell et al. 2003). The new femininity gives girls the licence to engage in practices and display attitudes previously reserved for men. McRobbie (2000) explains this shift through two factors. Firstly, the emergence of AIDS, a mostly sexually transmitted disease, has necessitated a more explicit sexual culture in which sex and sexuality are openly talked about to provide information about infection and prevention of the disease. Secondly, the new sexuality has been ushered in by feminism and its insistence on gender equality. However, this new femininity is not displacing conventional femininity. McRobbie herself maintains that teenage magazines continue to reinforce a conventional femininity in many ways: for example, they continue to emphasize the importance of relationships and physical beauty and reinforce heterosexuality as the norm; but they now offer an alternative femininity marked by assertiveness, freedom and pleasure which has become a viable choice for girls. Hence femininity is diversifying in popular culture, providing girls with a wider range of identities.

Teenage magazines are, of course, only one, albeit an important, aspect of popular culture. Many cultural texts are very critical of the new femininity which McRobbie identifies. For example, the television programme *Ladette to Lady*, which has become very popular since its first airing on ITV in 2005, with several series broadcast in the UK, the US and elsewhere, revolves around the premise to teach women who 'behave like men' to become more feminine. Behaviours such as having casual sex, displaying no manners or drinking excessively are identified as masculine and therefore abnormal and inappropriate for females. Similarly, conservative newspapers, which dominate the market in the UK, label such women as unfeminine by describing them as 'ladettes', a linguistic derivative of the male 'lad' which constructs women as manly (Whelehan 2000) and by proclaiming the 'death of femininity' (Taylor and Courtenay-Smith 2006) in headlines of articles focusing on female drinking. Moreover, many UK newspapers continue to represent women whose behaviour infringes the norms of conventional femininity as deviant and problematic. Debates around teenage pregnancy, abortion, binge drinking or drug taking illustrate this clearly: girls who have casual sex or drink to excess are criticized as behaving deviantly and irresponsibly. Binge drinking is a popular-cultural term which refers to the sessional consumption of large quantities of alcohol in a relatively short space of time, where drinking is an end in itself and getting drunk is often the intended outcome (Lyons et al. 2006). In the UK, binge drinking is a common cultural phenomenon which large numbers of people across socio-economic, age and gender backgrounds engage in (Measham and Brain 2005). It is associated with loudness, excess, pleasure, rudeness and aggression, which means that it infringes both conventional femininity – marked by moderation, quietness, being nice – and generally held social norms of behaviour. Female binge drinkers are classed as worse, as more deviant and more of a problem, than their male counterparts because they are 'double deviants' (Heidensohn 1985). An article in the *Daily Mail*, the UK's second biggest-selling daily newspaper, illustrates this clearly as female drunkenness is framed as particularly disturbing: 'They are so drunk they can barely stand. Everywhere they tread, there are pools of vomit or broken glass. Shouting, screaming teenagers tramp the streets throughout the early hours, and fights start to break out beneath the blinking neon lights of an otherwise empty city. And, *most disturbingly*, virtually all of this binge-drinking army are women' (Harris 2005, emphasis added). Moreover, women who socialize and drink excessively are criticized much more than men: for example, for endangering the 'health of the nation' by possibly damaging their reproductive organs (Day et al. 1994) or for delaying commitment to family life: 'Figures released yesterday reveal an epidemic of binge drinking that experts put down to the low cost and availability of alcohol, and the tendency for women to have families later in life. . . . Experts also say women who now have greater disposable incomes are *putting the good life before family life*' (Grant 2006, emphasis added). Women who delay settling down and having children are portrayed as selfish here for putting their own desires and pleasures first and for enjoying their financial means. An equivalent critique of men – that their socializing, drinking and the delaying of fatherhood are selfish – is non-existent and unthinkable. This is because being sensible, family-orientated and selfless are aspects of conventional, emphasized femininity and therefore expected of women, but not of men. We can see in these examples that the tendency of the media, and wider culture, to hold women more responsible for their behaviour than men continues, despite girls and women increasingly claiming and engaging in traditionally masculine behaviours (Hey 1986; Tincknell et al. 2003). From a feminist point of view the intense critique of women represents an exercise in patriarchal control: if women do not conform to behaviours prescribed as appropriate by emphasized femininity, then they will be symbolically punished. This symbolic punishment or 'keeping in line' of women is not uncommon and is to some extent grounded in the target audience of the media. Estella Tincknell et al. (2003) point out that while media targeted at female consumers, such as girls' and women's magazines, promote a new femininity, media targeted at general audiences, such as newspapers, present this new femininity as a problem and threat. Looking across popular culture, it seems that the new femininity remains deeply contested.

Despite the new femininity, romance, relationships and men remain central issues. Diane Negra (2009) has analysed the ways in which popular-cultural representations of women strongly revolve around time and segment women's lives into distinct stages. These are marked by normative milestones which women should achieve: finding a man, getting married and having children. Time is generally framed as a threat and being feminine means living in a state of crisis, trying to combat the problems associated with advancing time and an ageing body, such as faltering looks or the biological clock which sets limits on childbearing. These threats are related to a larger, overarching danger: the spectre of being single. Singledom intensifies these threats as women are presented as running out of time to achieve the things that matter, namely getting married and having children. Moreover, it spells failure as the normative stages of the female lifecycle have not been achieved. The assumption that all single women are desperate to be in a relationship reinforces the centrality of finding a man in women's lives. These ideas are reinforced across popular culture in various ways. Mainstream cinema, for example, has produced a plethora of romantic comedies where the plot revolves around single women desperate to find a man, such as *Bridget Jones's Diary* (2001) or *The Wedding Planner* (2001). Television reality series such as the American *#1 Single* or the British *Mr Right* focus on single women attempting to find a man to settle down with. Drama series such as *Sex and the City* – which is progressive in centring on women's lives and depicting them as intelligent, witty human beings with good careers, financial independence and a close circle of friends – ultimately end up portraying love, romance and lasting relationships as the source of meaning and happiness in a woman's life. In *Sex and the City*, both the TV series and the two movies (2008, 2010), this is exemplified in the protagonists' search for 'Mr Right'.

Women's magazines do increasingly acknowledge that women desire and manage careers, financial independence, their own homes and circles of friends, but all of these always remain secondary to romantic relationships (Ballaster et al. 1991). Relationships, as a code-word for men, are the key issue which is endlessly analysed and takes up a large amount of space by cropping up across all sections, from problem pages to sex advice, from human interest stories to special features (Ballaster et al. 1991). And indeed even teenage magazines, which promote the new femininity and endorse sexuality outside relationships, continue to present permanent romance and relationships as the ideal (Tincknell et al. 2003).

Self-help literature, which has proliferated enormously since the 1980s, centres on several areas of life where it is deemed possible for individuals to improve their conditions. Some of the most popular subjects are careers and work success, self-esteem and assertiveness, and sexuality and relationships (Simonds 1992). Self-help literature is a mostly female genre, especially when it takes the form of relationship and sex advice, instructing women on how to either find or maintain relationships. Hence alongside the new femininity, the ideology of romance and the centrality of romantic relationships to femininity continue to thrive. This is highly ideological in that it reinforces heterosexuality, with its milestones of wedding, marriage, pregnancy and childrearing. Moreover, it essentializes women as a natural species driven by inherent, uniform needs and desires, as sharing a 'women's world' (Ballaster et al. 1991: 129). The ideology of romance reinforces a limited, dependent femininity. Femininity remains dependent on male opinion and approval because being able to attract a man as a romantic object and partner is central to 'normal' femininity (Tincknell et al. 2003). Women's self-identities remain relational in the sense of being tied to and defined by others, most notably men and children, in their capacities as lovers, partners, wives or mothers. This contributes to the maintenance of a culture in which autonomous and full selfhood is not immediately or easily available to women (Simonds 1992).

The new independent, self-consciously sexy and fun femininity identified by McRobbie (1997) is certainly on offer in popular culture, but it appears to be countered by the persistence of conventional notions of femininity centred on romance. Femininity has diversified; there are multiple femininities on offer today. But two points have to be raised. Firstly, it is noticeable that McRobbie identifies the new and free femininity in teenage magazines. This raises the question whether new behaviours have become acceptable for women of all ages or only for younger women, where they can be framed as part of a rebellious phase in life. Is romance no longer the main goal, or has it simply been put back to a later stage in life, allowing younger females to experiment openly with sex, drink and drugs, as long as they eventually come back into the conventional fold and opt for long-term relationships and settling down? Ballaster et al.'s (1991) research suggests that glossy women's magazines such as *Cosmopolitan*, which are aimed at younger, professional women, mirror the teenage magazine's new femininity by endorsing the figure of the free, young, single woman who enjoys her freedom by going out with friends, engaging in consumption and having sexual encounters. However, being single is always framed as a temporary condition and long-term romantic relationships are emphasized as the most fulfilling context for sexual expression and, ultimately, for life.

Secondly, Negra (2009) suggests that since the 1990s, popular culture has been saturated with post-feminist themes and debates which reinforce conservative and conventional norms of femininity as 'the ultimate "best choices" in women's lives' (Negra 2009: 4). This post-feminism asserts that feminism has misled women into thinking they can 'have it all' and imposed desires and life choices – e.g. having careers, settling down late in life, being socially and financially independent – which are ultimately against their 'feminine nature' and make them unhappy. The post-feminist narrative promises to counter this by encouraging women to 'come home', which literally means bringing women back to a conventional femininity where they find fulfilment in domesticity, marriage and children. Negra identifies these post-feminist themes in a range of popular cultures, from chick lit and films to advertising. Of course, the post-feminist vision of femininity is just as socially constructed as other types of femininity, but by presenting itself as 'natural', post-feminist femininity denies the structural and historical processes which underlie its formation (Skeggs 2001). The recourse which post-feminism takes to very old, conventional, traditional characteristics and values of femininity arguably helps its claims to represent a return to 'nature', even though in reality we witness merely a return to earlier ways of thinking about femininity. Returning to our discussion about the diversification of femininity, it seems that the emergence of a freer femininity insisting on equal rights, opportunities and pleasure seeking is coupled with a return to and strengthening of conventional femininity across popular culture. Hence women are given more options of identity, but at the same time the conventional feminine identity is often framed as the most valid, appropriate and good one.

The Body and Physical Appearance: 'Looking Good'

Women in popular culture have always been closely associated with and scrutinized in terms of their physical appearance, for example the size and shape of their bodies, their hair, the age of their appearance or the condition of their skin. Women are defined by their physical appearance in a way that is simply not the case for men. A key theme in teenage and women's magazines is how to look good (Ballaster et al. 1991; McRobbie 2000; Tincknell et al. 2003). A large proportion of each edition is taken up by fashion, cosmetics and beauty products. The beauty ideal is very narrow: girls should be small, thin, have silky hair and be conventionally pretty. Girls and women are encouraged to compensate for natural deficiencies in their appearance through cosmetics and fashion in order to measure up to the ideal standards. There is a paradox, though: while the use of fashion and cosmetics is advised, 'natural' beauty is proclaimed the ideal and what men want (McRobbie 2000). Girls are told to self-improve, but in moderation, to achieve a 'natural' look – in effect they are told to go along with what men, presumably, want. The amount of effort which this beautification entails is presented as worth it, as time well spent, because getting a boyfriend or husband is the ultimate quest in life. Ultimately, 'looking good' is a case of 'looking good for men', which intricately connects physical appearance back to romance. The ways in which teenage and women's magazines constantly seek male approval of female beauty sits uneasily with and undermines any messages about a new femininity marked by confidence and independence (Tincknell et al. 2003).

As physical appearance continues to be of crucial importance to femininity, there has been a widespread rise in cosmetic surgery, including procedures such as breast enlargement, lifting and reduction; liposuction; rhinoplasty; face lifts; dental veneers; and even vaginal surgery (Tebbel 2000). Advertising for cosmetic surgery allows us to explore some of the ideological consequences of 'looking good' for femininity, such as stereotyping and the nature of the beauty ideal. The classified adverts sections at the back of many women's magazines are a key space where clinics offering a range of cosmetic surgical procedures advertise (Image 1).

Advertising is an industry rife with stereotypes, including gender stereotypes (Lindner 2004). The 'dumb blonde' is a popular female stereotype with a long history (Greenwood and Isbell 2002). The dumb blonde is characterized by her hair colour, sexuality and lack of intellect (Perkins 1997). She is blonde (usually peroxide rather than natural), sexually attractive in conventional and obvious ways (e.g. slim, young, tanned, big breasts, long hair), possesses a voracious sexuality but is incredibly stupid. This stereotype is commonly constructed through blonde hair, slim bodies, large and visible breasts or cleavage, as well as skimpy, figure-hugging clothes which sexually display the body. Cosmetic surgery adverts imply that models desire and obtain 'better' bodies, especially bigger breasts, which sums up their aspirations and reinforces the message about limited intellect.

Gender stereotypes are still widespread across popular culture. For example, dumb blonde jokes continue to be told, illustrated in cartoons and laughed about (Greenwood and Isbell 2002). Moreover, the stereotype of the dumb blonde features in television soap

Image 1   Selection of classified advertisements in *Marie Claire*, May 2011.
(Photograph: Anneke Meyer)

operas such as the British *Hollyoaks* (character Carmel McQueen),
television drama series such as the American *Baywatch* (Pamela
Andersen as C.J. Parker and Erika Eleniak as Shauni McClain) and
Hollywood films (e.g. Reese Witherspoon as Elle Woods in *Legally
Blonde*). Media celebrities, such as 'It girl' and model Paris Hilton,
ex-glamour model Jordan or ex-Big Brother contestant Chantelle
Houghton are portrayed as dumb blondes but also actively model
themselves in this way. In the post-feminist decades since the 1990s,
stereotypes of women have resurged, reviving essentialist 'truths'
about women (Negra 2009). The twist is that these stereotypes are
now perpetuated by women as well as men, often in 'ironic' ways.
In some cosmetic surgery adverts, for example, the choice of model
can be read as humorous because it conforms so closely to the stereotype that it almost becomes a parody of itself. Stereotypes are also
presented as instances of free speech, constituting a freeing of oneself
from the 'political correctness' engendered by a bunch of humour-
less and quarrelsome feminists (Negra 2009). All of this does not
make stereotypes any more acceptable or less derogatory; in fact, it

enhances their ideological effectiveness by showing (limited) awareness of their faults and pre-empting critique.

Gender stereotypes are highly ideological in nature. The figure of
the dumb blonde reproduces several gender ideologies, such as the
feminine beauty ideal being characterized by big breasts, long hair,
flawless skin, wearing make-up, slimness and youth (Bartky 1990).
Jean Kilbourne (2003) has argued that it is thinness above all which
is valued as girls and women are constantly encouraged to reduce
their physical size and be(come) small and thin. The stereotype of the
dumb blonde also reproduces gender ideologies by defining women
through their appearance and bodies rather than their occupations
or achievements. A woman might have a successful career, but this
does not construct her feminine identity, which is largely based on
looks (Kilbourne 2003). This is linked to another aspect of gender
ideology which presents women as the emotional rather than cognitive sex and therefore intellectually limited in comparison to men.
Taken together, this gender ideology constructs femininity as inferior
to masculinity, which always inhabits the opposite domain; women
have beauty but men have character, women look good but men
have careers, women are in tune with their emotions but men have
the brains. This highlights that stereotypes such as the dumb blonde
are also ideological in the sense of serving those in power, who, in a
patriarchal society, are men. By defining women via their appearance
and making them look unintelligent, these stereotypes reaffirm men's
intellectual superiority and legitimize their dominance.

Stereotypes such as the dumb blonde are also ideological in that
they hide the truth. For example, cosmetic surgery is on the rise,
and this needs sociological investigation and explanation. But the
cause is not a rise in the number of 'dumb blondes' who simply opt
for surgical make-overs, such as breast enlargement or liposuction,
whenever they can afford to. One of several factors driving the rise
in cosmetic surgery concerns women feeling compelled to live up to
beauty regimes (Kilbourne 2003; Tebbel 2000). The beauty ideals
of contemporary culture have become increasingly unrealistic and
unachievable in a 'natural' way while costs for surgical procedures
have decreased (Bartky 1990). In popular culture there is a constant
theme of women improving their looks and staying youthful by off-
setting the impact of the ageing process through various measures,
such as dieting, clothes, cosmetics, hairstyles, exercise, botox injec-
tions and cosmetic surgery (Negra 2009). This trend can be observed
across popular culture: for example, in advertisements for anti-aging
products, celebrity trends such as fashion diets or personal trainers,

or the continued emphasis and practical instructions on 'how to look good' across all types of women's magazines (Ballaster et al. 1991) and the explosion of television make-over programmes designed to make individuals – mostly but not exclusively women – look 'better' in the sense of conforming to conventional beauty standards, which inevitably means slimmer, younger, more expensive clothes, whiter and straighter teeth, fewer wrinkles, tighter stomachs and firmer breasts. While some of these programmes, such as *What Not to Wear*, *How to Look Good Naked* and *Snog Marry Avoid?*, are limited to non-surgical measures, many others, such as *10 Years Younger* or *The Swan*, do include surgical procedures, most commonly liposuction, breast enlargement or lifting, face lifts and dental surgery. These programmes are deeply moralistic and harsh, castigating individuals for failing to maintain ideal looks and graphically parading their shortcomings to the audience with close-up and near-nude shots. All these developments suggest that, historically speaking, the pressure on women to look good has, if anything, intensified and the image of ideal feminine beauty has become even more narrow. The pressure has been extended to men as well, because in the late modern era focused on aesthetics, self-identity has become increasingly based on appearance (Roberts 2007). However, Martin Roberts (2007) notes that the requirement to look good does not hold quite the same power over men as women. So, for example, as shows like *What Not to Wear* are extended to men, male subjects reveal themselves to be more resistant than female subjects to fashion rules and advice given by the presenters. Male subjects often adopt a joking, less serious attitude. These responses are more difficult for women, for whom physical appearance is too high a stake to be joked about.

Negra (2009) points out that pressures to look good have not only been extended to men but also to groups of women previously thought of as asexual, such as mothers or older women. This is a double-edged sword. These women are no longer considered beyond the pale of attraction, but as a consequence of this, they, too, face the pressures to conform to a certain look. This look is essentially a young, 'girlish' look, as femininity and feminine beauty are associated with youth (Wearing 2007). Hence we see mothers desperate to return to pre-pregnancy bodies as soon as possible and older women baring it all on make-over shows. Popular culture is obsessed with youth, especially as far as women are concerned, yet age has increasingly become a topic. Make-over shows express this trend most glaringly. The popular *10 Years Younger* centres on middle-aged and older participants and aims to make them look younger. Ageing is treated as a pathology which can be cured by making the right lifestyle and consumer choices regarding diet, exercise, cosmetics, hairstyles, clothes, teeth, skin condition and body shape (Wearing 2007). These consumer choices are guided by 'experts' and include various non-surgical and surgical procedures. As youth is framed as a matter of consumer choice, it becomes an individual responsibility. Programmes like *10 Years Younger* shame their participants as individuals who have morally failed to maximize the appearance of their bodies (Wearing 2007). Sadie Wearing (2007) has pointed out that discourses about age and youth are intricately linked to femininity. Youth is central to conventional notions of feminine beauty and indeed to femininity itself, because femininity is so defined by physical appearance. Hence to be appropriately feminine, one has to be, if not young, then at least youthful. The conflation of youth and femininity becomes very apparent in make-over programmes like *10 Years Younger* where the make-over essentially consists of making women appear more conventionally feminine. Any 'masculine' clothes, hairstyles or behaviours are challenged and removed as women are turned into girls.

For women of all ages, and to a lesser extent for men, the stakes of looking good have been raised in the last decade as new surgical and non-surgical procedures have been invented and become more affordable. For example, botox and face lifts have added wrinkle-free skin to the list of desirable features, while tummy tucks and liposuction have made flat stomachs a must. But just as teenage magazines advise girls that their make-up should look natural because men do not like obviously 'made-up' girls (McRobbie 2000), so adult women are faced with popular-cultural norms which oblige them to conform to conventional beauty ideals through a variety of regimes and actions yet to 'efface the signs of their own labour' (Negra 2009: 126). Women who do not manage to do this, and where the effort or procedure of beautification shows, are criticized. For example, older women who wear clothes strongly associated with youth, e.g. miniskirts or leggings, are seen as growing old disgracefully or as 'tarty', while those whose faces show signs of face-lift surgery or botox, e.g. tight skin or limited muscle movement, are described as fake because they are not in line with their 'natural' age (Wearing 2007). This is, of course, contradictory and means that women are put in an impossible position of having to look young, yet being criticized when they obviously try to do so. This critique is linked to the deeply classed notion of genuinely passing for something. Middle-class notions of taste and style are marked by understatement and effortlessness, which means that any immediately apparent signs of making the body look more youthful are classed as cheap, fake and inappropriate (Skeggs 1997; Wearing 2007). As a consequence, middle-class women, who are more familiar with these ideals and less likely to need intensive intervention because of their affluent lifestyles leaving fewer marks on the body, are less likely to fall into the trap than are working-class women.

To return to our initial argument, gender ideologies around beauty ideals are one factor driving women into cosmetic surgery, and advertising is one aspect of popular culture which reinforces these ideals and creates pressures for women to look a certain way. Yet advertising is ideological in that it hides this fact. Of course it can be argued that only certain women are targeted by cosmetic surgery adverts and that many women will not identify themselves with the stereotype of the dumb blonde. But Judith Williamson (1978) has shown that ideologies in advertising work by making viewers participate in the structures of meaning which have been set up. Even those female viewers who recoil in disgust at the type of woman who has her breasts enlarged are decoding the meanings and messages 'correctly': that is, in line with dominant gender ideologies. Moreover, these reactions reinforce the cultural double standards regarding anti-ageing regimes in general and cosmetic surgery in particular, which maintain youth as a central requirement of beauty yet criticize those who defy age in this way as disingenuous (Wearing 2007). As youth is especially central to conventional notions of feminine beauty, it is mostly women who are affected by these double standards. While only a small group of women may actually be targeted by cosmetic surgery adverts as potential consumers, the stereotype of the dumb blonde draws on and reinforces wider aspects of traditional femininity, such as women as 'naturally' emotional rather than intellectual.

Women at Work and at Home

The areas of work and the domestic have long been central to women's positions and representations in society. Conventional ideology of gender difference revolves around a strict dichotomization, where men and women are essentially different species who inhabit different spheres of life. While men are associated with the public domain and the world of work, women are associated with the private space of the domestic. According to the gendered division of labour, husbands are in paid employment to support their families financially, while wives are engaged in the unpaid labour of childcare and domestic chores. Feminism has fought against these ideas and arrangements which significantly disadvantage women, for example by making them financially dependent on their husbands and by limiting their options in life to domestic family duties. Getting women educated and out to work and into good jobs has therefore been at the heart of the feminist struggle. Financial independence is fundamental to leading an independent life and pursuing one's own goals and desires rather than those of men.

Of course a lot has changed since the 1950s. In modern societies today, it is common for women to achieve educational credentials, have careers and remain in work after having children. However, women continue to earn on average less than men and are much more likely than men to be in part-time and low-paid jobs with few career prospects. Moreover, women continue to do most of the childcare and domestic duties even when they are in full-time employment. So the situation of women in the world of work has not improved as much as feminists had hoped for and has left many women, especially those from lower socio-economic backgrounds, disillusioned. There is also sense in which women remain tied to the domestic sphere in a way that men are not: the home might not be a woman's only place these days, but it continues to be seen as a feminine sphere where the chores it entails are women's duties. In this section we want to look at how women are represented in popular culture in relation to work and the home and examine the ways in which such representations may shape social trends.

In contemporary women's magazines, it is acknowledged that most women are working. Weekly magazines which are relatively cheap and aim at older, often working-class women, such as the British *Bella* or *Women's Weekly*, continue to portray jobs as jobs, rather than careers (Ballaster et al. 1991). This indicates that paid work is a means to an end rather than a source of fulfilment and secondary to women's primary careers as carers, wives and mothers. In contrast, monthly magazines which are expensive, glossy and aimed at younger, professional readers, such as *Cosmopolitan* or *Marie Claire*, devote much more space to work and value the notion of a career. They promote the figure of the energetic, assertive, successful career woman. Nevertheless, careers remain secondary in importance to romance and relationships, which dominate the pages. Appearance is still central for all women, including career women, who have to prove their femininity, not least because feminine looks are crucial to attracting a sexual partner. This is reinforced in narratives across popular culture where it is not a woman's career success and confidence that attract a man, but her prettiness and lack of confidence. *Bridget Jones's Diary* is a case in point (Tincknell et al. 2003).

Many films and dramas show women in low-paid and low-status jobs, such as waitress, shop assistant or housekeeper (S. Leonard 2007). Whilst this reflects the reality of many women's real-life situations, it is noticeable that these female characters usually have no career ambitions and are often paired with male protagonists who occupy superior positions (Negra 2009). For example, in *Along Came Polly* (2004), Jennifer Aniston plays a waitress who gets together with Ben Stiller, who is an insurance underwriter. Or in *The Pursuit of Happyness* (2006), Thandie Newton and Will Smith play a couple trapped in dead-end jobs and debt. As they split up, Newton moves to New York to take up a job in a pizza parlour, while Smith begins a career as a stockbroker. Of course there are also many films, series and dramas which have to acknowledge social change and portray women who have successful careers and occupy professional jobs. Negra (2009) argues that this presents a problem in the sense that these images do not fit conventional femininity. Popular culture deals with this through several strategies, two of which we want to highlight here. Firstly, popular culture tends to delegitimize career women and their lives by presenting them as unhappy, problematic and unfulfilled. For example, the increasing equality between men and women is often portrayed as causing romantic conflict. Chick lit books and films tend to link men's sexual irresponsibility to women's success in the world of work (Tincknell et al. 2003) or present women's devotion to their careers as standing in the way of their femininity and, therefore, marital happiness (S. Leonard 2007). Films such as *Miss Congeniality* (2000), *The Wedding Planner* (2001), *Life or Something Like It* (2002), *Mona Lisa Smile* (2003) or *The Proposal* (2009) are cases in point (S. Leonard 2007). Another example of delegitimation concerns work being presented as a place which facilitates women's extramarital affairs, for instance in *American Beauty* (1999) or *The Good Girl* (2002) (S. Leonard 2007).

The second strategy to 'resolve' the conflict posed by successful working women is to minimize their professional roles. This works through the narrative scenario of 'retreatism' (Negra 2009). Hollywood films, especially romances, and television family dramas 'regularly include a retreatist epiphany in which the professional woman comes to realize that the self she has cultivated through education and professionalization is in some way deficient unless she can rebuild a family base' (Negra 2009: 21). This means women are shown to be working and even having careers and high-powered jobs – such as fashion designer (Reese Witherspoon in *Sweet Home Alabama* [2002]), journalist or fashion magazine editor (Anne Hathaway and Meryl Streep in *The Devil Wears Prada* [2006]) – but these careers do not satisfy them and they retreat. Witherspoon retreats from her career and relationship in New York to her childhood sweetheart and home state of Alabama; Hathaway quits her promising journalist job and decides to stay in New York with her boyfriend instead of going to Paris. In these narratives the end is that female protagonists 'go home'. This is a metaphor for retreating from professional jobs or ambition back to their original, good character, which is symbolized by rural places and hometowns, long-standing boyfriends and childhood sweethearts. The moral character of the protagonists is portrayed as an essentially good one, marked by love, care and tenderness, but one which has been corrupted by or cannot be sustained in the world of work. This is highly ideological. The retreatist narrative 'solves' the complex problems and situations of contemporary women in simplistic and romanticized ways by suggesting they leave and return to their point of origin (Negra 2009). This is highly passive, too: instead of facing problems and changing the world, women retreat from it. Moreover, women are essentialized as they are portrayed as possessing the same, inherent nature, marked by conventional ideas of femininity as caring, emotional, loving and considerate. These female attributes are positive qualities, while the world of work is associated with negative qualities such as greed, superficiality and ruthlessness. However, retreatist narratives do not advocate that women bring their 'inherent qualities' to bear on the workplace to make it a better, more 'feminine' place. Instead, women are portrayed as incongruent with work so that the only option for 'real' women is to retreat. We say 'real' women because these films often make a distinction between 'real', read conventionally feminine, women and women who are 'unreal' because they behave in ways which are traditionally considered masculine. Unreal women are portrayed as extremely tough, inconsiderate, ambitious and ruthless, to the point of being caricatures. Meryl Streep's character in *The Devil Wears Prada*, high-powered fashion magazine editor Miranda Priestly, is an excellent example. Man-women like her never retreat because they are compatible with and excel in the world of work, being more male than female. These figures only serve to emphasize that 'real' women are incompatible with the world of work and need to retreat.

The retreatist narrative is a powerful way to minimize women's professional roles and status discursively. But depending on the plot, it is not always an available or credible strategy. Another technique of minimization concerns narratives of 'adjusted ambition', which 'discredit the meaning and value of work in the heroine's life or at least to insist that it be made secondary to romance' (Negra 2009: 88). For example, in the 2009 film *The Proposal*, Sandra Bullock plays the executive editor-in-chief of a major book publishing company. She is portrayed as career-driven, hard-working, professionally efficient and powerful, taking decisions which make or break writers' careers. She is also shown to be extremely hard, blunt and ruthless to the point of appearing inhuman, and for this reason is universally feared and disliked by staff. This hardness extends to her social life: she seems to have no friends or family, certainly no love relationship, and is living on her own. She devotes her entire life to work and has no human connections or social life. The plot sees Bullock being threatened with deportation for being Canadian and saved by her assistant, played by Ryan Reynolds, who agrees to marry her so she can stay in the US. He takes her to his native Alaska to be introduced to his family; here Bullock's character encounters human values such as family love, care and affection and she is transformed into a better person. This better person is in essence a more conventionally feminine person: softer, caring and loving. Consequently, Reynolds and Bullock genuinely fall in love and get married. While the narrative and persona of Bullock would make a full retreat, in the sense of her giving up work, too far-fetched, the film employs the strategy of adjusted ambition instead, showing Bullock to realize the limited importance of work in comparison to love and become less career-focused. Moreover, the film resolves the tension of a female being in a professionally superior position to a male – Bullock is Reynold's boss – by showing him to have written a brilliant novel which is immediately published. This elevates him from the subordinate position of assistant to an equal position in a different, creative field.

However ambivalent its portrayal, the figure of the working woman has entered popular culture. At the same time, there has been a renewed focus on the domestic. For example, television has been marked by the rise of genres which focus on different aspects of the domestic sphere, including childrearing (e.g. various *Supernanny* series, *Honey We're Killing the Kids*), cooking (an explosion of cookery programmes, both by professional chefs and by laypeople), nutrition (e.g. *You Are What you Eat*), cleaning (e.g. *How Clean Is Your House?*) and home improvement (e.g. *Changing Rooms*). The domestic has become a topic of interest. With the exception of cooking, which is dominated by male chefs and has in the process become elevated, at least in the media, to an art form rather than a daily chore (Feasey 2008), such programmes tend to feature women as central personas. This means both the experts who come to teach participants how to clean their house, eat healthily and raise their children, as well as the laypeople who open their houses and lives to the scrutiny of television cameras. Hence the domestic is reaffirmed as the realm of responsibility and expertise of women. Many of these programmes play on shock and disgust, inviting viewers to be horrified by excess and extremes, marvelling at just how dirty houses are, how badly behaved children are and the sheer amounts of junk food people eat. There is a clear class element in these programmes as the laypeople tend to be working- or lower-class women, who are instructed on how to look after the domestic by educated, middle-class females. Depending on class, there are different kinds of domestic femininity portrayed: one of expert, the other of failure. This class dimension clearly shows in the domestic reality television show *Wife Swap*, which has become a huge success on both sides of the Atlantic. The show centres on women as they swap families to go and live with the other's husband and children for two weeks. For the purpose of gripping and conflictual television, producers pit very different women against each other, most often in terms of class. As the series continued to run, the format was expanded to juxtapose families along alternative lines, such as politics (conservative vs liberal) or faith (religious vs non-religious), but the paradigm episodes pit working-class women against middle-class women, with the former being exposed as deficient by being shown to rely on pre-cooked meals or leave their children to go to the pub. This highlights that much of conventional femininity is bourgeois femininity; the ideal of woman as a domestic goddess, devoting herself to the care of the family home, the children and her husband, has never been realistic for many working-class women. Reality television shows set up working-class women (and men) to emerge as inadequate and valueless as they are measured by middle-class standards which inevitably find them wanting, in terms of their existing culture and subjectivity and in terms of insufficient drive to invest in and 'improve' themselves (Skeggs 2009).

The nature of domestic female figures in popular culture has changed in recent decades. The sphere of the home has become aestheticized and with it the role of women: instead of being domestic workers weighed down by a range of not very glamorous tasks, such as cleaning, ironing, washing up, women are now often portrayed as homemakers (Negra 2009). The homemaker is the person responsible for turning the house into a tasteful, aesthetic and comfortable sphere, complete with fresh flowers, colour-matched carpets and walls, plumped-up pillows and fresh scents. Television home makeover shows, such as *Changing Rooms* or *60 Minute Makeover*, which have become so popular since the 1990s, prescribe this aesthetic in detail. Women's magazines have refashioned domestic labours as leisure and consumption: for example, cooking or equipping the house with consumer durables and furniture have become matters of style and taste and therefore forms of self-expression (Ballaster et al. 1991). Of course, the dirty, boring tasks have not gone away, but today either they do not feature in popular-cultural texts – e.g. women's magazines will discuss home furnishing but not cleaning – or they are remodelled to fit the new aesthetic of the homemaker. For example, cooking is associated with sociable and fun occasions such as family meals or dinner parties, while soap adverts show washing clothes to take place in bright, clean, tasteful houses where it becomes part of the overall aesthetic.

Motherhood is perhaps the key role which continues to tie femininity to the domestic sphere. Parenthood has historically been understood as motherhood in the sense that bringing up children is a woman's job. As a consequence, motherhood is important to women's identities in a way that fatherhood is not for men. Women who have children are very much defined by this; they are first and foremost mothers (Lawler 2000). Motherhood occupies a contradictory position in contemporary culture. On the one hand, motherhood continues to be undervalued. For example, having children is seen negatively by employers and often impacts adversely on a woman's career; childcare is no longer provided by the state but has to be paid for by parents; mothering is considered a dreary, uninspiring and mentally unchallenging task. But, on the other hand, it has been elevated and aggrandized, especially in recent years, as mothering has been reframed as not only the most important job in society but also the most fulfilling. Several Hollywood films, such as *Raising Helen* (2004) or *No Reservations* (2007), portray motherhood as life-changing, as bringing meaning to a woman's life and transforming her into a better person (Negra 2009). Other films, such as *Changeling* (2009), show mothers utterly devoted and ontologically bonded to their children. Generally speaking, motherhood has become fashionable. Celebrities now raise their own children in the limelight and show them off in exclusive magazine deals; pregnant celebrities proudly show off their bumps; adopting children from developing countries has become the latest celebrity trend. Hence, motherhood is both idealized and devalued, sentimentalized and sneered at.

Susan Douglas and Meredith Michaels (2004) call the idealization of motherhood in contemporary culture the 'new momism'. New momism is itself contradictory. It pretends to, and on the surface does, celebrate motherhood by suggesting that mothers do an enormous amount of unpaid work, that they are altruistic beings who devote themselves entirely to their children and that they give up many of their own dreams and desires in the process. However, this new momism also creates new standards of perfection which mothers have to achieve in order to be 'good mothers' (Lawler 2000). It is not enough to feed, clothe and care for children; good parenting now includes exposing children to a range of social pursuits and skills, from music lessons to football practice and helping them maintain friendships. It also requires parents to ensure their children obtain the best possible education, for example by getting them into the best schools or helping them with their homework, and to keep their bodies healthy and fit through nutritious food and sufficient exercise. As children are perceived as constantly at risk from a range of threats lurking in late modern society, from paedophiles to knife crime, good parents have to engage in continuous protectiveness (Meyer 2007). This has resulted in constant supervision of children and drastic changes in childhood. Child play has moved from the streets to private spaces; child leisure time has become much more structured as parents arrange organized activities; and the vast majority of children are now taken to school by their parents (Valentine and McKendrick 1997). This new protectiveness is linked to the predominance of the discourse of innocence, which frames children as innocent, naïve, vulnerable and therefore in constant need of protection, and to the elevation of children to 'sacred' beings who are the centre of family life and adult meaning (Zelizer 1994). There are two points to note here which are particularly important with respect to gender. Firstly, it means that parenting has become a much more intense business as parents have constantly to organize and supervise children's lives, from school runs to supervising homework, from driving them to football practice to never leaving them on their own. Secondly, the responsibility for this 'intensive parenting' (Furedi 2001) mostly falls onto women. Despite an increase in fathers' engagement with their children since the 1960s, women are still the main carers in the vast majority of families and continue to be defined through their relationship with their children. Mothers are therefore not only the ones doing the work, but the ones set up to fail by the increasingly unattainable standards of perfection. Mothers can never quite be 'good enough' as there are always additional sacrifices they could be making for their children (Lawler 2000). And as mothering is seen as a labour of love, steeped in pure altruism, they are not allowed to complain about duties either. It is in this sense that motherhood has undergone an ambivalent cultural development, being elevated to a new level yet becoming a highly prescriptive and moralistic tool which makes enormous demands on women while setting them up to fail.

Sexuality, Morality and Violence

Sexuality and morality have vastly different meanings and implications for femininity and masculinity. For women, respectability has always been fundamentally tied to sexuality (Skeggs 1997). In order to be 'appropriately' feminine, women have to be respectable, and in order to count as respectable, they have to be sexually innocent, shy or modest. Openly and confidently sexual women, for example those with multiple sexual partners or those who emphasize their sexuality through 'sexy' clothes or demeanours, cannot be respectably feminine. This dichotomy is reflected in cultural representations which tend to categorise women as either 'vamps' or 'virgins', as 'madonnas' or 'whores' (Benedict 1992). Sexuality is therefore central to women's standing. Asexuality and chastity are key virtues which indicate respectable femininity, while sexual activity, availability and promiscuity are vices which construct women as unrespectable vamps. While the new femininity expressed in teenage and women's magazines seems to challenge this dichotomy, it is still alive and powerful in popular culture. Lads' magazines, for example, allow men to be both openly sexual and morally responsible and conservative, to objectify women by visually consuming their largely naked bodies while claiming the moral high ground (Tincknell et al. 2003). Phil Hilton, former editor of the UK's largest weekly lads' magazine, *Nuts*, conceptualizes the magazine's readers as socially conservative young men who want to look at and have sex with women, but would not like their girlfriends to be the ones who parade their sexuality or behave in 'unfeminine' ways (*Sex in the Noughties: Nuts vs Zoo* 2007). Tincknell et al. conclude that '[g]irls cannot be both morally responsible and hedonistically pan-sexual with their own bodies because the social consequences are too punitive' (2003: 58). Yet men can. One of the punitive consequences for women is disparaging critique. The importance of sexual morality to femininity is exemplified in the long list of derogatory words which exist in the English language to label women who are sexually available or active, such as 'tart', 'slut', 'slag', 'whore', 'hooker' or 'prostitute'. This language denigrates women by presenting them as unrespectable, cheap and worthless. There are no equivalent terms for men, suggesting that sexual morality is not as central to masculine identity and that discourses of sexual morality are deeply gendered. Men can be sexually promiscuous and still have a high moral and social standing; in fact, this can be seen as making them even more masculine as a strong, 'natural' sex drive is part of hegemonic masculinity.

The madonna/whore complex is most clearly at work in the media coverage of rape. Rape is a deeply gendered crime which is committed by men against women (Walby and Allen 2004). Helen Benedict's (1992) analysis of US newspapers shows that coverage perpetuates several 'rape myths': that is, widespread but false representations and beliefs regarding rape. The newspapers link sexuality to blame by constructing female victims as either innocent virgins or vamps who brought it on themselves. We can illustrate the contemporary currency of some of these myths by looking at how the *Daily Mail* represents cases of rape involving alcohol: that is, cases where the victims, and sometimes the perpetrators too, have been drinking significant amounts of alcohol before the attack. This serves as a useful example because the involvement of alcohol has led the media, especially conservative ones like the *Daily Mail*, to openly perpetuate rape myths, clearly believing them to be acceptable.

'Asking for it': drunken women as vamps

One myth pervading media coverage of rape stipulates that women are to blame for rape because they are 'asking for it' (Benedict 1992), provoking rape through their clothes or behaviours such as drinking alcohol on a night out:

> If a woman goes out half dressed, exchanges raunchy sexual banter with eager young men, drinks ten large vodka and Red Bulls, takes someone home and snogs him enthusiastically, she should not be staggered if he gets the wrong idea. . . . If a girl wants to dress and behave in a sexually provocative way, she should not be thunderstruck if an immature young man thinks she is behaving in a sexually provocative way. (Dudley Edwards 2006)

This myth frames men as passive and naïve victims of women who mislead them. This image of men is constructed through adjectives such as 'young', 'immature' and 'eager', which indicate a lack of experience and savviness. According to the *Daily Mail*, men who rape do not misinterpret women's behaviour on purpose but rather men's actions are caused by women deliberately leading them on. Misleading practices include flirting ('exchanges raunchy sexual banter'), drinking alcohol ('drinks ten large vodka and Red Bulls'), dressing in a 'sexual' manner ('half dressed') and kissing ('snogs him enthusiastically'). Women who do these things are classified as sexual vamps who are 'asking for it' because they 'behave in a sexually provocative way'. The above quote goes so far as to equate flirting, drinking, dressing up and kissing with consent to sex by stipulating that if a woman does all these things, 'she should not be staggered if he gets the wrong idea'. According to this logic, once a woman has engaged in any of these everyday practices she has effectively agreed to sex and therefore cannot complain of rape.

The rape myth of women 'asking for it' can be seen as a clear example of ideology. It is a false belief which misrepresents reality. The scenario of rape painted is one of ambiguity: men are not quite sure what women mean and rape almost 'by mistake'. In reality, rape is a violent crime which involves a man forcing a woman into sexual intercourse. He ignores and knowingly acts against her wishes. Men are not passive victims, but active criminals. Moreover, women's actions such as drinking, kissing or dressing in a certain way do not constitute consent to sex. To say that they do means effectively to disallow these behaviours to women unless they are prepared to accept rape as a consequence. Men are not asked to modify their behaviour. In fact, research has shown that women's behaviours are not the reason they are raped, for example rapists tend not to notice what victims wear, but that rape is a crime of opportunity where women become victims because they are in a certain place at a certain time (Benedict 1992). The 'asking for it' myth is also flawed because it holds women responsible for men's behaviour, when individuals should be accountable for their own actions.

This myth highlights the double standards regarding popular attitudes to rape. Research (Finch and Munro 2005; Kramer 1994) has shown that the wider public as well as the media consider rape victims more blameworthy when they have been drinking, while rapists under the influence of alcohol are more readily excused. Victim blaming 're-genders' the social problem of rape by framing women's excessive drinking rather than male violence as the cause (Meyer 2010). Men rape women but the real problem is that drunken women cannot defend themselves. This refocusing process has a long history: for instance, 'drug rape' discussions often blame the drug and take the emphasis off men (Berrington and Jones 2001). This excuses male behaviour, frees men from taking responsibility and obscures the real, underlying problem which made women's drinking an issue in the first place: male rape.

Sex gone wrong vs 'real' rape: women as virgins or vamps

While rape victims who have been drinking are portrayed as vamps, other rape victims can be classed as virgins and are treated much more sympathetically by the media.

Benedict (1992) shows that women deemed 'asexual', such as mothers or older women, tend to be defined as virgins. Their asexuality signifies their innocence, and as innocent, 'real' victims they will not be held responsible for their rape. Hence the categories of virgin and vamp illustrate that blame is directly linked to female sexuality. However, while 'asexuality' is a necessary criterion for qualifying as an innocent victim, it is not in itself sufficient. Women also need to be a victim of a specific type of rape which conforms to the media's definition of 'real' rape (Estrich 1987). The following extract illustrates this well:

> Even to use that word [rape to refer to rape involving alcohol] is to insult those women who have genuinely been subjected to the terror and degradation of a sexual assault under threat of physical harm. Women like Jill Saward, who was repeatedly raped and assaulted by three strangers who broke into her father's Ealing vicarage, wearing balaclavas and carrying knives. HOW can you possibly compare what Jill endured to an encounter that takes place between two adults who flirt together, drink together and then have sex together, but which one of them later claims took place against her will? (Platell 2006)

Jill Saward is presented as a virgin victim here. As the daughter of a vicar, she clearly comes from a religious family background. Further, she was present in the sanctity of the family home, rather than, say, an 'immoral' and 'dangerous' public space such as a nightclub, when she was attacked. These two things mark her out as chaste and innocent and therefore a blameless victim who deserves sympathy. But it is equally important that she was the victim of a type of rape which the media recognize as 'real' rape: that is, a stranger attack which involves weapons and inflicts visible injuries. The media construct the notion of 'real' rape in opposition to the wide category of 'not real' rape, which includes all cases of acquaintance rape where perpetrator and victim know each other (Meyer 2010). The media often label this type of rape 'date rape', with the term 'date' implying that women have consented to sex by agreeing to meet a man (Lees 1995). The rape which ensues is presented as a misunderstanding, as 'sex gone a bit wrong', rather than an act of aggression and violence (Benedict 1992). The media do not recognize this type of rape as 'real' rape and tend to trivialize it. For example, the *Daily Mail* calls men who rape drunken women after a night out 'pathetic scumbags' (Dudley Edwards 2006) who are 'leading women astray' (Platell 2006) or 'acting in an ungentlemanly way' (Doughty 2006). Such language is highly ideological because it exonerates men by omitting their violence and trivializes the criminal nature of rape involving alcohol by using nebulous and euphemistic expressions. It inaccurately represents men who rape as being badly behaved and immoral, rather than violent criminals. It underplays the misuse of power in the form of coercion and violence and the ways in which men use rape to dominate, terrify and humiliate women.

The categories of 'real' and 'not real' rape map onto the categories of 'virgin' and 'vamp'. Categorization leads to declaring victims either innocent or guilty and is central to the perpetuation of a hegemonic ideology on rape. Since the 1970s, feminists have publicly criticized rape myths and made them less acceptable. But it seems that the hegemonic ideology has remained powerful by adapting to social and cultural changes. This adaptation process is known as 'co-option' and takes the form of making distinctions between different types of rape and rape victims. While representations of stranger rape of 'asexual' women make concessions to the feminist critique, other types of rape committed by acquaintances against 'sexual' women are represented in ways which reinforce the old rape myths (see Lees 1996; Meyer 2010). Categorization aids the manufacturing of consent to hegemonic ideology and rule, especially from women. Women may perceive themselves as potential victims of sexual violence and disagree with victim blaming. But categorization of rape and victims justifies critique by presenting it as rational and grounded in specific reasons, rather than a blanket condemnation. Moreover, it allows women to see themselves as part of a group of deserving, blameless victims who would not be criticized.

Media coverage of rape is just one example of how women are judged by popular culture and how important sexuality and morality are to these judgement processes. Especially conservative media such as the *Daily Mail* disapprove of the new femininity which involves casual sex and excessive drinking, hanging onto notions of such behaviours being 'unfeminine' and morally dangerous. This is not unexpected as the media tend to frame women who pursue individual autonomy as a threat to the moral order of society (Tincknell et al. 2003). In practice, of course, we see millions of women in the UK and elsewhere ignoring such attitudes; however, behaving in 'unfeminine' ways comes at a heavy price. Parts of the media symbolically punish women through relentless critique while the criminal justice system legally punishes them by making rape convictions difficult to achieve (Meyer 2010). In May 2011, the UK justice secretary and former practising lawyer Ken Clarke caused controversy when insisting in an interview with BBC radio station 5 Live that there is a difference between 'serious rape' and 'date rape' (BBC 2011). He defined serious rape as involving 'violence and an unwilling woman', suggesting that there are forms of rape which are not serious and involve women who 'want' to be raped. This attitude is a clear indication of the prevalence, durability and power of rape myths over time and across society.

Conclusion

The representation of women in contemporary culture is a complex issue. There are historical changes and continuities, differences across different media, and analyses have to be specific to the particular aspects of women's lives which are represented. Nevertheless, there are a few general points with which we can conclude. The most overarching one is that representations matter: they are not 'only' words and images, but reflect and encourage certain ways of thinking about and acting in relation to women. This applies whether women continue to be seen as carers of children through their role as mothers, whether they are judged by their physical appearance regardless of other achievements or whether they are denied victim status because they have been behaving in 'unfeminine' ways. Representations of women have undoubtedly diversified, taking into account new roles and offering new identities, but traditional images and norms continue to exist and exert powerful influence. This is not surprising as social change is a continuous process full of twists and turns. A full understanding of representations of women can also only be gained in conjunction with an analysis of representations of men, and the ways in which they compare. This is what we will turn to in the next chapter.

5
Representing Men

Discourses of Masculinity

Having discussed popular-cultural representations of women in the previous chapter, we now want to turn to men. There is no one, unitary masculinity; rather there are several masculinities in contemporary Western culture which are constituted through diverse and changing systems of representations of men (Nixon 1997). Like femininity, masculinity has undergone drastic changes since the 1960s and diversified. There are three key discourses of masculinity which will inform the discussion and analysis of representations in this chapter: the 'old man', the 'new man' and the 'new lad' (Edwards 2003). Theses discourses are chronological in the sense of emerging in different historical periods: traditional masculinity is the 'original' type of masculinity strongly associated with the 1940s and 1950s; the new man emerged in the 1980s; and the new lad appeared in the 1990s (Edwards 2003). Despite the chronology of emergence, all three types of masculinity continue to coexist; the genealogy of masculinity is not a matter of one type supplanting any other(s) (Gill 2003). All discourses of masculinity continue to change, too, not least because they interact with and define each other. As Tim Edwards put it, 'a New Lad is precisely a New Lad as he is not a New Man and vice versa' (2003: 139). All versions of masculinity discussed here are a 'reality' in the sense of referring to actual men as well as concepts with which to analyse masculinity. This is why they are best thought of as discourses which are produced not only through media language and images but also through men's everyday practices (Gill 2003). In this chapter we want to provide a brief outline of the three key discourses of masculinity and then analyse their relevance in relation to men's bodies, sexuality, work and domesticity in contemporary culture.

The discourse of traditional masculinity: the old man

The discourse of traditional masculinity refers to those values and behaviours which have traditionally been seen as typically male, as defining men. As part of this process they have been naturalized, which means that the 'typical' characteristics and practices are identified as inherent aspects of men, grounded in their biological make-up. This is an essentialist understanding of social life which conceptualizes men and women as inherently different species. It is not surprising, therefore, that traditional masculinity, more than any other type of masculinity, directly juxtaposes men and women. Men are presented as strong, active, powerful, authoritative, hard, aggressive, violent, competitive and rational, and lacking sensitivity and emotions, while women are conceptualized as soft, weak, passive, submissive, powerless, peaceful, sensitive, emotional and caring. Traditional masculinity is the oldest type of masculinity discussed, with the emergence of the old man being located in the 1940s and 1950s (Edwards 2003). But the old man is also old in the sense of being the least modern or progressive of all types of men (MacKinnon 2003).

Strength and power are key characteristics of traditional masculinity (MacKinnon 2003). Physical strength derives from possessing a strong, large and muscular body and a tough mental attitude, while social power is institutionalized through men's financial income and independence and their position as head of family and household. Depending on social class and occupation, social power also refers to authority over others in the workplace, the authority to make important decisions in the public realm and directly shape society. Whether in manual or professional employment, the old man primarily defines himself through his work; his contribution to society in the realm of production is his source of identity (Edwards 2003). Consumption is not central to traditional masculinity; women are the ones responsible for household consumption and the traditional male has little interest in or knowledge of things such as shopping, fashion or beautification. His attitude to consumer items, from clothes to furniture, is functional. Similarly, appearance, aside from physical strength, is not key to traditional masculinity: looking good, beautifying yourself and being sexually attractive is the realm of women, not men. However, Edwards (2003) and Osgerby (2003) have pointed out that this denial of fashion and consumption as male concerns is too simplistic a view of history. Even in the era dominated by traditional masculinity, some old men – e.g. gangsters or playboys in the 1940s and 1950s – showed considerable interest in fashion and consumption. However, because these realms are traditionally associated with women, men could only be stylish if they proved their heterosexual masculinity in other areas, for example through violence (the gangster) or promiscuity (the playboy).

Traditional masculinity is staunchly and unambiguously heterosexual, focused on the sexual conquest of women. Heterosexuality is understood as natural and grounded in a strong sex drive which has to be continually satisfied (Firminger 2006). Women are seen not so much as partners or friends but as sexual objects which satisfy these desires. The old man believes in the ideal of marriage but can simultaneously be a promiscuous playboy who satisfies his sex drive outside it (Edwards 2003). Homosexuality is deemed feminized and unnatural. The old man is homophobic as well as sexist.

Cognitive skills, especially scientific reasoning and rationality, are further attributes of traditional masculinity. Men are associated with possessing information and knowledge, thinking logically and solving difficult mental tasks. They are seen as competitive and driven, aiming to win and succeed, whether at work or in their personal lives. As a consequence, the traditional male emerges as an uncompromising and ruthless figure, who looks after his individual interests first and foremost. Traditional masculinity is associated with not expressing any emotions, considering them the realm of women rather than men (Firminger 2006).

In its origins, traditional masculinity is very much tied to an age of clear gender roles and family structures, where women were responsible for childcare and domestic chores while men were the sole breadwinners who went out to work. With the profound socio-cultural changes of the 1960s, most notably in terms of gender relations, this outlook started to be questioned by feminists and other social movements, such as the gay movement and the peace movement (Gill 2003). The old man has been called the 'unreconstructed male', meaning the male of the past who has not been modified by these societal changes (MacKinnon 2003). In some ways, then, the old man is a throwback to an older era – but social change is never neat or complete. Many aspects of traditional masculinity still resonate and are continuously scattered throughout contemporary popular culture. And while the old man may be unreconstructed, he is not totally divorced from the society that surrounds him. Some aspects of traditional masculinity are more acceptable today than others and more commonly revived. The idea of a naturally high male sex drive is a case in point, being constructed across a range of sites from talk shows to films and women's and men's magazines. Moreover, some relatively unacceptable elements, such as open sexism, have found a new life in the discourse of the new lad. Rosalind Gill (2003) has argued that since the 1990s we have witnessed the rise of a new social Darwinist trend in psychology, which explains male and female behaviour through evolutionary principles. This trend has legiti-mated the revival of traditional masculinity as it reinforces the notion of men and women as different species.

The new man and the metrosexual

A new type of masculinity emerged in the 1980s which has been termed the 'new man' to emphasize its differences from traditional or old masculinity. According to John Beynon (2002), there are two different strands within this new type of masculinity, namely 'new man as nurturer' and 'new man as narcissist'. In contrast to traditional masculinity, the new man as nurturer is in touch with his feminine side. He is caring, sensitive, emotionally skilled and shares household duties, including childcare. He is usually middle class and well educated, liberal in his political outlook and sympathetic to the feminist cause. The new man is non-sexist, believes in gender equal-ity and relates to women as human beings rather than sex objects. He is heterosexual but capable of having female friends and interested in female sexual pleasure as well as his own. Within popular culture, this is the less popular of the two strands and often confined to certain groups of men, such as environmentalists, hippies, charity workers or human rights activists. Rowena Chapman (1988) argues that this is because the new man as nurturer cannot be as easily incorporated into a consumerist ethos.

The second strand of the new man as narcissist represents men as fashion-conscious and health-conscious consumers. The new man knows the value of appearance; he is well groomed and looks sexy. He possesses a fit and muscular body, achieved through regular exercise and diet regimes, wears expensive and stylish clothes, has a trendy haircut and uses beautification products such as moisturizers or hairwax. He openly displays sophisticated cultural tastes, from drinking in stylish bars to going to the theatre. He is an avid consumer and constructs his masculinity through consumer style and taste. The importance of work or social class as a source of identity has declined. The new man is career-minded and successful, yet also has a *joie de vivre* and enjoys partying and spending his money on socializing and consumer items. He works hard and plays hard.

We can see major differences compared to traditional masculinity here, revolving around an increase in the importance of consumption, culture, appearance, sexuality and emotions for men. As these were traditionally the realms of women, the emergence of the new man seems to have 'femininized' masculinity. Masculinity and femininity are still binary opposites, but there is much more common ground. Of course the new man did not emerge overnight and there are several structural conditions which have made this new type of masculinity discourse possible. The most important ones include changes in gender attitudes thanks to the feminist movement (Beynon 2002; Chapman 1988), the new materialism and individualism of the 1980s and the growth of the consumer society (Edwards 2003), the increasing profile of the style press (Nixon 1996), as well as a new popular psychology of masculinity and the rise of gay liberation (Gill 2003).

The new man has always been a controversial figure in popular culture, being criticized, for example, for being narcissistic, effeminate, fake and inauthentic (see Edwards 2003; Gill 2003). In the 1990s, the metrosexual emerged, which can be seen as a refashioned version of the new man because the two share many characteristics (Cohan 2007). The metrosexual is young, middle class, trendy and lives in major urban areas. He invests considerable time and money in his appearance and has extensive knowledge of fashion trends and styles, characteristics which were previously attributed to gay men only (Cohan 2007). But the metrosexual is heterosexual and indeed comfortable enough with his sexuality to play with the rules of traditional masculinity, for example by being friends with gay men, visiting gay venues, openly performing masculinity through consumer choices and even wearing ambiguous clothing (Kimmel 2006). The metrosexual believes in gender equality and is prepared to take on greater roles in the domestic sphere, for example as an active father or someone interested in the sexual pleasures of his partner. David Beckham has often been identified as the embodiment of this metrosexual. But it should be noted that, pursuing the ultra-masculine occupation of a professional footballer and being the partner of a former popstar, Beckham can adopt the metrosexual image without being in danger of being identified as 'really gay'. The public outcry over his wearing of sarongs also suggests that there are limits on even his ability to play with gender roles.

The new lad

The 1990s arguably witnessed the (re)emergence of a third discourse of masculinity, dubbed the new lad. The new lad can be seen as a response to the new man and growing gender equality of the 1980s and 1990s (Beynon 2002; Edwards 1997) and as a backlash against feminism (Gill 2003). The figure of the new lad is particularly associated with British culture. However, since the late 1990s it has also gained ground in the US (Atkinson 1999), and the existence of lads' magazines across the globe– e.g. the Swedish *Moore* or the Mexican *H para Hombres* – suggests that this figure is no longer confined to the English-speaking world. The new lad is characterized by his interests, namely football, drinking and sex, which are often enjoyed in a loutish and aggressive manner (Beynon 2002). His attitudes to women are marked by sexism and objectification: women are seen as sex objects to be conquered rather than human beings to have relationships with. Summing this up, Imelda Whelehan defines the new lad as 'part soccer thug, part lager lout, part arrant sexist' (2000: 58). His sexism forms part of a general conservativism, which sees the new lad in favour of, and nostalgically yearning for, traditional and stereotypical gender roles and acting defensively heterosexual (Whelehan 2000). In all these respects the new lad is a fallback to traditional discourses of laddism with their machismo, misogyny, womanizing and drunken rowdiness (Edwards 1997). But the new lad is also marked by some additional features which make for his newness. For example, he and his mates interact in a juvenile way through sexualized banter, joking and pulling pranks (Beynon 2002). This 'humour' is linked to the dumbness of new lad culture, marked by the absence of serious conversations or relations. Like a child, the new lad does not think or talk about profound issues but simply wants to have fun. The pervasiveness of 'humour' means that sexism and homophobia usually feature in the form of jokes and irony, allowing the lad to be bigoted and offensive while claiming it is all just one big laugh and those not laughing with him are up-tight losers (Whelehan 2000). The new lad is new not just in the sense of having juvenile humour, but also by retaining, against all odds, some element of the new man (Edwards 1997). Like the new man, the new lad is a style-conscious and self-conscious consumer; he is aware of what he is wearing and likes labels and brands. The difference is that instead of the new man's sophisticated, expensive and trendy clothes, the new lad opts for mid-range labels of trainers, t-shirts and tracksuit tops such as Lacoste, Ben Sherman or Rockport (Edwards 1997). For both new men and new lads, consumption rather than production is the source of masculine identity, albeit of a different kind.

Discourses and history

All three discourses of masculinity continue to exist, but often not in as pure a form as they have been described here. We have seen that all discourses of masculinity are multi-faceted, revolving around a range of issues, themes and behaviours. It is therefore not surprising that representations of men and maleness in popular culture are often partial, never incorporating all the elements, and that they mix elements from different concepts of masculinity. Feona Attwood, for example, has found a mixing of old and new elements in contemporary men's magazines which she describes as constructing a 'very contemporary form of masculinity' which nevertheless is a 'bricolage of those familiar and rather old-fashioned signifiers of masculinity, "tits and ass and porn and fighting"' (2005: 97). One thing which unites all discourses of masculinity is heterosexuality: masculinity is always straight and defined by sexual attraction to women. For the remainder of this chapter we will illustrate how masculinity is represented and constructed across popular culture by looking at the key themes of body and appearance, sexuality and work and domesticity.

The Body and Physical Appearance

Bodies and physical appearance are central to contemporary representations of masculinity – whether we talk about traditional men, new men or new lads. This has arguably been ushered in by the rise of the new man, specifically the new man as narcissist. Sean Nixon (1996) traces this emergence in 1980s advertising, fashion magazine photography and menswear retailing. He notes that men's bodies start to become objects to be displayed and looked at by spectators. Popular culture represents male bodies which are highly muscular, lean and sculpted, and increasingly naked. The ways in which they are lit and positioned invites a desiring gaze and sexual appreciation; male bodies are now made to look good and sexually attractive. Such display and gaze sexualize and fetishize male bodies in a way which was previously only the case for women. The specifics of gender beauty ideals differ, though, for while feminine beauty revolves principally around thinness, the ideal male appearance emphasizes the importance of a highly muscular physique (Hatoum and Belle 2004; Kilbourne 2003). Looking at fashion photography and advertising, Nixon (1996) suggests that the look of the new man is signified and constructed through the combination of several signs, such as faces, body shape or clothes, which give him a contradictory 'hard–soft' look. The new man is sensual yet tough, masculine in both an old and new way. This 'hard–soft' look is illustrated particularly well in a series of popular Calvin Klein adverts. In the example reprinted here (Image 2), the male model combines 'soft' or feminine features – e.g. longish hair, shaved chest, pretty face, high cheekbones, sensual lips – with 'hard' or masculine features – e.g. strong angular jaws, muscular physique, defined pectorals, confident look at the camera. It could be argued that the 'hard' features guard against an interpretation of the male viewer's gaze as homoerotic.

The image of the new man is by no means confined to advertising but can be found across popular culture. Until the 1980s, consumption was largely the preserve of women and gay men, but this changed with the arrival of the fashion-conscious new man who wants to look good and will consume in order to achieve this. We can witness this in the proliferation of new and innovative designs in menswear and emergence of menswear shops in high-street stores such as Next or Top Shop and designer stores such as Armani or Paul Smith (Nixon 1996). Fashion trends now exist for men as well as women, whether we look at skinny jeans or the return of cardigans. Make-over style programmes on television, such as *What Not to Wear*, feature male as well as female subjects, and some programmes, such as *Queer Eye for the Straight Guy*, are explicitly make-over shows for men (Cohan 2007). There has been an explosion in men's beauty products, ranging from hair-styling products and aftershaves to moisturizers and body lotions (Mort 1996). Style magazines for men first appeared in the 1980s, such as *Arena* (now defunct) or *GQ*, which contained fashion photography, plenty of stylish advertising and advised men on a range of style issues, from haircuts to fashion trends (Edwards 1997). *FHM*, a glossy monthly launched in 1994, is a hybrid magazine, straddling lad culture and the new man culture. In this vein it retains a considerable concern with fashion. For example, one of its nine content categories is called 'style', which contains articles on fashion trends and grooming products. In 2009, four *FHM* editions featured special guides on how to dress, which gave style advice on things such as essential items of clothing for men's wardrobes, which types of jeans to wear with different types of trainers, and

Image 2   Calvin Klein advertisement (www.lambre.by).

which colours suit different skintones. Moreover, there are fashion photography spreads of clothes modelled by famous men. Such photography and advice are very reminiscent of women's magazines; however, in *FHM* they sit next to traditional 'men's topics' such as cars, gadgets and women. Looking across popular culture illustrates that the new man is reflected in and has engendered the growth of consumer markets for men and that despite substantial criticism (see Edwards 2003; Gill 2003), the new man has left a legacy requiring men to look good and look after themselves. Contemporary male make-over shows such as *Queer Eye for the Straight Guy* indicate this well. They invite viewers to marvel, in a humorous yet critical way, at how unfashionable, unhygienic, 'un-groomed' and out of shape some men are, presuming a wide audience consensus that such a lack of concern and attractiveness is unacceptable for men. Moreover, the creation of a beautiful and stylish appearance is presented to men in the same way as it has been presented to women for decades, notably as a matter of consumption rather than hard, routine work, and, as such, a source of pleasure (Feasey 2008).

The focus on men's bodies and appearance entails objectification and sexualization; men have become sexual objects to be looked at, judged and desired for their beauty and aesthetics (Nixon 1996). As this sexual objectification is traditionally associated with women and gay men, it threatens to undermine masculinity – which is premised on heterosexuality – by feminizing and homosexualizing it. Nixon (1996) argues that there is a difference in the cultural representation of male and female bodies: while representations of women have always been targeted at male spectators and pleasure, the representation of male bodies invites a 'masculine–masculine gaze'. The new man is primarily there to be looked at and admired by other men, for his muscular physique and his stylishness. In doing so it draws on a gay accent which accompanies the sexualization and fetishization of male bodies. Yet this does not preclude a female gaze. Men's bodies are offered for female consumption and pleasure, too, which means that men have become objects to be looked at by women, inverting the traditional relationship of male viewer (subject) and female object (Moore 1988). A case in point is the series of Diet Coke adverts in the 1990s which featured a male manual worker baring his muscular torso, to the delight of a group of female office workers. What is important here is that masculinity has to reassert itself against the twin threats of feminization and homosexualization and prove its heterosexuality (Attwood 2005). In men's magazines, this is done by strongly emphasizing the heterosexuality of their readers (Edwards 1997). Attwood (2005) identifies two strategies of emphasis. Firstly, she notes that all men's magazines, from the more style-driven ones such as *GQ* to the more laddish ones such as *Nuts*, incorporate sexualized, soft-core pornographic images of women which are offered for the sexual pleasure of readers. Men's magazines might put the male body on display, but images of female bodies continue to dominate. Peter Jackson et al. (2001) explain this through the success of *Loaded*, the original lads' magazine launched in 1994, which pulled the entire men's magazine market downwards, away from style and fashion and towards sex. The difference now seems to be one of degree of focus and nudity: pure lads' magazines *Loaded*, *Zoo* and *Nuts* are the only magazines to feature topless photographs and they devote a much bigger percentage of their content to images of women than do more general lifestyle magazines such as *GQ* and *Maxim* and the hybrid *FHM*. In terms of visual images of the other sex, men's and women's magazines are very different. The former are saturated with sexual photographs of women, while the latter rarely feature sexual images of men.

The second strategy to reassert the heterosexuality of readers revolves around body maintenance. Many men's magazines, including *Men's Health*, *GQ*, *Maxim* and *FHM*, subscribe to a regime of body maintenance where men have to work on their physique to maintain and improve it through dieting, exercise and beauty products. In essence this is similar to women's magazines. However, there are differences regarding attitudes to these regimes and their purported aims. Attwood (2005), drawing on Jackson et al. (2001), argues that while women's magazines present body regimes as pleasurable activities which result in beautiful physical appearance, men's magazines present such regimes as hard work informed by scientific knowledge which aims to counter physical decline. This is well exemplified in *FHM*, where articles on fitness, exercise, diet and nutrition feature in a content category entitled 'Upgrade: Live Long and Prosper'. Men's magazines present male bodies not as aesthetic objects but as machines which are to be maintenanced. Presenting bodies as projects to be worked on is not only a strategy to reassert heterosexuality and counter the 'feminization' of men, but also opens the body up as a site of identity (Jackson et al. 2001). Work has historically been the main source of masculine identity, but it has become increasingly unstable and fragmented in late modernity. In this context the body emerges as an alternative site where men can fashion a sense of masculinity by subjecting their bodies to regulatory regimes, disciplines and restraint such as regular exercise, fitness programmes and controlled diets (Jackson et al. 2001). Michael Kimmel (2006) argues that men's bodies have always been symbols of masculinity by signifying power and strength, but he agrees with Jackson et al. (2001) that contemporary men achieve muscular bodies by working out rather than through physical labour. Nevertheless, it could also be argued that the difference in attitudes to looking good, notably its presentation as a pleasurable activity to women and as hard work to men, are not clear-cut and depend on the particular aspect analysed. Dieting and exercise, for example, are often presented as necessary labour rather than fun in women's magazines, too. After all, restricting amounts and types of foods you can eat is difficult to sell as pleasurable. Conversely, grooming products or clothes are not really identified as hard work in men's magazines either. Indeed, television male make-over shows such as *Queer Eye for the Straight Guy* portray looking good as a fun activity which consists of consumption rather than work (Feasey 2008). Part of the show's point, in fact, is to convince heterosexual men of this pleasure. Hence it is true that looking good is more easily presented as fun for women because there is a long history of this, yet the aspects of looking good which are grounded in shopping rather than physical exercise and control are increasingly fashioned as fun for men, too.

Bodies and physical appearance have even come to pervade popular-cultural texts which represent some form of traditional masculinity. Detective films, especially the sub-genre of the cop action film, serve as a good example because they continue to be a male-centred genre (Gates 2006). The 1980s were the height of the cop action film; major successes included *Lethal Weapon*, starring Mel Gibson, released in 1987 and with sequels in 1989, 1992 and 1998, and *Die Hard*, starring Bruce Willis, released in 1988 and with sequels in 1990, 1995 and 2007. The protagonists in such films are cops and action heroes, using detective skills as well as physical force and violence (Gates 2006). Heroism is a strong feature of traditional masculinity, presenting men as engaged in heroic activities, ranging from the winning of medals in sport to saving the world through fighting and struggle (Benwell 2003). In cop action films there is an emphasis on physicality, in terms of both violence and bodies. The job of a cop action hero is hard physical labour and the protagonists display hyper-masculine physiques marked by extremely muscular, large, strong bodies which are constantly on show (Gates 2006).

Die Hard is the most successful Hollywood cop action film and its character John McClane, played by Bruce Willis, the embodiment of the action cop. McClane is a detective in the New York Police Department fighting a group of terrorists. The plot sees terrorists invading a high-rise plaza in order to rob its vaults and hold those in the building, including McClane's estranged wife, hostage. McClane single-handedly defeats the terrorists and rescues the hostages through a series of physical and often violent actions, such as man-to-man fights, climbing up and down the occupied building, throwing bombs, destroying buildings and cars, and shooting people. In the end he is reunited with his wife and has won back her love through his tough, heroic actions. While action cops largely draw on traditional masculinity, focusing on physical strength, tough attitudes, fighting and violence, they are also sexualized through the display of their bodies. According to Philippa Gates (2006), these two elements come together in a spectacle of hyper-masculinity: films such as *Die Hard* continuously showcase a hard and muscular male body which becomes the main weapon in the fight against crime. The focus is on physical power and strength, toughness and action; McClane solves his problems, notably the threat of losing his family, through action and physical defeat of the enemy. Like other action cop heroes, McClane is white, working-class and presented through his body. This is accentuated through his clothes: tank tops, which display bare arms, khakis and bare feet signify a no-nonsense fighter and visually emphasize his muscular body. At the same time they fetishize and sexualize his body, indicating that traditional masculinity, too, has become sexualized.

The new lad occupies an ambivalent relationship towards bodies and appearance. On the one hand, Edwards (1997, 2003) has noted that the lad is a fashion-conscious consumer who wants to look good. He is concerned about his appearance and invests considerable time and money to present himself in a particular way. Lad culture is associated with a particular style of clothes marked by trainers, jeans and shirts. This may be a casual style, but the clothes are branded and not cheap, with popular brands including Adidas, Kappa, Rockport, Ralph Lauren and Ben Sherman. Everyday grooming regimes, such as hair styling, the use of beauty products, moisturizers and aftershaves, are an intrinsic part of laddish masculinity. In contrast to the new man, the new lad does not opt for the stylized, trendy or sculpted look, but rather goes for the no-nonsense, casual-but-smart look, which nevertheless signifies a concern with physical appearance. Yet while 'laddishness no longer signif[ies] an absence of concern with bodily maintenance' (Jackson et al. 2001: 86), this concern tends to be downplayed as it is rarely openly voiced or discussed, but rather silently accepted. This is illustrated in the content of lads' magazines *Loaded*, *Nuts* and *Zoo* and the hybrid *FHM*. They mostly focus on sports, media, sex, fun, gadgets and women rather than fashion, beauty or style (Attwood 2005). Edwards (2003) has argued that style and fashion, because they are traditionally associated with femininity, threaten to undermine masculinity by revealing it as 'effeminate'. The new man, being overtly style-conscious and sexually ambiguous, never managed successfully to displace the resulting unease. According to Edwards, the success of the new lad lies in his ability to reconcile, at least artificially, the contradictions between masculinity and consumer culture by displaying a 'no nonsense, don't care' approach to fashion and subscribing to heterosexual promiscuity: 'New Lad iconography, centred upon shirts with logos, premium lager and sport, although equally commodified, invoked none of the sexual uncertainty of the New Man. . . . In short, it let young working-class men use moisturisers, dress up and go shopping without appearing middle-class, effeminate or homosexual' (Edwards 2003: 144).

However, it is noticeable that since the time of Edwards' writing, there has been an intensification of lad characteristics in the more recent lads' magazines, *Nuts* and *Zoo*, which were launched in 2003 and 2004, respectively (Attwood 2005). Compared to the older lads' magazines *Loaded* and *FHM*, *Nuts* and *Zoo* concern themselves even less with grooming and style. Today editions of *Nuts* and *Zoo* devote two out of one hundred pages to fashion and style and the focus is usually on clothes. Men's bodies are rarely visible in these magazines, while women's bodies are constantly on sexualized display. In contrast to men's style magazines, lads' magazines show little concern with body regimes and maintenance and instead subscribe to a hedonism marked by a range of excessive activities such as binge drinking, casual sex, extreme sports and adventures and drug taking (Jackson et al. 2001). Paired with this is a fascination with all things extreme and grotesque, from extreme physical wounds to eating bugs and dogs, from disfigured faces to cars destroyed in crashes (Attwood 2005). Masculinity is here constructed through excess and being able to 'take it', literally by engaging in excessive activities such as binge drinking or metaphorically by being able to stomach looking at images of extreme damage. The traditional masculine attribute of toughness is applied to late modern culture and constructed through leisure and consumer pursuits. Attwood argues that this "laddish" rejection of body maintenance and objectification' (2005: 89) is most pronounced in *Nuts* and *Zoo*. They carry no articles at all on health, exercise or grooming and feature no problem pages. Advertising for grooming products is usually couched in term of conquering females. While the new lad clearly cares about his appearance, there is an increasing pretence that he does not or only despite himself in order to attract females and get laid. This represents a return to disavowal of all things 'feminine' as a strategy to reassert heterosexual masculinity. Edwards (2003) has suggested that the success of the lad is grounded in its resolution, albeit artificial, of the tensions between fashion/style and masculinity through means of 'not caring' and promiscuous heterosexuality. But the move away from fashion and style in recent lads' magazines invites the question whether this artificial solution has started to dissolve. The tension between the requirements to look good and to not care about one's looks continues to exist at the heart of contemporary masculinity (Cohan 2007).

Sex, Sexuality and Relationships

In chapter 4 we have seen that sex and sexuality are central to the representation of femininity and that the emergence of a new feminine sexuality, which actively seeks pleasure and is comfortable with casual sex, is paired with a more conventional approach, which associates femininity with the desire for love, romance and long-term relationships. Nowhere is this more visible than in women's and girls' magazines, where sex and sexuality are constant topics and tend to be talked about in terms of relationships. For example, feature articles and experts' columns offer advice on how to find romance, achieve sexual pleasure, be sexually attractive, improve sex in relationships, and so on. Men tend to be framed as romantic ideals rather than sex objects. In men's magazines, sex and sexuality are equally important for constructing masculinity, but this takes quite a different form. Attwood argues that '[a]cross the spectrum of magazines for men, women are objectified to embody sex' (2005: 91). We can see this in the plethora of sexualized images showing scantily clad women in seductive poses, in the popularity of articles inviting readers to rate women in terms of their sexual appearance, or in articles about sex being nearly always accompanied by sexualized images of women in some state of undress (Taylor 2005). Indeed, a historical analysis shows that since the rise of men's magazines in the 1980s, there has been a continuing increase in the amount of space devoted to sexual imagery of women (Mooney 2008). This preoccupation and objectification is exemplified in both *Nuts* and *Zoo* dividing their content into four categories, namely 'girls', 'news', 'features' and 'sport'. Sexual images depict not only celebrities or professional models but increasingly ordinary or 'real' women who are encouraged to send in pictures of themselves to be judged for their attractiveness (Mooney 2008). Tellingly, *Nuts* calls its 'girls' category 'Real Girls UK'. The format of rating women for their looks has proved so popular that it has been taken outside the traditional print context. For example, *Nuts* has organized 'beach babe' competitions in beach resorts in the UK (*Sex in the Noughties: Nuts vs Zoo* 2007). Both *Nuts*' and *Zoo*'s websites ask women to upload pictures of their breasts so they can be given marks by viewers. On *Nuts*' website this feature is called 'Assess My Breasts', and on *Zoo*'s website there are several features which allow readers to rate topless women for their appearance and post comments, including 'Rude List' and 'Real Girl of the Year'. Hence in men's magazines sex is associated not with the domestic sphere of relationships and romance, but rather with sexual conquest in the public arena. Masculinity is about looking at women, judging them for their physical appearance and attracting them in order to get sex rather than love or relationships. This link between the sexual objectification and the sexual conquest of women manifests itself particularly clearly in *Nuts* and *Zoo*, which saw their sales figures slump when they started using A-list celebrities (*Sex in the Noughties: Nuts vs Zoo* 2007). Lads' magazine editors believe that readers prefer to see images of and rate 'ordinary' women – i.e. non-famous women and Z-list personalities such as Abi Titmus, glamour models or reality television contestants – which allow them to maintain the illusion of actual sexual conquest (*Sex in the Noughties: Nuts vs Zoo* 2007). Annabelle Mooney (2008) has argued that the increase in sexualized imagery and the move towards 'ordinary' or 'real' models constitute a normalization of pornography: showing pictures of non-famous women in a state of undress which invite a sexualized gaze has become part of the everyday and is rendered unremarkable.

Sex, sexuality and relationships feature as topics in most men's magazines, but they are not as big a concern as in women's magazines and they are treated differently. *Men's Health*, *GQ* and *FHM* contain more or less serious sections on sex problems and advice. In *FHM*, sex and relationship advice features as part of the content category 'Miss *FHM*: What Makes Women Tick'. This title declares sex and relationships the realm and responsibility of females and suggests the reason they feature in a men's magazine is that men need to 'work women out' in order to attract and have sex with them. The advice given is very much in this vein: an all-female team of experts tells ignorant male readers how women's minds and bodies work to improve their sex lives. Laramie Taylor (2005) has shown that in the US versions of *FHM*, *Maxim* and *Stuff*, sex(uality) as a topic is not confined to advice pages and that the most popular content category of articles about sex(uality) is 'What Women Want'. But just like the advice pages, these general articles are about male rather than female sexual pleasure. Male readers are told that taking 'what women want' into account will lead to more and better sex for them. Taylor concludes that articles about sex(uality) in these men's magazines reinforce a traditional view of gender and sex where 'women's sexual experience serves as a pathway to the fulfilment of men's sexual goals' (2005: 162). She notes that this orientation is visually reinforced through the sexualized images of semi-naked women which tend to accompany these articles, signalling woman as sex object. Hence, it is not the case that men's magazines do not concern themselves with sex, sexuality and relationships as such, but these matters are framed very differently. While in women's magazines these topics feature within a narrative of romance and relationships, in men's magazines the focus is on getting more and better sex, whether inside or outside relationships.

Pure lads' magazines *Loaded*, *Nuts* and *Zoo* have to be differentiated from the glossier men's magazines just discussed. *Nuts* and *Loaded* contain no articles whatsoever on sex and sexuality which centre on relationships or advice. *Zoo* contains a one-page feature called 'Sex School with Madison' which offers sex tips. However, both questions and answers are not real or serious, centring on male fantasies such as threesomes and S&M and always using a humorous tone. For example, a man who in the initial stages of dating has pretended to be a racing driver and now wonders how to tell his would-be girlfriend is advised, 'If you tell her, she's sure to lose her hard-on.' Whether this is a real or made-up dilemma, it is clearly not taken seriously and the advice given is neither considered nor sound. Jackson et al. (2001) argue that articles on sex and relationships in men's magazines maintain a distance between these topics and the readers through tone of address, which is often 'ironic' and takes the form of 'male banter', turning everything into a jokey rather than serious affair. This maintains distance not just from issues such as sex and relationships, but also from women, whose domain these issues are traditionally seen to be. In many men's magazines, and especially in lads' magazines, there is simply no space for taking responsibility for serious things such as emotions or relationships as masculinity remains a phase of 'extended adolescence' (Tincknell et al. 2003: 50), a 'pubescent world of masturbation and drunken one-night stands' (Edwards 2003: 139). The men in men's magazines never seem to grow up and remain limited to interests in boys' toys and 'having a laugh'.

Overall, it seems, then, that men's magazines have taken on the traditionally female topics of sex and sexuality but are less concerned with relationships. Concurrently, high-quantity and high-quality sex, rather than romance, are goals. This trend has been coupled with a return to elements of traditional masculinity, especially in lads' magazines and hybrids such as *FHM*. These define masculinity via hedonistic, commitment-phobic lifestyles, where a strong male sex drive is satisfied via continuous casual sex rather than relationships (Attwood 2005). In fact, Estella Tincknell et al. (2003) point out that lads' magazines do not simply not talk about or not advocate committed relationships, but they actively present them as undesirable and dangerous things which men have to make sure they do not get trapped in. While singledom is associated with autonomy and fun, long-term relationships embody boredom, constraint and undesirable responsibility (Jackson et al. 2001). Of course, episodic and hedonistic sex is also part of the new sexuality which is central to the new femininity (McRobbie 1997), allowing women to seek sexual pleasure in multiple, casual and fleeting encounters rather than committed relationships. However, the difference is that women's magazines continue to present long-term relationships as the ultimate goal, while in men's magazines casual sex is the goal and commitment an infringement on masculine autonomy and fun. In relation to men's magazines, Gill (2003) has argued that this represents a return to a 'libidinous heterosexuality' focused on men having as much sex as possible with many different women. Men's magazines portray this as a return to nature, to men's true, essential being, which is directly opposed to the 'feminization' associated with the new man (Gill 2003). Of course, the new lad is as socially constructed as any other type of masculinity; this becomes most obvious in the self-presentation of the lad through certain types of fashion, style and activities. Jackson et al. (2001) argue that the new man failed to become the hegemonic version of masculinity because it was identified as fake and unreal, never managing to displace the common-sense understanding that 'real' men simply do things rather than reflect on their personal style or social behaviour. It is this 'reality' that the new lad taps into. While being 'natural' tends to have positive connotations in contemporary culture, there is a dangerous slippage from 'natural' to 'old-fashioned' or even 'backward'. Tincknell et al. (2003) point out that men's magazines guard against this slippage through women's complicity in their objectification. If women reveal their bodies and let themselves be photographed in sexualized poses, then this is presented as evidence of a liberated, modern woman who is exercising her right to do whatever she wants to do: '[S]exual availability is effectively recast as autonomy' (Tincknell et al. 2003: 52). Of course, this complicity is really an example of the workings of hegemony as women consent to patriarchal gender norms (Mooney 2008).

The discursive shift towards a more 'natural' masculinity maps onto post-feminist conceptions of femininity which also attempt to counter feminist ideas of femininity by criticizing them as going against women's 'true' nature. Hence a picture emerges of considerable social changes in representations of femininity and masculinity since the 1970s. Initially these changes took the form of questioning traditional and essentialist gender images and norms, but since the late 1980s there has been a return to elements of traditional and essentialist conceptions and a corresponding critique of the movements which questioned them in the first place. The elements of initial change which have survived to this day tend to be the ones associated with consumerism or at least capable of being incorporated into it. For example, women's equality is often reduced to vacuous notions of 'girl power', which amount to little more than women wearing what they want, spending their wages how they wish, drinking to excess and having sex with whomever they want. There is some empowerment and equality in this, but the real political fight for equal rights is fundamentally 'unsexy' and has been sidelined as too serious, boring and unnecessary (Negra 2009). Moreover, it is this shallow understanding of equal rights as a series of consumer choices that has led to a situation where women posing in semi-naked and seductive ways for male sexual pleasure can be read as an exercise of individual autonomy rather than sexual objectification and exploitation. The elements of the new man which have not been challenged for being too 'feminine' include hedonism, consumption and sexualization. Men spend more money than ever on fashion, cars, gadgets and grooming. But in many other ways, masculinity in the noughties has turned away from the new man and back towards traditional masculinity, as evidenced in sexist attitudes, treatment of women as sex objects or refusal of commitment. It is therefore too easy to recount social change as a movement towards greater gender equality and erasure of gender difference (Edwards 1997); there have been elements of this, but they have been coupled with a renewed emphasis on gender difference and inequality in recent decades. Consumerism has played a double-edged role in this, both helping along and hijacking the serious critique of social movements.

Contemporary representations of masculinity and femininity suggest that the two genders are not really compatible when it comes to love and relationships: women are constructed as wanting romance and long-term commitment, while men are portrayed as focused on casual sex and avoidance of commitment. This incompatibility is striking given the centrality of heterosexual love and relationships in popular culture. It seems to suggest the impossibility of a 'happy ending' because men and women are simply too different; yet so much of popular culture is devoted to and dependent on this happy ending, from the wedding industry and the romantic comedy genre to women's magazines and love songs, that these differences have to be resolved. Antony Easthope (1992) has pointed out that the problem in this respect is traditional masculinity. He argues that the discourse of love in contemporary culture envisages an equal relationship based on mutual trust, respect and deep, shared emotions. Love is a very desirable and highly valued concept, but many elements of traditional masculinity and new laddism do not fit, such as the unwillingness to commit, the sexual objectification of women or the denial of emotions. Hence, while contemporary femininity fits the discourse of love, contemporary masculinity in many ways does not. The 'solution' of much of popular culture to this lack of fit is to separate 'good men' from 'bad men' and to suggest that women have to make sure they choose the right one (Firminger 2006). Romantic comedies are one genre particularly reliant on such a 'solution' because they are in the business of presenting heterosexual love as the ultimate goal. *Bridget Jones's Diary* (2001) and its sequel, *Bridget Jones: The Edge of Reason* (2004), which are among the most successful romantic comedies of the noughties, illustrate the dynamics well.

The films' protagonist, played by Renée Zellwegger, is a 33-year-old woman living in London who works in publishing and television. She is frustrated about still being single and her main aim in life is to find Mr Right and eventually settle down, marry and have children. She keeps a diary recording her efforts, successes and disappointments in finding Mr Right (Spicer 2004). Throughout both films, Bridget Jones is torn between her on–off relations with two men, Mark Darcy, played by Colin Firth, and Daniel Cleaver, played by Hugh Grant. Both films centre on her finding out which of the two is her Mr Right.

Mark Darcy and Daniel Cleaver are totally opposite characters. Daniel Cleaver, who is Bridget Jones's boss, is classically handsome with a well-toned body and trendy haircut. He is witty and intelligent, outgoing and charismatic, confident, cultured and fun to be with. Bridget Jones fancies him and the two constantly flirt at work and start dating. However, he is a sexual predator and womanizer who flirts, dates and sleeps with many women, often at the same time. For him these women are sex objects who fulfil a function, namely to satisfy his sexual desires. It is clear to viewers that he is not Mr Right, being too fickle and capricious to ever commit exclusively to Bridget Jones. In contrast to Daniel Cleaver, Mark Darcy, a successful lawyer, is less strikingly handsome. He is good-natured but dour, slightly nerdy and dull, and a sensible person who does not stimulate enthusiasm (Spicer 2004). Unlike Daniel Cleaver, he is not openly highly sexed, believes in marriage and the nuclear family and is ready to commit to Bridget Jones and marry her. This is suggested in several ways, for example through commitment shown in a previous marriage (which only ended because it was broken up by Cleaver) or his genuine love for Bridget Jones. He is socially rather unskilled and finds it difficult to express his emotions and sensitivity, but this is presented as more desirable than Cleaver's shallowness and actual lack of profound emotions and sensitivity. Mark Darcy's love as well as his willingness to take on the traditional role of head of the family who provides for wife and children structurally set him up as Mr Right – even though Andrew Spicer (2004) notes that the dullness of Mark Darcy's character, especially when contrasted with Daniel Cleaver's charisma, makes for a somewhat 'imperfect' ending.

The 'solution' to the problem of masculinity's incompatibility with love is therefore the splitting of men into good ones and bad ones. This is by no means confined to romantic comedies. Teenage magazines tell their readers that they must learn to distinguish the 'bad boys' from the 'good boys' (McRobbie 2000) and either avoid bad boys or change them into good ones (Firminger 2006). In these scenarios the bad ones are those that only want sex, while the good ones are ready to commit to a long-term relationship and delay sexual contact. This splitting is highly contradictory, unrealistic and ideological as it banishes all the undesirable characteristics of masculinity, from sexism to commitment avoidance, to 'bad' people and leaves traditional masculinity as such unquestioned. Men's magazines, especially lads' magazines, offer no 'solution' because the lack of fit is not recognized as a problem. Relationships and love are constraints to be avoided rather than goals to be desired. What they do not address, of course, are the downsides of perpetual lack of commitment: for instance, how emotions such as care, belonging and security are to be found and nurtured if not in a relationship (Jackson et al. 2001). In a traditional fashion, love, emotions and commitment are silenced as male needs and presented as things that only women want.

Men at Work and at Home

The absence and presence of work

Work in men's magazines is conspicuous by its absence. Upmarket *GQ* contains a small number of articles on work-related issues or occasional specials, for example a Business Special section in April 2010. *FHM* used to contain a one-page regular feature called 'Good Job/Bad Job' in 2009, which briefly outlined two very different kinds of jobs. Tellingly, this feature was hidden away on the very last page of the magazine and by 2010 it had disappeared altogether. *Maxim*, *FHM*, *Loaded*, *Nuts* and *Zoo* do not tend to feature any articles on work. This is remarkable given the centrality of work to masculinity. It is a source of identity for men who define themselves via paid employment performed outside the home. This invites the question why there is such a lack of interest and concern in contemporary men's magazines. Jackson et al. (2001), drawing on Beck's (1992) work, locate the reasons in the condition of late modernity. In the late modern period, work has become less stable, more fragmented and more risky. The concept of one-job-for-life has disappeared, an increasing number of jobs are temporary, part-time and casual, and the constant drive towards greater profits through downsizing, lean management and technological innovation means that many skills and jobs are at risk of becoming redundant. Work is therefore no longer a stable source of identity and Jackson et al. (2001) suggest that, as a consequence, a new, more secure source of masculine identity is sought in the body. When you invest in the body, for example through exercise and nutrition regimes, you can at least be sure that it pays off. The argument is not that the body has replaced work as a key source of identity, but that it has emerged as an alternative site.

Jackson et al. (2001) argue that men's magazines aim to provide their readers with a 'constructed certitude' in the face of changing social conditions in late modernity; as work is no longer a plausible field for doing this, the magazines focus on the body. However, lads' magazines contain either very little (*FHM*) or nothing at all (*Loaded*, *Nuts* and *Zoo*) on body maintenance. They seem to provide constructed certitude through naturalizing gender and sexuality difference. Patricia Holland (2004) notes that sexualized images of women have become very visible in popular culture, most notably lads' magazines, at precisely a time when there is a general trend towards increasing gender equality, for example in areas such as education or employment. She suggests that the lads' magazines' sexualization of women is a response to more equal gender relations. As women become economically, socially and personally more assertive, more successful and more demanding, lads' magazines resort to constructing gender difference, and by implication female inferiority, by asserting the 'natural', biological and therefore permanent nature of sexual relations, roles and identities. These essential gender differences not only justify gender inequality and sexism, but also offer men the illusion of stability and superiority. Moreover, lads' magazines can be seen to provide certitude to their readers through the establishment of a sense of community. This, Mary Talbot (2007) argues, is achieved through the simulation of friendship and reciprocal discourse. For example, pronouns such as 'you' or 'we' are frequently used, which directly speak to the reader and suggest that readers and magazine producers share a like-mindedness. The choice of obviously laddish language – e.g. 'wicked', 'get in' or 'birds' – is another way of creating this sense of community. Lads' magazines frequently use utterances which demand responses from readers

– e.g. commands like 'Try this!' or questions like 'Need you know more?' – which suggest the existence of common interests, tastes and values (Talbot 2007). Further strategies to construct this sense of community and group-belonging include the exclusion of absent others, notably women, through pejorative talk and the use of irony which presumes readers to be in the know.

Just as work does not feature in men's magazines, neither does the domestic. Most domestic issues, from cooking to home furnishing, and domestic roles, such as husband or father, are conspicuous by their absence. The coverage of sex and sexuality is rarely framed in terms of relationships, but rather focuses on the pursuit of women in public spaces. This suggests that we have to look elsewhere for representations of masculinity in the world of work and at home. While men's magazines do not concern themselves with either, work at least remains central to representations of masculinity in other major forms of popular culture such as television or film (Feasey 2008). Domestic roles may be less frequent, but there is a trend towards men moving into the domestic sphere. Moreover, the strict boundaries of public (work) and private (home/family) have become blurred in the process, which is why we examine them in conjunction.

Television and film are vast and complex media which encompass a range of different genres and programmes. To make matters even more complex, both television and cinema film have witnessed a proliferation and diversification of images of masculinity (Feasey 2008; Spicer 2003). This analysis, because of space constraints, will focus on television programmes. While cinema-going remains popular and of course films are shown on television, too, since the 1970s, television, with its range of programmes specifically made for the medium, has become the most popular cultural medium (Spicer 2003). This popularity and importance have arguably been intensified in the last two decades through the invention of new technologies which make watching television programmes more convenient. For example, television set-top boxes (e.g. Freeview+ Box, Sky Digibox, TiVo) allow viewers to record television programmes and watch them at a time of their choosing. The internet now contains various platforms and websites, e.g. YouTube or the BBC iPlayer, which allow users to watch television programmes on their computer at any time. These technological developments have uncoupled television programmes from the medium of television and have made them easily and continually accessible for audiences. For the remainder of this chapter we will investigate the place of work and home in the representation of masculinity by looking at a range of very popular television genres, namely hospital dramas, crime dramas, soap operas and cooking programmes.

Hospital dramas: men as doctors

Television hospital dramas are an excellent case study for examining the role of work in the representation of contemporary masculinity as well as understanding historical shifts and changes. This is because they have a long history going back to the 1950s, yet continue to be a very popular genre in the UK and the US today (Jacobs 2001). Moreover, the role of the doctor is socially esteemed and lends itself to a traditional view of masculinity as marked by professional skills and knowledge and the exercise of power and authority.

Hospital dramas of the 1950s and 1960s revolved around an inevitably male doctor-hero who is the centre of power and authority in the hospital (Feasey 2008). He possesses amazing and infinite medical skills and knowledge, which save lives on a day-to-day basis. Doctors in these dramas were never shown to lose patients or to fail through misdiagnosis or a lack of answers. The doctor is almost god-like in his omnipotence and not only widely respected but worshipped. He is an infallible hero who represents an infallible masculinity (Jacobs 2001). In the 1950s and 1960s, female doctors simply did not feature; women were confined to the role of nurse, a profession associated with care rather than knowledge. This has changed, and contemporary medical dramas, whether the British *Casualty* or *Holby City* or the American *ER*, all feature female doctors. However, Rebecca Feasey's (2008) analysis shows that the vast majority of doctors continue to be male and that male doctors continue to be the centre of most narratives. Since the 1970s, the portrayal of these (largely male) doctors has considerably changed. It has become more realistic and less reverent, showing doctors making mistakes, facing limits in their medical knowledge and power, failing to cure patients and sometimes even inadvertently causing their death (Jacobs 2001). Moreover, there is now a new focus on doctors' private and emotional lives, where they face struggles such as divorce or depression. The doctor-hero in contemporary hospital dramas is no longer infallible and much more vulnerable, no longer god but human (Feasey 2008). These changes reflect wider social changes, notably a disenchantment with science and a recognition of its limits, as well as changes in masculinity. Neverthless, male doctors continue to be presented as having incredible expertise, skills and knowledge, as doing a very important job of saving lives and curing diseases, all of which associates them with a traditional masculinity marked by hard skills and competence, rationality and power. Of course, the doctor role is ideal for constructing this traditional masculinity, because in real life the job requires considerable education and expert knowledge and is one of the most high-status occupations in society.

But Feasey (2008) observes that the contemporary doctor-hero is also often, if not always, compassionate and caring, which illustrates the changing expectations of ideal masculinity ushered in by the new man, such as being in touch with their 'soft' side, admitting weakness and expressing emotions. Overall, contemporary male doctors are still portrayed as heroes, but what makes a hero has changed as the focus shifts to morality and character. Male doctors are represented as dedicated to the cause of medicine and demonstrate their commitment through long working hours and spending all their energy on saving lives and caring for their patients. They are morally principled and sincere, wanting the best for their patients and fighting against hospital bureaucracy. Characters exemplifying this type include *ER*'s Dr Kovac, played by Goran Visnjic, and *Holby City*'s Mr Griffin, played by Hugh Quarshie. They are honest, principled and highly capable heroes (Feasey 2008).

Crime dramas: men as crime fighters

One of the most popular and male-dominated television genres is the crime or police drama (Cooke 2001). It has been identified as a genre which is very much suited to producing traditional masculinity because of its focus on the male world of work and the simple formula of policemen fighting criminals (MacKinnon 2003). This still holds true despite considerable historical changes. Police dramas of the 1950s featured the male 'bobby-on-the-beat', who was a hardworking, honest and decent man committed to dealing with crime and protecting the community to which he belonged. The crimes featured tended to be very low level. These dramas were marked by moral certainty, with a clear line being drawn between the good policeman and the bad criminal (Cooke 2001). But this rose-tinted image of crime fighting gradually disappeared as the nature of policework and the characters of policemen became more violent, professional, maverick, challenged and personally flawed (Feasey 2008). By the 1990s, policemen are often specialized agents who come in from the outside. Moral certainty persists in those dramas, which portray policemen as personally flawed but fundamentally decent characters who demonstrate their professional commitment to the cause of fighting crime. These dramas show policemen using aggression, force and violence, and breaking the rules, but justify these behaviours through images of an increasingly lawless society and an overworked police force. There are many contemporary examples of this kind of drama, from the British *Taggart* to the Swedish *Wallander* series. Feasey (2008) notes that crime dramas only broke with this certainty in the 1990s. Series such as the American *The Wire* or *24* challenge the clear line between heroes and villains by portraying criminals in a more sympathetic light and showing policemen engaged in misdemeanours such as corruption, brutal violence or racism. Across the decades, crime fighters have always tended to be men. Cop shows are a male genre; the few exceptions tend to compromise female police officers by aligning them with gendered crimes such as rape or showing them preoccupied with their private lives. Masculinity is central to the crime drama. The emphasis on fighting and triumph, the assertion of power and authority, the increasing focus on violence, aggression and breaking the rules to get the job done – all these core elements neatly fit with traditional masculinity but not with femininity or indeed homosexual masculinity. Therefore it is unsurprising that the crime drama remains a largely male heterosexual domain.

Feasey's (2008) analysis of contemporary crime drama series shows that one of the most central and recurring themes is sacrificing the family. She states that 'police and crime dramas routinely show male police constables, detectives and special branch officers ignoring the needs of their family in favour of the force, sacrificing their personal life for the good of wider society. In short, their success in the public sphere seems to demand a sacrifice in the private realm' (Feasey 2008: 84). Because this sacrifice is portrayed as for the greater good of society, the policeman does not come across as a selfish individual pursuing his career at the expense of his partner and children, but as an altruistic person who puts society first and himself last. Feasey (2008) demonstrates these points by looking at two of the most popular recent crime series in the US and the UK, namely *24* and *Spooks* (*MI5* in the US). The main character in *24* is Jack Bauer, played by Kiefer Sutherland, who works as an elite field agent in the Los Angeles Counter Terrorist Unit. His work is extremely demanding and requires long hours, which is reflected in the title. He certainly has no time for his family, not even in times of crisis such as his daughter being wrongfully charged with kidnap. But this is presented as a positive thing. Bauer's wife and children are seen to get in the way of his extremely important job of protecting national security, while he emerges as the hero and martyr who puts his country above all else. Feasey sums this up writing that

> because Jack works tirelessly to stamp out threats to national security and protect the status quo we are asked to see a man of strength, bravery, integrity and honour, . . . to overlook this man's motives, his recklessness, his disregard for his family and his inability to face up to his personal responsibilities in favour of positioning him as a hard-boiled hero. (2008: 89)

This reinforces the notion of primacy of the public sphere over the private sphere: private lives are expendable but professional work is not. Men, who are traditionally associated with the public sphere and who continue to occupy most of positions of power, emerge as more important and indispensable than women. Crime dramas therefore continue to represent a very traditional kind of masculinity built around work and the exertion of power, control and authority to make an important difference in the world. There is very little of the new man in here: the crime fighter is tough, ruthless, aggressive and even violent, and certainly does not express any emotions. While the male doctors of contemporary hospital dramas struggle with their emotional and private lives, usually in the hours outside work, and show professional compassion, the policeman has literally and metaphorically no time for such things.

Soap operas: men in work and at home

Soap operas are the most popular television genre in terms of viewing figures. They have historically been identified as a female genre because of their focus on domestic issues and their popularity with female viewers. However, in recent years soap operas have tried to broaden their appeal by introducing a greater number and more diverse range of male characters (Feasey 2008) and dealing with traditionally 'masculine' themes such as business, crime and violence (MacKinnon 2003). While hospital dramas clearly align men with power and knowledge by locating them in the world of work and positioning them in the prestigious role of the doctor, no such easy assessment can be made of men in soap operas. This is because soap operas blur the boundaries of work and the domestic, of the professional and the personal (Geraghty 1991). Of course, soaps feature places of work – usually pubs and clubs, cafés and restaurants, market stalls, bookmakers, garages, factories – but in these places domestic dramas are played out and intimate, personal conversation are engaged in, most commonly about finances, love, childrearing and extramarital affairs. There is no distinct private sphere because there is no real privacy: everyone always overhears and knows about other people's conversations (Feasey 2008). But equally there is no real public sphere because public places are saturated with private concerns and professional relations are translated into personal ones. Those with jobs constantly spend their time at work talking about their private troubles, whether the bar staff in a pub or mechanics in the garage. The cause for the blurring of boundaries is the genre of the soap, which relies on talk, rather than action, to develop characters and storylines (Gledhill 1997). Indeed Christine Gledhill (1997) emphasizes that talk in all its forms, i.e. conversation, gossip or confession, is the action of soap operas. As a consequence, male characters are drawn into the traditionally feminine activity of talking and thinking about personal and domestic affairs, even though Feasey (2008) shows that men are still frequently represented as unable to communicate their true feelings and inept at dealing with emotional and personal crises. There is no purely public sphere of work where men can make their mark. They have jobs but work is of secondary importance to the character. Moreover, except for a few high-power positions such as owners of nightclubs or factories, the types of jobs available in soap operas are largely working-class and service sector jobs. These jobs are low in social status and power and often involve the provision of services to customers, putting the workers into a subordinate position. Hence, most of the jobs featured in soap operas do not lend themselves well to the construction of traditional masculinity marked by expertise, hard skill and authority.

Because of soap opera's focus on the domestic sphere and personal relationships, we would expect it to be a genre which shows men in their roles as husbands and fathers. And this is indeed what has happened. Fatherhood has moved to the centre of narratives, for example through storylines about single fathers or mysteries about paternity. In some ways this reflects social changes and especially the impact of the new man, which position fatherhood as an important element of men's lives and require them to get involved in childrearing. In some ways these depictions can be read as a move towards greater gender equality as men become associated with the traditionally feminine sphere of the private and the personal, which is no longer purely a women's responsibility. But on the other hand, Feasey (2008) has argued that these shifts have often resulted in establishing men as taking control of the domestic sphere, resulting in an increase of male power and authority. For example, in paternity mysteries, female characters are in control because only they have the power to name the father of their child. However, once revealed, storylines usually end in reconciliation as fathers bond with their children, take on the responsibility of looking after them and re-establish their family unit. In this sense they ultimately establish control over the private, domestic sphere and become masters of their own homes. Hence soap operas tend to both challenge and reinforce the idea of male patriarchal power through the figure of the father.

Lifestyle shows: men as chefs

Since the 1990s there has been an explosion in lifestyle programmes on television which deal with domestic tasks, such as home improvement (both DIY and decorating), cooking, fashion and dressing, gardening, cleaning and childrearing (Negra 2009). While most of these tasks have traditionally been seen as a woman's responsibility, this new breed of lifestyle programme is increasingly headed by male presenters and features male experts and laymen. This may be interpreted as going some way towards breaking down the traditional boundaries between the private and the public onto which femininity and masculinity are commonly mapped, asserting male responsibility for the domestic and the chores it entails. However, both Negra (2009) and Feasey (2008) caution against this by pointing out that not all areas of the domestic have seen an equal influx of men as they have been turned into lifestyle programmes. Childrearing and cleaning programmes, for example, remain female-dominated. Moreover, the ways in which men are represented in lifestyle programmes differ significantly from the way that women are represented. We want to explore this in some detail by looking at cooking programmes, because they feature a large number of male chefs.

There are female celebrity television chefs. Delia Smith is the UK's longest-running television chef, with programmes going back to the 1970s (e.g. *Family Fare*, *Delia Smith's Cookery Course*), and continues to be prominent today (e.g. *Delia*). Nigella Lawson is another famous female chef with her own television shows (e.g. *Nigella Bites*, *Nigella Feasts*, *Nigella Express*). But a much larger number of celebrity television chefs are male, including Jamie Oliver (e.g. *The Naked Chef*, *Jamie's School Dinners*, *Jamie's Great Italian Escape*, *Jamie's Ministry of Food*), Gordon Ramsay (e.g. *Ramsay's Kitchen Nightmares*, *Hell's Kitchen*, *The F Word*), Rick Stein (e.g. *Rick Stein's Mediterranean Escape*), Gary Rhodes (e.g. *Rhodes around Britain*, *Saturday Cooks*), Ainsley Harriott (e.g. *Ready Steady Cook*, *Ainslie's Barbeque Bible*),

The Hairy Bikers (e.g. *The Hairy Bikers' Cookbook*) and Hugh Fearnley-Whittingstall (e.g. *River Cottage*). Jamie Oliver and Gordon Ramsay have become famous outside the UK. Many of their programmes have been aired across the globe, and several series are set in the US, including *Jamie's Food Revolution Hits Hollywood* (simply known as *Jamie Oliver's Food Revolution* in the US), *Jamie's American Road Trip* and *Ramsay's Kitchen Nightmares USA*.

Feasey (2008) suggests that there has been a shift in lifestyle programmes away from instruction and towards consumption. In cooking programmes, audiences are no longer given detailed advice on how to cook certain dishes or master particular kitchen techniques; instead they are addressed as consumers of a lifestyle such as travelling (e.g. *Jamie's Great Italian Escape*, *The Hairy Bikers' Cookbook*) or organic living (e.g. *River Cottage*). Feasey also notes that this shift concerns especially programmes with male chefs. While female chefs such as Delia Smith and Nigella Lawson continue to present themselves as educators and nurturers of the audience, male chefs emerge as lifestyle gurus rather than cooking instructors. This is one way for men to negotiate the domestic sphere of the kitchen. As the kitchen has traditionally been seen as a woman's domain and cooking a woman's duty to her family, male chefs have to counter this feminization and assert their masculinity. Looking at Jamie Oliver's show *The Naked Chef*, Feasey identifies several discursive techniques which distance him from the feminine sphere of the domestic and therefore ensure his masculinity. One such technique is vagueness or imprecision. Oliver's cooking programmes do not tend to feature detailed instructions or prescriptions, for example regarding the quantities of ingredients, heat settings or the order of preparation. Instead, his approach to cooking is portrayed as spontaneous, random, impulsive and instinct-driven. His colloquial language and unspecific comments, e.g. talking about 'chucking things in' or 'smashing up herbs', add to this impression that he improvises as he goes along rather than follows precise rules. Traditionally, cooking has been perceived as a dreary chore, as a part of a woman's routine and mundane domestic labour. But Oliver's vague, impulsive and improvised approach refashions cooking as a fun activity and a social pleasure, and in this way it serves as a distancing technique from the feminine sphere of the domestic as a space of labour. To maintain this image of cooking as leisure, all aspects around cooking are presented as fun: for example, Oliver's food shopping trips involve strolling through the streets, chatting to shopkeepers and are interspersed with window-shopping of clothes. Those aspects of cooking that cannot be recast as 'fun' because they are too obviously mundane, routine and unpleasant chores, e.g. tidying up the kitchen or cleaning appliances, do not feature in the programme (Hollows 2003). A second distancing technique concerns Oliver presenting himself as an 'ordinary bloke' who does not quite know the exact protocols of cooking, takes short cuts, gets things wrong and loves 'simple' food. His youthful, laddish masculinity, marked by laddish language (e.g. 'pukka') and demeanour (e.g. up for having a laugh), add to this image of him as 'one of the boys'. Oliver's 'incompetence' is no more credible than his 'imprecision', given that he is trained and works as professional chef, but it serves again to distance him from the feminine sphere of the domestic by adhering to the traditional image of the incompetent male in the kitchen (Hollows 2003).

While Hollows' (2003) and Feasey's (2008) analyses are very insightful and accurate, they necessarily miss the slightly new direction which the Jamie Oliver brand has taken in recent years. This began with *Jamie's School Dinners* (2005) and has crystallized in *Jamie's Ministry of Food* (2008) and his American *Food Revolution* series (2010, 2011). The new image of Oliver is less fun-seeking lad and more serious campaigner, who is set on changing a nation's food and cooking habits. The twin aims are to teach people a love of food and to get them to eat more healthily by cooking from scratch and with fresh ingredients. In this vein, Oliver teaches school dinner ladies (*Jamie's School Dinners*) and working-class parents (*Jamie's Ministry of Food*) how to cook nutritious and healthy meals on a budget. There are, of course, tensions in his aims, as home-cooked and healthy do not necessarily go together and Oliver's fondness for drizzling everything with olive oil may not be the best way to combat obesity. But our main point is that this move towards campaigning for healthy eating and changing the habits of a nation has necessitated a shift for Oliver towards a more instructive style of cooking as he teaches detailed recipes. Nevertheless, he remains removed from the feminine realm of cooking as a domestic chore by being firmly placed in the public sphere: the cooking education takes place in public places such as schools, companies and community centres and his job is a public mission which he carries out for the greater good of society. He may aim to change the private sphere, notably improving parental cooking at home, but does so from a position of public health campaigner and instructor. Moreover, Talbot (2007) has pointed out that *Jamie's School Dinners* strongly demarcates cooking expertise along gender lines. The real-life dinner ladies featured in the programme may cook for a living, yet Oliver is set up as the expert who teaches, monitors and instructs them. He continually asserts his authority and professionalism by listing their shortcomings, criticizing the poor quality of their performance and expressing frustration regarding their lack of skill. The way in which Jamie Oliver is presented in his shows demonstrates that while men may now host programmes involving traditionally feminine activities and domains, these are reinvented in new ways to de-feminize them and thereby assert the masculinity of their presenters. This suggests that men entering women's spheres still produces anxieties over the blurring of gender difference and that the media respond by asserting difference through other discursive strategies such as style and image building. Nevertheless, such programmes do open up the domestic space as a space for men and thereby challenge traditional masculinity, which would outrightly reject activities such as cooking as a woman's work.

Conclusion

Representations of men are diverse and marked by both historical continuities and changes. The new man ushered in major changes in masculinity in the 1980s and has left a significant legacy in terms of appearance, sex(uality) and relationships. Even though men are still not objectified to the same extent as women, contemporary men are required to look good and adhere to standards of style and bodily appearance. Moreover, men are expected to have a soft side in terms of sex and relationships. However, there has been a backlash against these new versions of masculinity, best embodied by the figure of the new lad and the insistence on the 'natural' difference between men and women. This development is concomitant with post-feminism's backlash against new versions of femininity and suggests that representations of masculinity and femininity have undergone broadly similar historical trends. Challenges to traditional concepts of masculinity and femininity in the 1970s and 1980s have been followed by a critique of these challenges. This has led to a situation where traditional and progressive representations of masculinity and femininity coexist. The issue of work illustrates this well for masculinity. Consumption has become a major new source of male identity, but work is still central to masculinity. Men in popular culture are nearly always working men and tend to dominate high-status, powerful working roles such as doctors or crime fighters. But men have also entered the traditionally feminine sphere of the domestic, blurring traditional boundaries. Nevertheless, the domestic is not as defining for male as for female identity: men may increasingly be shown as fathers, but they are always still in full-time work and it is the latter which tends to define them. Moreover, men tend to take on domestic tasks such as cooking in professional capacities, which distances them from women, who tend to fulfil domestic tasks in their private capacities as mothers or housewives. These mixed trends suggest that the struggle over gender relations continues, driven by traditional and progressive forces, and that any converging of masculinity and femininity still has the power to generate anxieties about insufficient difference between genders, especially the 'feminization' of men.

PART III

Consumption, Gender and Popular Culture

Introduction to Part III

In this final section we move our focus onto gender and the consumption of popular culture. Chapter 6 begins with an overview of literature on gender and cultural consumption, looking at how people make sense of and respond to media texts and asking which role gender plays in these processes. The literature on active audiences, encoding/decoding and the polysemic nature of texts is surveyed and critiqued. Moreover, the chapter examines the consumption of media in relation to the production of gendered identities. What impact does our media consumption have on the ways in which we perform our gender? Finally, chapter 6 investigates case studies from new media, such as video and online games and erotic adult internet sites. Whilst cyberspace offers some potential for the reconfiguring of traditional gender categories and characteristics, 'real world' gender differences continue to be at play in the virtual world.

Chapter 7 moves the discussion of consumption and gender into a different terrain by focusing on space and place. Rather than looking at how men and women consume media and popular-cultural texts, this chapter examines public consumption spaces. We consider the limits to women's consumption of urban space in the city of modernity. Our analysis then moves on to look at girls' roles within youth subcultures; subcultures not only have a strong spatial element but are arenas in which cultural production and consumption take place. In our analysis we consider whether subcultures allow girls space to be active consumers and, sometimes, cultural producers. The final case study examines issues around gender and the consumption of contemporary urban space. Here we use the example of gay leisure spaces to consider a range of power struggles over consumption in urban space.

Whilst chapter 6 deals predominantly with private, domestic consumption, chapter 7 deals with gender and consumption in public space and points to how women are themselves consumed and gazed upon in urban spaces. As we have argued throughout this book, there are interlinking chains between production, representation and consumption. Consumption itself can be a highly productive act; it can produce meaning, identities and subjectivities.

6
Consuming Popular Culture

The Role of Gender

In chapters 4 and 5 we have discussed the ways in which women and men are represented in popular culture. Such investigations raise the question of how consumers actually respond to the representations that they read, listen to and view. In the discipline of cultural studies, consumption is understood as a process of 'making sense' of cultural texts. So, in what ways do consumers make sense? Do they uncritically absorb, totally reject or ignore representations? Does the gender of consumers matter in this respect: that is, do men and women make sense of texts in different ways? The answers to these questions are central to issues around the power of media discourses and ideologies about gender, because in order to be powerful, they have to be taken on board by consumers. But conceptualizing consumers as makers of sense and meaning also necessitates affording them a genuinely active role and asking what consumers do with cultural texts and what role gender might play in this. For example, do men and women consume different types of cultural texts or do they use them in different ways? In what ways can cultural consumption be a way to construct feminine and masculine identities? This chapter delves into theory and research on cultural consumers and 'media audiences', as they are often labelled, to answer these questions.

Theorizing Media Influence and Audiences
Media effects

Media and cultural studies have historically led the way regarding enquiry into the nature and consequences of cultural consumption. A key concern has been to establish how consumers respond to the messages and images circulated in the mass media. This approach has become known as media audience research or media reception research. Since the 1930s, several grand theoretical models have been developed to conceptualize how audiences respond to the media. These general models have increasingly come under critique for being insufficiently detailed and complex, which led to the 'ethnographic turn' in academia in the 1980s. Since then, many academics have carried out ethnographic studies of particular instances of media consumption and discovered intricate knowledge about the process.

The earliest theoretical model attempting to understand the power of the media to affect the beliefs, knowledge and behaviour of audiences is the 'direct-effects theory', also known as the 'hypodermic syringe model' (Livingstone 1996). It stipulates that media texts contain certain representations and messages, which are directly, uncritically and passively absorbed by the audience. Hence the media directly affect audiences, who simply believe what they are told and shown. This theory is based on a linear model of mass communication: sender (media)–message–receiver (audience) (Seiter 1999). The model of power underlying this theory is simplistic and one-dimensional as the media have all the power to impose their messages on an entirely powerless audience (Gauntlett 1997). Despite this, the direct-effects tradition has appealed to many social scientists on both the left and the right. Most notably, the Frankfurt School in the 1930s wedded Marxism to the newly emerging popular culture and theorized the media as an instrument of mass deception (Adorno and Horkheimer 1993). The media were seen as owned by a dominant economic elite who use them to disseminate ideologies which dupe audiences into a state of 'false consciousness'. In this state, audiences come to accept and believe opinions and facts about the world which are actually inaccurate and work against their own interests. While the Frankfurt School conceptualized its ideas on the basis of social class, feminists have later applied its approach to the study of gender and media consumption. Early feminist researchers into gender and the media in the 1970s, such as Germaine Greer or Gaye Tuchman, saw the mass media as maintaining patriarchy by indoctrinating women with stereotypical images and narratives which construct femininity as different and inferior to masculinity (Ang and Hermes 1996). Similarly, genres mostly consumed by women, such as soap operas, romance novels or women's magazines, are systematically devalued as low culture (Strinati 2004). The assumption of such research is that female and male audiences simply accept these messages and thereby become complicit victims of the sexist media. This is, of course, simplistic and presumptious; the direct-effects model presupposes a uniform and passive audience who unthinkingly absorb media messages.

Research has shown time and again that consumers are neither uniform nor passive in their responses. For example, Rosalind Ballaster et al.'s (1991) research with female readers of women's magazines has found that many women are very critical of the ways in which these magazines present women. The narrow feminine beauty ideal reproduced in images and descriptions is rejected by many readers as stereotypical, objectifying and unrealistic. Moreover, these consumers self-reflexively interrogate their relationship with these magazines and demonstrate clear awareness of their motivations for reading them: for example, because they offer fantasy and escapism or because magazines reflect a certain stage of their lives. This active, critical and reflexive engagement is a long way from the unconscious, uncritical reader who simply absorbs media messages. Research by Rosalind Gill et al. (2000) into men's responses to the media's male beauty ideal illustrates well that audience responses tend to be varied rather than uniform, with different individuals responding in different ways. For example, while some respondents aspired to the male beauty norm of a toned, slim and muscular body, others rejected such desires as shallow. A third group considered such ideals irrelevant to their lives because they were in a long-term relationship and no longer had to compete in the marriage market. Gill et al. also demonstrate that individuals themselves often respond in more than one way: that is, they hold several views simultaneously and these views may even be conflictual. For example, some respondents criticized media concern with male body appearance as shallow, yet aspired to a good body and achieved this through regular exercise. As we can see from these contemporary examples, research into media effects continues, but any media influence is conceptualized in much more open, indirect, complex and sophisticated ways than the direct-effects model suggested (Kitzinger 1999).

Active audiences: meaning production, polysemy and resistance

In response to the conceptual shortcomings of the direct-effects theory, sociologists and media and communication scholars have developed the notion of the 'active audience' to explore the engaed and powerful role which audiences may play in the process of consumption. Audiences are conceptualized as active in two ways, both of which break with fundamental assumptions of the direct-effects tradition. Firstly, media audiences are conceptualized as actively involved in the process of meaning production (Fiske 1989b). Rather than seeing the media as producers of meaning and the audience as passive receivers of meaning, this idea suggested that audiences actively interpret and make sense of what they see, hear and read. In this process of making sense they create meanings. Therefore we can see meaning as the outcome of both the media and the audience. The active role of the audience in the process of meaning production is highlighted when different individuals interpret the same media text in different ways. These different interpretations are possible because of the polysemic nature of cultural texts. The concept of polysemy stipulates that all texts contain multiple meanings and are open to be interpreted in different ways (Fiske 1989b). Polysemy is different from the idea of multiple messages in that it focuses on the different ways in which the same message or representation can be interpreted by different individuals. According to John Fiske (1989b), the condition and possibility of polysemy of cultural texts derive from semiotic excess: that is, an excess of meaning. He argues that in a cultural text, several semiotic elements – such as words, images, colours or characters – come together to create the overall meaning producers want audiences to get. This overall meaning would be what Stuart Hall (1980) calls the preferred meaning. However, Fiske argues that there are always elements around the edges of a cultural text which are not part of the overall meaning or do not quite fit. This leaves the text open to different interpretations by the audience. For example, in chapter 5 we have discussed how television cooking programmes employ several strategies to distance male chefs from something traditionally conceived of as a female task and a mundane chore. In Jamie Oliver's shows one major strategy is his lack of precision and guidance when it comes to cooking. He never mentions quantities of ingredients, temperatures of cooking or explains the necessity of any order of preparation or cooking. This helps create an image of Oliver as someone who improvises as he goes along, as an artistic and instinctive chef with flair rather than a dull educator, and concurrently portrays cooking as an art form and lifestyle rather than a routine task. However, viewers may also read this lack of precision and education as indicative of incompetence, as Oliver not providing detailed information and explanations because he is not familiar with them. Or viewers may read the programme, and by implication Oliver, as simply useless because it does not meet their expectations of providing detailed guidance on how to cook. Whatever the response, this example illustrates that audiences actively produce meanings in the process of cultural consumption because they make sense of texts. Not all of these meanings are intended by the programme's producers; the polysemic nature of texts allows consumers to (re)interpret them in various ways.

The concept of polysemy represents a fundamental break from the hitherto dominant notion that media texts contain one meaning which the audience get. This raises an important question: if texts are polysemic, do cultural producers like the media have any power to influence the meanings which the audience take away? Or can consumers read whatever they want into a text? Can the media close down the range of interpretations and steer the audience towards one particular meaning – or are cultural texts completely open to interpretation? Cultural populists, such as Fiske (1989b), take the concept of polysemy to its extreme and suggest that there are barely any limits on audience interpretation because meanings, unlike goods or financial capital, cannot be controlled. Therefore the power lines between producers and consumers are not as firmly entrenched in culture as they may be in the economy. In fact, the lines become blurred as consumers also become producers of meaning in the process of consumption. In this version, power shifts away from the media to the audience, who become the ultimate point at which meaning is produced. The result is the near-reversal of the direct-effects model: now the audience appear as more powerful than the media.

The concept of the active audience breaks with the direct-effects tradition in a second fundamental way: it envisages audiences as actively and critically thinking about cultural texts and engaging in interpretive resistance (Croteau and Hoynes 2003). This means audiences can consciously deconstruct media texts to resist and reject their predominant messages or to actively reinterpret them in contrary and subversive ways. Such interpretive resistance is often social and collective, as well as individual, as audiences draw on alternative cultural resources, such as alternative knowledge or discourses, to resist. For example, Ballaster et al.'s (1991) research into consumers' responses to women's magazines found that the readers who reflected on and criticized women's magazines' images of femininity as stereotypical and objectifying were part of two social groups – notably students and youth workers – who are familiar with feminist critiques. However, we have to be careful not to overestimate or overvalue resistance (Kitzinger 1998). Rejecting media meanings is an act of symbolic resistance; this is important but does not necessarily feed into material resistance in the form of direct actions. For example, many readers might find images of femininity in women's magazines objectionable, but this does not fundamentally change the structure of society or encourage them to take action to initiate social change. Moreover, it is important not to make a simple equation between media messages as bad, manipulative, wrong and regressive and resistance to media messages as good, right and progressive (Kitzinger 1998). For example, in Gill et al.'s (2000) research, some respondents criticized popular-cultural images of men perpetuated in the media as narcissistic, vain, self-obsessed and self-loving because of the focus on bodies and the importance of looking good. This critique could be seen as liberal and progressive. However, Gill et al. show how this opinion is related to discomfort with the figure of the new man, especially male concerns about appearance, and to a traditional attitude to masculinity which makes these respondents see contemporary media images as inappropriately effeminate and homoerotic. In some cases, this traditional view of masculinity also translated into homophobia. Taking this broader picture into account, the respondents' media critique does not appear enlightened but rather based on regressive, traditional and illiberal attitudes.

Encoding/decoding

Stuart Hall (1980) developed the encoding/decoding model of the media in order to overcome the respective weaknesses of direct-effects models and the concept of the active audience. The model intends to capture the complexity of the production and consumption of media texts. It strikes a balance by accounting for the power of the media to endow texts with meanings as well as the power of the audience to interpret and respond to these meanings in multiple and critical ways. The production of media meanings is a complex process which necessarily involves media producers and audiences, or readers, as Hall calls them, in active roles. According to Hall's model, the media as producers have the power to encode a text with particular meanings and messages. The meaning which they intend the audience to get is called the preferred meaning. When audiences read media texts, they engage in an active process of decoding meanings and messages. This means they can read or interpret the text in different ways. Hall identifies three major reading positions: that is, positions members of the audience can adopt in the process of understanding and evaluating a text's meanings. The preferred reading position means that the reader agrees with the preferred meaning produced by the media, whilst an oppositional reading position indicates the reader's rejection or reinterpretation of it. In the negotiated reading position, readers work with the preferred message to accept some elements of it and reject others.

We can use Peter Jackson et al.'s (2001) focus group research into how men respond to men's magazines as an example of how different readings would work. We have seen in chapter 5 that men's magazines, especially lads' magazines, objectify women by constantly depicting them semi-naked and in sexualized poses. The magazines justify this objectification by presenting it as just a bit of 'harmless fun' and by insisting it demonstrates their love and appreciation of women. This, using Hall's (1980) model, would be the preferred meaning which magazines want their readers to adopt. Jackson et al. (2001) found that the vast majority of male focus group participants went along with this and believed sexualized images of women to be acceptable and inoffensive. They engaged in a preferred reading where the reader decodes the message in the way intended by media producers and agrees with it. However, a few male focus group participants were hostile to the magazines and outrightly rejected their depictions of women as shocking, sexist and objectifying (Jackson et al. 2001). These participants engaged in an oppositional reading where the reader understands but rejects the message and reinterprets the facts in a way which is opposite to how the media intended it. In the negotiated reading position, the reader adopts a 'pick and choose' approach and accepts certain aspects of the message while rejecting others. Or, to put it slightly differently, the reader adjusts the preferred meaning so that it fits his or her worldviews and interests, for example by ignoring or explaining the elements that s/he finds undesirable. In Jackson et al.'s (2001) study we can see a negotiated reading at work in focus group discussions about the 'honesty' of lads' magazines. Many male participants assert that lads' magazines are honest, up-front and unpretentious about men's true interests: women, sports and entertainment. Sexual images of women are not necessarily seen as a positive or right thing, as magazines are described as stooping to the lowest common denominator and catering for the unacceptable face of masculinity, but they are considered an honest reflection of what men want. This would be an example of a negotiated reading where readers downplay, explain and legitimize those elements they see as disagreeable.

Hall's approach is clearly influenced by Gramscian thinking about power and especially Gramsci's notion of hegemony (Seiter 1999). The encoding/decoding model paints a picture of a continuous power struggle over meaning. The media send out messages but they have to struggle to get audiences' agreement. Readers can be critical of particular messages yet media producers privilege certain interpretations over others in the first place and thereby set the framework of meaning with which consumers have to engage. This balanced and nuanced account of power struggles over meaning has made Hall's model extremely influential in cultural and media studies, informing major pieces of empirical research (e.g. Morley 1992). It is certainly the most sophisticated of any grand theory developed to conceptualize the relationship between media producers and media audiences. Despite this there are several downsides and shortcomings. These are related to the sheer complexity of media texts and audiences' responses which a general theory cannot fully capture.

The complexity of media texts complicates the ways in which we can understand consumption and its consequences. Hall's concept of the preferred meaning suggests that there is one meaning which the media promote at the expense of others. However, the media are not a monolithic whole which constructs one set of representations and messages; instead they are large and complex institutions marked as much by diversity as by similarity. There is an enormous variety of types and genres of media with different political outlooks and agendas, which portray quite different images and messages. For example, chapters 4 and 5 have revealed substantial differences between men's and women's magazines' representations of intimate relationships. While women's magazines portray long-term relationships based on love and commitment as not just desirable but the ultimate goal in life, men's magazines, especially lads' magazines, frame relationships as something to be avoided, a trap which gets in the way of life's purpose of having fun, going out and getting laid. Of course, we could say in Hall's defence that the preferred meaning does not have to be produced across different types of media but only within one given media text or type. Yet even when looking at one specific media publication, e.g. one newspaper or one type of women's magazine, we find diversity of meaning. Consumers tend to be presented with multiple and complex representations and messages, and indeed ambivalence, incoherence and contradictions. For example, chapter 4 has shown that glossy women's magazines targeted at young, professional women, such as *Cosmopolitan*, embrace a new femininity which allows women to enjoy their single life by going out with friends, going shopping, drinking and clubbing, having casual sex and multiple, non-committal relationships. But at the same time, these magazines still portray long-term relationships and love as the ultimate goal, the most desirable way to live your life. The status of singledom continues to carry some of the old connotations of being sad, lonely and left on the shelf. This suggests that even looking at one media brand or publication, we cannot find just one, straightforward preferred meaning. Multiple messages and representations allow readers to accept some and reject others, to pay attention to some and ignore others, to take different things from the media and to find those which suit them or confirm already held beliefs. Indeed, Fiske (1989b) points out that multiple and incoherent messages are useful and encouraged by the media because they broaden their appeal to diverse audiences and may therefore increase sales. But this diversity presents problems for any theory of media consumption or audience reception as it renders unstable the very texts upon which theories are premised. In relation to Hall's model it poses the question: if there is more than one preferred reading, how do we know which ones the audience respond to and in what ways?

Nevertheless, we do not want to paint a picture of complete diversity of meaning in the media. Hall (1980) is right to emphasize that there are limits to differences and diversity in the mainstream media. For example, chapter 4 has outlined how the conservative *Daily Mail* opposes and criticizes female binge drinking as a contravention of appropriate femininity. In contrast, the liberal *Guardian* is much more relaxed about this, seeing women as engaging in behaviours that have hitherto been open only to men. However, no British newspaper, whether left- or right-leaning, currently asserts that binge drinking is a good thing; it is widely problematized as unhealthy, expensive and socially corrosive. Hence there is diversity of meaning within and across the media but this is often diversity within limits; the mainstream media do not radically challenge the order of the day.

The encoding/decoding model remains useful for analysing media audiences, but shortcomings mean it is more suited to certain types of media texts and genres than others. It works best for analysing factual media with strong ideological and political messages, such as newspapers and news programmes, television documentaries, current affairs programmes, investigative magazine or newspaper reports. These factual media are designed, mostly if not exclusively, to inform and tend to contain clear messages which audiences can agree or disagree with. The *Daily Mail*'s coverage of binge drinking, for example, would make for a useful case study. However, several writers (e.g. Morley 1991, 1992; Seiter 1999) have pointed out that Hall's model does not work as well for fictional media. Fictional media mainly aim to entertain and may not contain any particular messages. This is a valid critique, even though we have to look at specific media before denouncing Hall's model as useless for the analysis of all fictional media. For example, we have seen in chapter 5 that entertainment programmes such as crime dramas contain strong discourses about normative masculinity. Similarly, soap operas or men's and women's magazines are far from devoid of political messages, even if they are not as ideologically driven as, say, a news programme. However, there are fictional media where we really cannot find direct and sustained political messages, for example sports programmes, reality television shows such as *Big Brother* or talent contest shows such as *The X Factor*. Similarly, Helen Wood (2006) has pointed out that while daytime talk shows may contain ideological and political messages, it is difficult to identify an overall connected meaning which could be identified as the main, sustained message: that is, Hall's preferred meaning. This returns us to the earlier critique of multiple messages which complicates the application of the encoding/decoding model.

The Complexity of Audience Responses: Gender and Beyond

How members of the audience respond to media texts and the meanings they promote depends on socio-individual factors such as gender, social class, age, knowledge, experience, political outlook, identity and many others. None of the theories discussed above can conceptualize how readers might be predisposed to one response rather than another depending on their social backgrounds and positions; yet empirical research has clearly demonstrated such links. For example, Gill et al.'s (2000) research has shown that aspirational responses are strongly structured by age and geographical location, with men in their twenties and from metropolitan areas being the most likely to aspire to the body beautiful depicted in the media. By contrast, desire was heavily structured by sexual orientation, with gay men being the ones openly to find male media models attractive and desirable. Jenny Kitzinger (1998) emphasizes that the factors shaping audience responses are not simply individual but socially patterned. She argues that individuals form part of interpretive communities, which comprise persons in broadly similar social positions who are likely to interpret media texts in similar ways. One major social structure is, of course, gender; this raises the question whether men and women form different interpretive communities and respond to media messages in different ways. This is impossible to answer per se. The notion of an interpretive community comprises several social factors, so gender alone is not a sufficient condition and we cannot privilege gender as being more important than other social factors. Moreover, gender may be a more or less influential factor shaping audience responses, depending on the text and the audience.

We can think through these complexities using heavily gendered media texts such as men's and women's magazines. Jackson et al.'s (2001) focus group research showed that most men see no problem with the sexualized images of women pervading men's magazines. Unfortunately the study did not include women's views on this. We may hypothesize that female readers may be more predisposed to resist men's magazines' legitimation of sexualized images as 'harmless fun' and 'celebratory of femininity' and be critical of them because they are part of the social group which is being objectified. This hypothesis is supported by related research. Many women in Ballaster et al.'s (1991) study are critical of the visual images of femininity in women's magazines, which they see as stereotypical and objectifying. These images are nowhere near as sexualized and objectifying as the ones reproduced in men's magazines, suggesting that many female consumers would find them objectionable and problematic. However, lads' magazines and their websites increasingly include images of ordinary women who have sent in erotic pictures of themselves, suggesting that many women do not resist objectifying messages about their gender. The point here is that as a major social structure, gender may predispose men and women to respond in different ways to gendered representations, but how this plays out and how gender interacts with other social factors in shaping responses cannot be assumed and needs to be studied in detail. Moreover, we always have to be careful and avoid essentialization; just because two persons share a gender does not mean they will have the same experiences or opinions.

Hall's model of multiple reading positions is, as noted, more sophisticated than any other grand theory of media audiences. Nevertheless, it simplifies the complex processes of audience responses and meaning production by condensing them into three reactions of agreement (preferred reading), disagreement (oppositional reading) and negotiation (negotiated reading). Jackson et al.'s (2001) research identified twelve major types of responses, or discursive dispositions, as they call them, among readers of men's magazines: celebratory, compliant, hostile, apologetic, deferential, defensive, vulnerable, distanced, refusing/rejecting, analytical, dismissive and ironic. Many of these responses could be seen as sub-categories of Hall's three reading positions: for example, a celebratory response could be an instance of agreement where the reader accepts the preferred meaning promoted by the magazine. However, this categorization does not work for all responses. For example, the ironic response of some readers mirrors the ironic humour used by the magazines themselves. But irony has a tendency to be double-edged: on the one hand, it has the potential to be subversive; but, on the other hand, it tends to reinforce the very old, conventional ways of thinking which it claims to be ironic about (Jackson et al. 2001). The 'irony' used by lads' magazines and its readers often serves to perpetuate sexism and homophobia, while denying that this is what is achieved by presenting it as 'all a bit of a laugh' (Benwell 2004; Mooney 2008). Our point here is that the complexities of such responses and discursive moves cannot be captured through a small number of fairly static reading positions. Further, audience responses in Hall's model revolve around the fairly clear-cut and coherent idea of (dis)agreement: readers either fully agree or disagree, with some in the middle who (dis)agree to some extent. But Jackson et al.'s (2001) research shows that most responses are marked by ambivalence and contradictions about patriarchal norms, gender relations, ideas of masculinity and indeed the magazines themselves.

All grand theories of media audiences discussed assume a particular kind of consumer and context of consumption. The terminology of 'reading' very much betrays this. The consumer is an individual, on his or her own, who reads/views/listens a media text in a deep, concentrated and interested way, who actively engages with the messages as he or she is absorbed and then produces a thought-through response (Morley 1991). This model has been borrowed from film studies' model of the cinema viewer, but cinema watching is arguably not a transferable model for all kinds of media consumption (Morley 1991). As far as magazines are concerned, studies of both women's magazines (Hermes 1995) and men's magazines (Jackson et al. 2001) have shown that most readers are casual readers who browse and flick through magazines rather than reading them cover-to-cover or in-depth, putting them down if more important tasks or issues arise. As far as television is concerned, research (e.g. Morley 1992; Seiter et al. 1991) indicates that television watching is often accompanied by other household activities such as ironing or cooking, especially in the case of women, for whom the private sphere of the home is also the sphere of work. These insights were produced by ethnographic studies of specific instances of audience consumption, rather than simple audience reception, and take into account the context of consumption, which is crucial to meaning production. The findings of ethnographic studies of television viewers and magazine readers have major implications for our understanding of the process of meaning production and the power of media messages. There are clearly different modes of consumption and levels of engagement: consumers can be concentrated or inattentive, meaning that media messages and meanings can be actively engaged with or not paid attention to. Different media may predispose different modes of consumption: for example, while the cinema context may encourage focused viewing of films, the domestic living room context may encourage an intermittent, diffuse and inattentive viewing.

Taking the context of consumption into account highlights that media consumption can be a collective as well as an individual act. For example, an individual may read a newspaper by herself at home or in the work canteen, where she discusses topics with colleagues. Television and video, in particular, are media where the context of consumption is usually social as they are watched in the home where other members of the household are likely to be present. Collective consumption is important in two respects. Firstly, it means that individuals do not simply consume what they want; there are social relations of consumption which affect negotiation and choice. Gender has been shown to be a crucial factor in these relations. For example, David Morley's (1992) study of family television viewing has found that men tend to be in charge of the remote control, which gives them greater power over what is being watched in the communal living room. Ann Gray's (1992) study of the domestic use of video recorders analyses how women's genres, such as soap operas or romantic films, are seen as trivial, which means that female viewers have constantly to fend off male critique and ridicule. As a consequence, women prefer to watch these shows in all-female contexts and refrain from pressing for their programme choices in mixed contexts such as the domestic living room. Secondly, collective consumption is important because it means that meaning production is often a collective process as groups make sense together by talking about what they consume. Many studies have shown this in relation to television (e.g. Seiter et al. 1991; Wood 2006) as viewers comment on and talk about what they are watching. It also applies to magazines: Mary Jane Kehily (1999) has found that girls tend to read teenage magazines collectively and that this often sparks off personalized discussions about topics mentioned in them. While collective reading can open up debates, it can also close them down through reactions such as derisive laughter or moral disapproval (Kehily 1999). In any case, meaning production is a social and ongoing process rather than an individual one-off event. This is especially true in a postmodern world where we are continuously bombarded with media texts and messages so that it becomes difficult to disengage yourself from them. This condition, Ien Ang and Joke Hermes (1996) point out, also makes it difficult for researchers to disentangle the influence of one medium from another. For example, readers of the *Daily Mail* have been offered plenty of coverage on the problem of binge drinking in the UK in recent years. But this highly topical issue is discussed across the British media, so readers will have been exposed to many other commentaries on it in television news, documentaries or magazines, which may reinforce or challenge the newspaper's discourses. In this scenario it becomes difficult to speak about responses or to draw out specific media texts as the source of attitudes because all we have is a diffuse media discourse.

Cultural Consumption and the Production of Gender Identity

Theories of media audiences now recognize consumers as active and thinking human beings, who nevertheless retain a certain passive edge by being conceptualized as respondents who react to the media. Ethnographic studies of media audiences have shown that audiences use the media for certain ends and do something with them. In the following sections we want to focus on the ways in which consumers actively use the media to construct gender identities. In chapters 4 and 5 we have discussed how work as a source of identity has relatively declined in importance in late modernity. Individuals increasingly fashion a sense of identity through a range of lifestyle and consumer choices, ranging from clothes and music to bars and newspaper readership. The proliferation of media since the 1940s has meant that late modern culture is very much a media culture; the media today are pervasive and inescapable. As a consequence, the media can be seen as central to the formation of self-identity. Here we want to explore interconnections of media and gender in the production of identity.

Genres, pleasure, subject positions and identity formation

What role do the media play in the formation of gender identity? This is a complex question which can be answered in multiple ways. On the most basic level we can say that many media products are gendered, although to varying extents. To say that media are gendered means two things. Firstly, it means that certain magazines, television genres, films, and so on, tend to be addressed to and mostly consumed by either men or women. Secondly, gendered media are those which concern themselves with issues and topics that are traditionally considered to be either women's concerns – such as love, romance, domestic issues or family relations – or men's interests – such as sports, cars, politics or finance. Given this, typical men's genres would include men's magazines, football programmes and TV car shows, while typical women's genres would include women's magazines, romantic novels and comedies, and soap operas. The consumption of such strongly gendered media texts can produce and reinforce a feminine or masculine identity, confirming women as women and men as men.

Heavily gendered media have led feminists to investigate why certain products appeal more to one gender than another. Feminist explanations have revolved around the concepts of cultural competence and referential consumption. These have been put forward in the context of research into soap operas, which attract a predominantly female audience. Charlotte Brunsdon (1981) has suggested that soap operas dramatize knowledge, experiences and meanings which real women are familiar with in their own lives. As a consequence, women have the cultural competence to read and enjoy the codes, conventions and narratives of soap operas. This cultural competence allows women to consume soap operas in a referential mode: that is, to relate textual content such as characters, storylines or events to their personal lives (Hobson 1991). Feminists see this referential viewing as a source of pleasure, a reason why women enjoy certain products of popular culture such as soap operas, romance novels or women's magazines. The same arguments regarding consumption, cultural competence, referential viewing and identity could be made about male genres and the production of masculinity. However, the role of the media in the construction of identities, or subjectivities as some thinkers call them, is arguably much more complex than this connection (Wood 2005).

Wood (2005) argues that academic research into and theories about audience responses and consumption always conceptualize individuals and media as separate entities which occasionally interact with each other. Wood suggests that this approach cannot capture the constant, multiple and dialogical ways in which viewers and the media relate. She proposes to study particular moments of viewing or reading to analyse the complex relations between media texts and subjects, to analyse 'texts in action' (Wood 2006). She argues that the role which media texts play in the formation of subjectivities, i.e. how the relations between texts and individual contribute to the construction of self and identity, is much more constant, direct and complex than the concept of referential viewing suggests. In her study of women watching daytime talk shows, she finds that in contrast to the common model of 'media message–audience responses' which media theories presuppose, there is a constant and genuine dialogue going on between the media text and the subject. Throughout the programme, individuals comment on discussion topics, the studio audience and the host and make links to their lives (Wood 2006). In Wood's words, media texts are 'in-action'. Through negotiation with the text and their real-life interpersonal relations, Wood argues, viewers construct their identity. They relate their own experiences and the situations of people they know to what is being said. Even if they personally have no directly relevant experience, they will use media texts and the experiences of those around them to position themselves in a particular way and create an identity. Wood uses the example of a gay, childless woman watching a talk show about father-hood, who uses experiences of friends and neighbours with families to position herself as liberal and unconventional. The advantages of Wood's approach are, firstly, that it investigates the continuity and complexity of relations between texts and subjects and how self-identity is formed in the process through a number of discursive moves. Secondly, while her research is on female viewers, her theory is not gender-specific and the production of subjectivity through subject–text relations can work in the same way for male and female identity. On the downside, this approach works well for talk shows which invite viewers to relate, comment and get involved, but may be less applicable to other genres such as news or film.

While Wood (2005, 2006) subjects the relations between texts and consumers to a more complex analysis, Wendy Hollway's (1996) work can be seen to complicate and elucidate the process of identity formation. Hollway shows that gender identities or subjectivities are formed through individuals taking up gendered positions, which are offered to them in discourses. She bases her argument on discourse theory, which stipulates that discourses entail and produce subject positions which individuals can adopt or reject to position themselves in particular ways. Hollway's research focuses on discourses of sexual-ity, but it can be equally applied to other discourses offering gender positions. Hollway suggests that multiple discourses coexist, which offer individuals a number of subject positions to take up and provide them with choice. Individuals decide to take up a certain position and reject others because of their investment in it; they have a stake in doing so and expect some kind of positive effect or reward. There is considerable pressure for men and women to invest in traditional femininity and masculinity as taking up clearly gendered subject positions is met with socio-cultural approval and confers some gender-specific power on the individual (Hollway 1996; Skeggs 1997). For women, for example, investments in traditional femininity can yield value and capital in institutions such as marriage and heterosexuality (Skeggs 2001). The *Daily Mail's* discourses on binge drinking are a useful example of these processes at work. In chapter 4 we looked in some detail at the newspaper's gendered coverage of binge drinking, which represents women who drink in very negative and moralistic terms, by suggesting they are sluts, deviants, unfeminine and asking for rape. This raises the question how female readers, as part of the social group which is heavily criticized, respond to such representations. The *Daily Mail* offers female readers the moral position of appropriate femininity, which is based on the rejection and disapproval of 'unfeminine' behaviour that is binge drinking. We may expect many female readers to take up this position because it is culturally valued and therefore confers power associated with being 'properly' feminine: for example, being seen as attractive to men or morally upright. In this case, taking up a subject position which is critical of a certain type of femininity can be a way for women to produce their own identity marked by 'appropriate' femininity (Ang and Hermes 1996). Of course, not all women automatically position themselves in this way. It also seems logical and intuitive to assume that women are likely to reject the *Daily Mail's* critique of female binge drinking as unfair and inaccurate because they themselves feel targeted. There is some research evidence (e.g. Kitzinger 1998) backing up this assumption, showing that social groups who are stereotyped or otherwise negatively portrayed are more likely to reject such media images. Alternative discourses and subject positions are available, and consumers of the *Daily Mail* can take up one of these (Hollway 1996). For example, female readers could draw on the feminist discourse and position themselves as social reformers and liberal-progressive thinkers who support gender equality and reject this kind of demonization of women. This discourse and positioning are certainly not promoted by the *Daily Mail*, a deeply anti-feminist paper, and its conservative readers are not very likely to go down this route. But as Foucault pointed out, all discourses contain the seeds of resistance and alternative thinking, and with this come alternative subject positions. Women can certainly seize this opportunity and use the *Daily Mail* against its intentions as a way to reaffirm a liberal, feminist identity.

The example of the *Daily Mail* shows not only that gender shapes our responses to media meanings, but also that consumption can be a way to actively construct a gender identity. The media are a key site for offering men and women discourses which position them in particular ways and invite them to take up gendered subject positions. This is a useful model which can be used in empirical research to analyse how actual individuals position themselves in relation to particular media discourses. Gender is, of course, only one important dimension which shapes the availability and uptake of subject positions; other social factors, such as social class, ethnicity or age, are equally important, and factors interact in complex ways (Hollway 1996). Ellen Seiter et al. (1991), for example, have conducted ethnographic research with female viewers of soap operas, testing Tania Modleski's (1982) claim that soap operas offer 'the ideal mother' as the prime subject position which female viewers can identify with and take up. The discourse of the ideal mother is marked by altruism and endless devotion to the family; the ideal mother has no needs of her own but constantly juggles the problems of all her children and husband and mediates conflicts. In the process she shows considerable common sense and infinite sympathy; she does everything out of love and without resentment. Her constant work and the prioritization of others' needs are a labour of love. Seiter et al. found that most female viewers not only did not identify with the ideal mother subjects, but actively responded with hostility and rejected them. This was particularly the case for working-class women, who identified with the juxtaposed female subject of the soap villainess instead. The villainess behaves in deviant and transgressive ways: for example, by destroying marriages, having affairs, committing crimes or being manipulative and self-interested.

These findings illustrate two important points. Firstly, despite certain subject positions being promoted in the media, viewers will not necessarily identify with them. They can and do take up other, more marginal and negatively coded subject positions instead. Secondly, Seiter et al. suggest that the processes of viewers making sense of a text and positioning themselves are shaped by an interplay of social factors. In their study, social class emerged as particularly important because, as they argue, the subject position of the ideal mother is very much marked by middle-class values and ideals which are unattainable for many working-class women. The tendency of the media to promote middle-class values and norms as universal results in working-class subjects appearing as deficient, inadequate and inferior to middle-class subjects (Skeggs 2009). This is particularly apparent in reality television programmes which revolve around the revelation and transformation of the self. Here working-class men and women tend to appear as lazy, unhealthy, untidy and dirty, bad mothers, selfish and superficial: that is, in need of a middle-class make-over. These programmes position the viewer as judge: '[A]udiences are offered the position not just of witness of the performance or collector of evidence but of juror, invited to assess the properties of the person, their investments and their relationships' (Skeggs 2009: 638). However, Beverley Skeggs and Helen Wood (2008) found that while middle-class viewers engaged in extensive critique of such television figures, many working-class viewers rejected the judgemental position offered by the media and instead identified with and defended the demonized subjects, such as Jade Goody or Jordan. The studies by Seiter at al. and Skeggs and Wood show that media consumption plays a role in the production of subject positions and the formation of plural gender identities, i.e. femininities and masculinities, which are shaped by interactions between gender and other social factors such as social class.

Performing gender and the role of the mass media

A slightly different way of looking at identity formation is through the idea that gender is performed and performing. In the introduction we outlined the differences between Goffman's (1959) concept of performance and Butler's (1990) notion of performativity. But an integrated analysis, which combines their respective strengths, is possible and arguably necessary to maximize their usefulness for the sociological study of gender (Brickell 2005). The work of Bronwyn Davies (2002), like Butler a post-structuralist, offers a useful integrative framework. The fundamental idea which Goffman, Butler and Davies agree on is that gender is not something that individuals are but something they do. Gender identity is a performance or performative construct, which consists of constant (re)production of individual practices and discursive positionings. Both gender and sex are social structures; they do not belong to and exist beyond the individual, yet are made up of individual practices (Davies 2002). In this sense, structure is performed by individuals. Social structures are always enabling as well as constraining, and gender illustrates this well. Dominant notions of femininity and masculinity restrict what men and women can do. In Western cultures, for example, men cannot wear skirts and women cannot go on stag dos, which are all-male celebrations of a groom-to-be's 'last night of freedom' before marriage. Men find it difficult to stay at home and look after their children because of a lack of financial support, while women find it difficult to obtain high-powered positions at work because of gender discrimination. However, gender also enables individuals to perform masculinity and femininity by providing them with knowledge of what counts as 'typical' feminine or masculine character traits, attitudes or behaviour. By adopting and performing these elements, individuals can position themselves as male or female (Davies 2002). For Goffman, individuals make conscious but not entirely free decisions about their performance, because they are constrained by frames: that is, principles of organization which govern events and social situations (Brickell 2005). Butler (1990) emphasizes that positioning and performances are not conscious but habitual and constant repetitions of the script of gender; femininity and masculinity are ways of re-enacting already-existing gender norms. She would speak of performative acts, which include speech as well as practices, rather than performances to emphasize the reiterative and unconscious nature of the acts. Whilst Butler rules out essential subjects existing prior to agency, the idea of a subject as such is not impossible (Brickell 2005).

If we conceptualize gender as performed and performative, the media play a crucial role in two ways. Firstly, in late modernity the media are one key source of information and knowledge about gender and in this sense can teach individuals how to do masculinity and femininity. For example, teenage television series such as *Hollyoaks* can provide knowledge on the latest appropriate fashions for young men and women. Secondly, certain media are heavily gendered: for example, while genres such as soap operas or romantic comedies are seen as women's genres, action films or car programmes are seen as men's genres. The very act of consuming or being a fan of these genres can be seen as performative of gender.

Both of these points can be exemplified in more detail by looking at Kehily's (1999) study into how teenage boys and girls consume teenage magazines. She has found significant differences in the ways that schoolgirls and schoolboys read such magazines, and argues that their different responses constitute performances of femininity and masculinity. The girls in her study tended to read magazines collectively and openly embraced them: for example, talking about the features they enjoyed and found useful. They used magazine content, especially the problem pages and topics such as sex, to generate discussions among themselves on many personal and intimate issues. In this way they performed feminine identities marked by talking and opening up, by asserting their heterosexuality and maintaining close friendships. However, the girls criticized one teenage magazine, *More!*, as inappropriate because of its sexually explicit material. This highlights the existence of multiple femininities: girls in the study performed a respectable femininity by rejecting magazines and images of femininity associated with promiscuity and sexual amorality. This suggests that the new femininity marked by assertive and open pleasure seeking and sexuality, which is offered by teenage and women's magazines today, is actively rejected by some female readers (Nayak and Kehily 2008).

In contrast to the girls, the boys read magazines individually. They also distanced themselves from the magazines through discursive moves such as denial of any real interest, emphasis on their reading being casual as well as humouring and pejorative talk. Magazine reading did not inspire any further talking about issues among boys, and in group interview sessions and in sex-education lessons they were extremely uncomfortable, uneasy and embarrassed about getting involved in talking about sexual topics. Kehily (1999) suggests that this distancing is a performance of hegemonic masculinity defined by knowledge – i.e. there is no need for men to talk – and toughness – i.e. there are no problems that need to be shared. Teenage magazines offer soft rather than tough, macho talk about sexuality and therefore run counter to hegemonic masculinity. As a consequence, teenage magazines come close to being unacceptable for boys to read and male readers need to distance themselves in order to perform masculinity, despite their apparent ignorance and vulnerability regarding sex and sexuality. Kehily concludes that '[t]he relationship between reading practices and gender differences indicates that acts of readership offer a sphere for producing and conveying sex-gender identities in school. ... [I]t is the meanings and associations ascribed to magazines by groups of boys and girls which produce public demonstrations of being and doing gender' (1999: 85–6). This illustrates our points about media consumption being one aspect through which gender identity can be performed. In some ways, individual boys and girls are active agents who exercise practices such as reading, talking or producing meanings. However, the gender identities which they perform have already been scripted, as the gendered meanings of magazines and their consumption are wider cultural meanings which predate particular individuals.

New media, gender identity and performance

So far our discussion has focused on gender in relation to the mass media, such as television or print. But the new media are one of the areas where the idea of performing gender identity becomes particularly important. The term 'new media' refers to ICTs (information and communication technologies) of the last two decades such as the internet with its websites, blogs and wikis, internet relay chat (IRC), networking sites, podcasts, but also email or iPods (Breen 2007). In contrast to the mass media, these new media blur the old communication model of one producer communicating content to a mass of receivers. Consumers have become producers of media content, too: for example, by leaving comments on websites, setting up their own personal wikis or blogs and creating and maintaining social networking sites through comments and photos. This means that for individuals the media are no longer just sources of information and entertainment, but also tools to interact with others, make their opinions heard and share photos. All this has rapidly changed the ways in which academics think about media audiences and consumption. As Henry Jenkins put it in 2006, 'The concept of the active audience, so controversial two decades ago, is now taken for granted by everyone involved in and around the media industry. New technologies are enabling average consumers to archive, annotate, appropriate, and recirculate media content' (2006: 1). This change is reflected in terminological changes as the terms 'consumers' or 'audiences' have been replaced by 'users'. As ordinary people increasingly use new media to produce their own content, tailor their consumption to personal interests and circumstances and interact with others, the new media are becoming an ever more important aspect of identity formation. This is particularly the case since the arrival of Web 2.0 in the mid-2000s, which has facilitated information sharing through easy uploading of images and text, user-centred design and interaction in a virtual community (Van Doorn et al. 2008).

The formation of identity, including gender identity, has occupied a central place in academic thinking and research regarding new media, especially the virtual world created by the internet. This world, often referred to as cyberspace, is 'composed of information rather than matter' (Donath 1999: 30). It is a disembodied space which does not contain real, physical bodies. This has led some thinkers to envisage the end of gender. The argument goes that in disembodied cyberspace, gender is no longer as salient a structural category because the physical markers of gender, upon which we rely in the offline world to categorize people as male or female, are no longer discernible (O'Brien 1999). This is seen as giving the internet a liberating potential; gender is no longer a necessary or fixed aspect of interaction and identity because it is not apparent online. Instead, physical anonymity means that individuals can hide, ignore or play with their gender by swapping or creating multiple identities. In a nutshell, in the virtual world where bodies are no longer an obstacle, we can be whoever we want to be; any identity is ours for the taking and making.

There is some truth in this. In cyberspace, individuals are freer than in the offline world to form and change identities because the absence of the body means there are fewer cues, allowing individuals greater power to manage the information they want to convey about themselves. However, fewer cues does not mean no cues. Moreover, there are limits to online identity construction, too. Just because the body is not physically present online does not mean that identity is free-floating; this logic would only work if identity was a single, fixed thing located in the physicality of the body (O'Brien 1999). But we have seen throughout this book that gender identities are matters of social construction and performance which involve the body but are not limited to it. For example, language and interactive practices are key aspects of gender performance, which can take place without the body being visibly present. In fact, these aspects of gender perform-ance are more rather than less important online because physical anonymity means that no one can rely on their body to do the gender work, so that even those who are 'natural, normal females' in real life 'must continually give the impression that they are female in order to be perceived as such' (Rodino 1997). The real question, then, is how gender identity is performed and constructed when the body is not available as a source of information to others.

Judith Donath (1999) uses Goffman to analyse how we leave gender cues in cyberspace. According to Goffman (1959), the per-formance of identity involves both expressions given – deliberate statements and actions designed to create a certain impression – and expressions given off – more subtle and at times unintentional actions which communicate meanings. The latter are much harder to control and sustain. Michelle Rodino's (1997) research into IRC mentions the example of one user who refuses to disclose his gender directly, yet unintentionally reveals it through giving off an impression of mas-culinity: for example, by speaking on behalf of men, using the male pronoun 'his' to refer to himself or using the username 'Mega-D', which has masculine connotations. Susan Herring's (1996) research has demonstrated that female and male users have different online styles, men often using competitive and adversarial language, while women tend to adopt a more supportive and consensual voice. These two pieces of research illustrate that the performance of a masculine or feminine identity has to involve continuously and consistently acting and expressing yourself in a way that fits the conventional script of gender (Donath 1999). Thus the performance of gender is not an easy feat; there are intricate rules and norms to be learnt and enacted, and, as a consequence, individuals may leave cues as to their offline gender in the online world (Donath 1999). Jodi O'Brien (1999) goes even further than this by suggesting that as gender is reinscribed into the amorphous space of the online world through language and social practices, it becomes even more reductive and stereotypical. She notes that in daterooms or chatrooms, in particular, gender stereotypes loom large as participants portray themselves as hyper-gendered Barbie or Ken types. Similarly Herring's (1996) research suggests that language use online reflects very traditional images of gender, with men being competitive and women supportive. According to O'Brien (1999), this reduction in the complexity of gender is caused by the absence of the body, which deprives us of a complex, nuanced tool of communication. Instead we reach for easy, quick solutions that can be textually communicated: stereotypes. In this scenario, rather than cyberspace offering a world where gender no longer matters, gender is reinscribed in even more narrow, conventional ways.

There are, of course, incidents of gender swapping in cyberspace as men present themselves as women and vice versa (e.g. Bruckman 1993). It is difficult to estimate how much this happens, but it is clearly easier to pass oneself off as the opposite gender from one's corporeal form in a context of physical anonymity. This gender swapping illustrates the argument about gender being something that we do, a performance, rather than a 'natural' category. Despite, or maybe because of, the possibility to gender swap, there is a constant concern with gender on the internet, especially in text-based forums. Niels Van Doorn et al.'s (2008) research into IRC shows that the initial stages of communication always involve enquiries about age, sex and location of users, while O'Brien (1999) analyses how individuals continually make reference to their bodies in ways which affirm their gender: for example, by talking about their hair, lack or presence of facial and body hair, body form, or sexual organs such as breasts or penises. Overtly masculine or feminine usernames can be created to indicate gender (Van Doorn et al. 2008). In these different manners, conventional gender classification schemes are transported online through the invocation of the body even if the body is not visibly present. The concern with gender also manifests itself in cyberspace constantly attempting to regulate gender identity in numerous ways, from websites requiring real names and addresses to register before use to constant suspicions being voiced in interactive forums regarding those who do not quite conform to the conventional norms of gendered communication (O'Brien 1999). Hence it may be easier to cross gender boundaries online, but these acts of transgression do not undermine the structural categories of gender; rather, they reaffirm the idea that masculinity and femininity are two distinct, opposite categories. Moreover, online content and interaction have recently become much more graphic and visual as Web 2.0 has facilitated easy uploading of photographs and videos and connecting to webcams. This means that a visual representation of the body, if not the physical body itself, is increasingly evident in the online world and is used by participants to 'prove' their corporeal gender visually (Van Doorn et al. 2008).

Consuming Gendered Media

Video and online games

In this section we discuss both video games – played on home computers or consoles such as PlayStation – and online games commonly known as 'massively multiplayer online role-playing games' (MMOs). Both types are media games, but the contexts of play may vary. Video games can be played on their own or with others, and, contrary to the popular image of the lone male gamer, a lot of video games are played in groups, while MMOs need more than one player to share the virtual space of the game (Yee 2008). Both video and online games are heavily gendered as they are predominantly male media. Despite a considerable growth in female players since the mid-1990s, games are much more popular with men and boys, who make up the vast majority of gamers (Kafai et al. 2008). Moreover, video and online games are associated with characteristics traditionally seen as male, such as competition and winning, action and heroism, killing and destruction, and technological skill and rationality (Walkerdine 2006). There are multiple reasons for girls' and women's relative lack of participation, including a dislike of pervasive violence and killing, a lack of female characters, the depiction of females as sexual objects and in generally stereotypical roles (e.g. as damsels in distress to be rescued by male heroes), as well as a lack of general experience with technology (Cassell and Jenkins 1998; Kafai et al. 2008). Yee's (2008) research into MMO players of the popular World of Warcraft has shown that female players are put off the game by being constantly reminded that the intended subject position of the gamer is male. For example, clothes often do not fit female avatars – characters which players can adopt as identities – and gaming culture is male-centred, which results in constant discrimination against openly female players, who are treated as incompetent and constantly sexually propositioned.

These patterns have initiated discussion about how games can be made more appealing to females. Common suggestions are to include more female characters, to create active and strong female characters, to invent game topics that appeal to women and girls or to develop narrative-focused games which require co-operation to succeed. But doing this successfully and consistently is not straightforward. For example, the popular game Tomb Raider features Lara Croft as a protagonist who is a tough, self-reliant, intelligent and violent female. This character offers a more active role for females, but there is considerable 'pandering to adolescent male interests in "tits and ass"' (Cassell and Jenkins 1998: 32) as Lara Croft has a very sexualized body with a slim figure, big breasts and bottom, all of which are scantily clad. It seems that even if the gaming industry is willing to produce more 'girl-friendly' games, it remains focused on male users, who are its biggest consumer group. On a theoretical level, the danger with developing 'girl-friendly' games is that this move reifies and essentializes the gender binary. The fallacy of this is highlighted by empirical research. For example, Diane Carr's (2007) study of teenage girls' preferences in video games has shown that girls are not one homogeneous category but actually like very different types of video games. Similarly Nick Yee's (2008) research has found that male and female players tend to enjoy the same kind of features in online games. Hence there cannot be categories such as 'girls' games' which appeal to all girls and girls only, and the same, of course, goes for 'boys' games'. Such categories would only reinforce the dominant yet erroneous idea that girls and boys are entirely different species.

If we understand gender in a constructionist way as a performative construct, then creating more 'girl-friendly' games would never solve the problem of gender division anyway. For example, Caroline Pelletier (2008) investigates the connections between gender and games by interviewing female and male teenagers about their gaming experiences and getting them to design their own games. Both girls and boys, Pelletier finds, use games to position themselves in gendered ways. Central to this is positioning is difference. For example, in group discussions, boys will make a point of opposing everything girls profess to enjoy in order to appear masculine. These tastes are revealed to be discursive strategies rather than realities as they are very unstable over time. In effect, boys use conventional gender norms to create their masculine identities. Perhaps the most striking example of this is the game design of one boy, Simon, who invents a game full of features which are commonly said to appeal to male gamers, such as formidable weapons, fantasy-based action and high-risk stakes where the player either wins or loses everything. Pelletier argues that this design is part of the performance of masculinity which works because it is recognized as such by others: 'It is precisely because members of the group will recognize and acknowledge an interest in weapons and ludic design as "male" interests, according to prevalent social norms, that Simon's game is effective as a statement of gendered identity' (2008: 155–6). This research suggests that creating 'girl-friendly' games in order to overcome gender divides would be ineffective, because the divide is not inherent in the games or their technological features, but created by the meanings ascribed to them.

Valerie Walkerdine (2006) argues that the solution of 'girl-friendly' games does not address the complex reasons behind the relative lack of girls' participation in gaming, which are to do with the deeply gendered nature of the medium and the performance of gender identity. Video and online games per se are a site for the production of masculinity because they are a male medium; they are associated with traditionally male ideals and characteristics, such as competition and fighting, and are predominantly played by boys. This presents a problem for female players because 'contemporary femininity demands practices and performances which bring together heroics, rationality, etc. with the need to maintain a femininity which displays care, co-operation, concern, and sensitivity to others' (Walkerdine 2006: 520). When operating in the predominantly masculine space of video games, females have to keep alive their femininity; they cannot be seen to be becoming too masculine. The management of femininity while gaming is a complex task. Walkerdine's ethnographic research with girls playing video games illustrates several ways in which girls perform and (re)assert their femininity. Firstly, they achieve this through detachment from the game. While some girls are very good players, they are rarely as skilled or as interested as boys. Becoming excellent requires a lot of practice and girls simply do not engage in this level of devotion, thereby remaining somewhat detached from the game and its masculine associations. Moreover, they remain detached during the game by disavowing their excitement of the game, which revolves around 'male' activities such as competition and killing. Secondly, Walkerdine shows that girls' two favourite avatars are cute, cuddly figures of ambiguous gender and cute-yet-powerful femme fatales. Both of these avatars allow girls to negotiate the masculine and the feminine, to adopt identities which contain attributes conventionally seen as masculine and thereby confer power in the game, but which at the same time allow the performance of femininity. Both boys and girls perceive female avatars as weak. When girls choose gender-neutral or ambiguous avatars such as animals or toys, they do not simply adopt these characters but position themselves as their carers and nurturers, thereby gaining a position of power and control (albeit limited), yet remaining in the classic female role of the carer. The female avatars which girls like display masculine attributes by being fighters, warriors or wrestlers, but are also distinctly feminine by being cute, pretty and girlish. Emerging from Pelletier's (2008) and Walkerdine's (2006) research is the insight that the consumption of video and online games, just like other media, serves as a way to perform gender identity and that this performance is more complicated for girls. This may be why they are not as enthusiastic about gaming as boys and means that a wide cultural shift, rather than a narrow technological one, is needed for fundamental change.

Gendered images: the male and the female gaze

In contrast to linguistic text, images provide a visual representation of male and female subjects. Media images can be heavily gendered by emphasizing the femininity or masculinity of those portrayed and they can sexualize men and women by showing them in sexually provocative poses, scantily clad or showing off sexual parts of the body. Sexual images of women are not limited to pornography but pervasive in mainstream men's lifestyle magazines. This raises the question of consumption: what are the reasons for and the consequence of the consumption of sexual images? Does it matter that men's magazines are full of them, yet women's magazines rarely portray male bodies?

To answer these questions, we need to look at Laura Mulvey's (2009) famous work on the male gaze. This is extremely useful because she attempted to understand not simply the process of consumption but its pleasures, in particular the pleasures derived from looking at something or someone (scopophilia). Analysing cinema film, Mulvey identifies three different types of looks, the most important one for our purposes being the look from the spectator to the screen action. According to Mulvey, there is a fundamental gender divide and imbalance in cultural texts because the pleasure of looking has been split between the active male subject who has the power to look and the passive, powerless female who functions as an object to be looked at. Who looks and who is looked at is not a neutral matter, but rather involves and reproduces power hierarchies because those who are looking are in control. Men, who are the ones who are looking, derive pleasure not just from the text they consume but from the fact that they are in control. As the subject–object split occurs along gender lines, the gaze is always and inevitably male and reinforces gender difference and inequalities which mark society generally. A good example illustrating the concept of the male gaze is a recent Stella Artois advert, shown on television and in cinemas. In this advert we, the spectators, see a man waiting in a bar for two things, a date to arrive and a beer to be served. A beautiful woman getting ready for her date and a glass of beer being pulled are shown in alternating shots, suggesting that these processes happen simultaneously and constructing equivalence between the two. Both the woman and the beer are objects of pleasure and consumption which the man is waiting for. And just in case this message has not become clear to all viewers, the final slogan, as the woman and the beer arrive at the same time, is 'She is a thing of beauty', the pronoun 'she' referring to both the woman and the glass of beer. This is an example of Mulvey's idea that the spectator position is a masculine one: male viewers can identify with the powerful gaze of the male character on screen, waiting for objects to arrive to satisfy his desires, while there is no space for an active female spectator.

Mulvey's work can help us understand men's lifestyle magazines. All magazines contain ample images of women which offer their bodies for male readers to look at and enjoy. The differences between magazines are matters of degree rather than principle. For example, the amount of space taken up by images of women varies, with downmarket lads' magazines devoting about half of an edition's space and glossy and hybrid magazines about a quarter to a third. There are also varying degrees of nakedness and sexual titillation: lads' magazines show women's breasts, nipples and bottoms and portray women in pornographic poses, while hybrid and glossy magazines stick to clothed, if scantily clad, women in sexually suggestive poses. The way in which more or less sexualized images of women dominate magazines for men indicates that men derive pleasure and power from looking at women who are offering their bodies for male consumption. The same cannot be said for women. Women's magazines contain far fewer images of men and never in the same sexualized poses, suggesting that there is no equivalent female gaze, at least not in women's magazines. The consumption of sexualized images of women can also be seen as an instrument with which to construct masculine identity, especially heterosexual masculinity, a process in which women only function as passive objects.

Drastic cultural changes since the 1970s, the time of Mulvey's writing, and theoretical shortcomings have led to critiques of the concept of the male gaze (see, e.g., Gamman and Marshment 1988). Most importantly, these critiques raise the questions whether the gaze is always male or if there could be a female gaze. And what happens when the spectator is a woman and the object a man? Suzanne Moore (1988) argues that there is an active female gaze in contemporary culture, which has been made possible by cultural changes in the 1980s which brought about the new man. She notes that in that decade, popular culture began to put male bodies on display and present them as objects of desire. As examples she cites films such as *American Gigolo* (1980) and *Top Gun* (1986) and adverts such as that for Levis 501 jeans, where cameras linger over men's bodies as they get (un)dressed and flaunt their semi-nakedness. Of course, men's bodies had been shown before in popular culture and there have always been male pin-ups. But two things fundamentally changed in the 1980s. Firstly, popular culture begins consciously to present male bodies as erotic spectacles for their audiences. The codes used to signal that men are there to be looked at are borrowed from eroticized images of women, such as sexual poses, slow and teasing removal of clothes, lingering camera shots or sultry looks. Secondly, this sexualization and aestheticization of the male body happens across popular culture, from men's magazines to films and advertising. According to Moore (1988), these cultural changes facilitate an active female gaze which allows women to become the subjects who look and derive pleasure and control from looking at men. However, whilst this analysis is certainly convincing, we have to emphasize that the female gaze is not the exact equivalent of the male gaze.

Firstly, while men increasingly care about their appearance and are judged by it, their desire to look good is mostly aimed at the mirror rather than women. The new man is narcissistic and primarily wants to look good for his own sake and be admired by the public rather than attract females (Moore 1988). This is illustrated by the kind of media in which images, erotic and otherwise, of men appear: mostly in men's magazines, rarely in women's magazines. As a consequence of this, the female gaze is not as powerful as the male gaze. Even in the role of objects, men are not as disempowered and passive as objectified women because they retain an active role in playing the game for their narcissistic egos. Secondly, while erotic images of men have become widespread, they are not as common as the semi-clad images of women. This is evident not only in comparisons of men's and women's magazines but also in societal reactions to sexual images of men. For example, since the 1980s, Diet Coke has run a series of adverts which involve a construction worker/delivery man/handyman taking his shirt off to reveal an extremely muscular torso to a group of female office workers drooling over him. The success of this long-running campaign is grounded in it being well known and memorable, providing a talking point by being different. This suggests that sexualized images of men are still not common or 'normal', which is why they provoke so much interest and attention. In comparison, when is the last time you actively noticed a woman's body being sexually shown off in an advert? Consumers do not tend to take note because it happens all the time. Hence there is a female gaze but it is not as prevalent or as deeply rooted in our socio-cultural fabric as the male gaze. It remains the Other gaze and lacks the power of the male gaze.

Support for this analysis comes from work on how the male gaze plays out in the new media. The new media are interactive, blurring the lines between consumers and producers. Arguably, this allows for the roles of subject and object to become less fixed as all participants are simultaneously looking and being looked at. Marjorie Kibby and Brigid Costello (1999) have conducted research into the adult section of the video-conferencing site CU-SeeMe. This adult section is in essence an interactive pornography site where users engage in visual and written erotic exchanges. They can communicate in public rooms with up to twenty-five participants or establish a private one-to-one interaction known as 'direct connection'. Users can chat, provide images and videos of themselves or put on so-called 'shows' in which sexual performances are visually displayed. There are two findings which we want to highlight. Firstly, Kibby and Costello argue that the interactive possibilities of the new media allow for the destabilization of the male gaze because both men and women 'construct positions that are simultaneously the subject and the object of the consuming gaze' (1999: 363). As the very foundations of the concept of gazing are shaken, relatively and theoretically speaking, the position of the male user becomes weaker while the female user becomes stronger. However, in practice the technological possibilities play themselves out quite differently. Kibby and Costello found that in heterosexual rooms on CU-SeeMe, the vast majority of shows are performed by single women and heterosexual couples. Single men rarely present themselves as sexual objects by putting their bodies performing sexuality on display. This means that men tend to remain in the position of the subject, looking on, as much as they can. Moreover, in shows performed by couples, Kibby and Costello note that '[m]ales in these couples often perform an active sexual role, positioning their female partner's body to the primary focus of the erotic display' (1999: 359). Hence, even if men put themselves on display, they act in ways which ensure that women become the primary object to be looked at. This indicates that the impact of technological developments and possibilities is always shaped by social context, in this case traditional norms around gender and heterosexuality. The male gaze commands considerable cultural authority and is difficult to destabilize in fundamental ways, even though the new media have certainly begun to initiate this process.

Conclusion

The complex and constantly changing nature of cultural consumption makes wide generalizations difficult, but we will attempt to offer a few concluding points. There is a balance of power between consumers and the media as they struggle over meaning. Consumers are neither passive dupes nor all-powerful producers of meaning. They are active, intelligent and diverse social groups who can critically engage with culture as they make sense of it. Yet the media are powerful social institutions which attempt to set the discursive frameworks of debate with which consumers have to engage.

Gender is an important factor shaping consumption. Many, if by no means all, cultural texts are gendered in the sense of being mostly addressed to and consumed by either men or women. But we have to bear in mind two important caveats. Firstly, gender is just one of a range of important social factors, which often interact with each other to shape consumer habits and responses. Secondly, there is always a danger in gender research to overplay differences and underplay similarities. In many ways, female and male ways of consuming are similar: for example, both men and women tend to flick through magazines rather than read them in depth, and men and women enjoy the same features of online computer games. In this chapter we have established that consumption is not only gendered but gendering: that is, that men and women use cultural texts to construct their masculine and feminine identities. In fact, these analytically separate processes often work together in practice: for example, if a cultural text is strongly gendered, then it lends itself to the formation of masculinity or femininity. The male genre of video games clearly illustrates this dynamic. Technological changes and the emergence of the new media have complicated academic thinking and research on consumption even further and call for more work. At present, it is interesting that many gender differences and inequalities persist despite the huge technological potential for drastic shifts towards a more equal playing field. This indicates the importance and power of socio-cultural meanings in the (re)production of gender identities, norms and relations.

7

Gender, Popular Culture and Space/Place

Space is never empty: it always embodies a meaning.

(Lefebvre 1991: 154)

It has long been acknowledged that there are significant gender issues when it comes to how we use space and, more importantly, how we are allowed to use space. There are spaces where men and women are regulated and kept apart (such as single-sex schools and single-sex toilet facilities) and spaces where self-regulation is in operation. For example, some women may feel conspicuous going for a drink alone in a bar, whilst some men might feel 'out of place' in a women's lingerie shop. Of course, there is nothing unlawful about a woman sitting in a bar unaccompanied or a lone man purchasing women's underwear, but a series of cultural and social rules may lead to gender-determined feelings of awkwardness or conspicuousness in these two consumption spaces. This is particularly the case because both examples also have potential sexual connotations. We innately learn cultural rules about gender and use of space and adapt our behaviour accordingly. It is the practices of self-regulation that are of particular interest from a socio-cultural point of view because the performativity of our gender is learned through our interactions with ideologically imbued texts.

There are numerous issues about power and gendered use of space which have an impact on people's everyday lives (see McDowell 1999; Massey 1994). In this chapter we take a series of case studies that focus on popular culture and space in order to examine the multifarious ways in which the colonization, design and response to different spaces and places are greatly affected by our gender and sexuality. As we have discussed in other chapters, women adopting 'male' drinking practices in 'male' spaces has been constructed as deviant behaviour in some discourses. The distribution of men and women in the spaces and hierarchies of the workplace can often be conceptualized using spatial metaphors, with men typically occupying 'higher' status positions. As we saw with some cultural industries, even these newer 'knowledge economy' jobs operate with firm gender demarcations in terms of use of space and distribution of power. A building site remains a firmly male-dominated workspace, a beauty parlour mainly female-dominated. Issues of gendered use of space (and place) affect our lives in ubiquitous ways. In the twenty-first century in advanced Western economies, a rhetoric of gender equality is frequently promoted – in spite of the fact that our daily lives are riddled with examples of things we cannot do, and places we cannot go to, because of being male or female.

In this chapter we look at three diverse case studies that allow us to discuss gender and popular culture in terms of the way we use socio-cultural spaces. Firstly, we look at the example of the modern city and the contrasting ways in which this space was accessed by men and women. Here also we will focus on the figure of the *flâneur*. This is the largest case study and provides a way of introducing some key theoretical debates about gender and space. We examine elements of gender and the city from the early city of modernity – the mid-nineteenth century – through to the mid-twentieth century – and in particular the debates about gender in terms of public versus private space. We then look at two further case studies that help examine the spatial dimensions of debates about gender and popular culture. The case studies are youth subcultures and space, and contemporary urban night-time consumption spaces. Each of these is strongly linked to popular culture. By looking at case studies from different time periods, we can discuss whether or not men and women's use of space has altered over time.

As a starting point, when thinking about gender and space, there is a very significant, but often overlooked, fact, which is that the majority of spaces that we inhabit have been designed and built by men. A rapid survey of town planners and architects from the nineteenth century to the present day will reveal that all but a handful have been male. What are the ramifications, then, in terms of gender, that the space that both men and women inhabit has been designed predominantly by men? Clara Greed argues that urban planning has been a key force in 'domesticizing' women, and that urban planning is 'one of the power structures which project patriarchal beliefs on urban space' (1994: 16). Likewise, the feminist geographer Doreen Massey

(1994) has written extensively on this subject of male domination of public and work spaces using examples such as municipal football pitches through to science parks to emphasize her arguments. This prompts some important questions. Do women face barriers when attempting to operate in spaces designed by men? Would/do women design space differently to men?

Space, Gender and Modernity

Although a subject of vast and overwhelming complexity that we can only briefly survey here, the emergence of the city of modernity provides some key theoretical work about the differences between men and women's use of popular cultural space. When using the term 'the modern city', we are roughly drawing on the period identified by Mike Featherstone (2007) as the late Enlightenment through to the late 1960s. As the physical site or manifestation of industrial capitalism, the modern city brought about new gender relations and new gendered uses of space. With the emergence of the 'shock city' of modernity came attempts to understand the huge societal changes that this new organization of space, work and leisure brought with it. However, as feminist theorists have noted, the issue of gender, or more specifically the relationship between women and the city, was an area that was overlooked until the latter part of the twentieth century. Much work about women and cities has been written retrospectively to compensate for women being 'hidden from history'.

In terms of gender and the modern city, a key theoretical focus has been on the city as an overwhelmingly male space. Men used the city as a workspace, a leisure space and a public space in terms of political debate (see Habermas 1989). Women, on the other hand, had restricted access to the city. Whilst there were some enclaves of urban life that women could participate in, feminists argue that women were largely excluded from politics and education, and from the public realm in general.

Marxist commentators have also acknowledged that capitalist modes of production functioned most efficiently with male workers being nurtured by female carers and that ideological state apparatuses were used to reinforce the 'naturalness' of this socially constructed relationship. Society was organized along patriarchal lines and involved the subordination of women and the separation of male and female roles, with men acting as the breadwinning head of household and women as homemaker and nurturer of the next generation of workers. The nuclear family has also provided the context for the successful reproduction of capitalist, bourgeois values – hard work, economic aspiration, punctuality, respect, diligence, and so on – so ensuring system stability. To effect continuity, modern women and men had essentialized gender characteristics more intensely ascribed to them, were more intensively ascribed with essentialized gender characteristics, and the language of biological necessity was widely invoked to explain away this new social construction. Modern societies were thus able to develop successfully through exploiting this 'natural' complementarity between male and female roles and ensuring continuity in the balance between the public and private spheres. Elizabeth Wilson argues that even the domestic sphere was not controlled by women. It was characterized as feminine but 'it was organized for the convenience, rest and recreation of men, not women, and it has been an important part of feminism to argue that the private sphere is the workplace of the woman' (1996: 65).

Furthermore, the dichotomy between the male/public sphere and the female/private sphere was not universal to all, as a high percentage of working-class women worked in mills and factories alongside men during the nineteenth and early twentieth century (even though they were predominantly excluded from politics, decision-making roles and most aspects of public life). In terms of debates about the public versus the private sphere, it is claimed that women, especially middle-class women, were increasingly shepherded to the private, domestic sphere of the home. It is perhaps if we look at leisure and public spaces in the city that the differences between male and female access to space become most acute.

The *Flâneur*: Gender, Public Space and the Early City of Modernity

The city of modernity brought about huge changes in relationships between people and public space. In terms of gender and space, a key figure associated with the city of modernity is that of the *flâneur*. Initially identified by the poet Baudelaire in the Paris of the 1840s, the *flâneur* is a man, usually wealthy and educated, who wanders the streets for pleasure, soaking up the sights, smells and atmosphere of urban space – one who goes 'botanizing on the asphalt' – a 'people watcher' in contemporary terms. According to Walter Benjamin, the *flâneur* is made possible because of the spaces and atmosphere of Paris in that period, which were very different to gloomy and overcrowded London, for example. Paris, under the edict of Napoleon III, was to undergo radical new city planning designed by Baron Haussmann. The crumbling, labyrinthine spaces of the medieval city were replaced with wide, airy boulevards, new parks and squares. It was the first example of an all-encompassing approach to urban planning, and Haussmann, the architect who implemented these radical plans, became a key pioneer of urban modernization. Sigfried Giedion describes how between 1853 and 1869 Haussman spent two and half million francs remodelling the centre of Paris, a large portion of which was spent 'on street construction and the demolition necessitated by the decision to run new streets through closely packed quarters. Paris in Haussmann's time was adapted to the totally changed conditions of the nineteenth century' (2008: 745). This was a radical approach to the design of urban space. The city was conceived of as one large system. Rational planning was imposed that took into account the entire infrastructure of a city: from housing and sanitation through to the flow of traffic and people. 'The technical aspects of town planning had never before been so systematically and precisely organized' (Giedion 2008: 765). This approach marked the beginnings of the town planning of the twentieth century, which is often criticized because of its brutal 'top-down' approach. Significantly, one of the first voices of dissent against brutal town planning came from a woman, Jane Jacobs (1961).

So the modern city brings about a new urban figure – one who proves fascinating to social commentators of the age. For Baudelaire there were intrinsic linkages between prostitutes and *flâneurs*, and both can be seen as key figures of the modern city – both walk the streets and gain knowledge of the dark recesses of urban life. Prostitutes had very specific, almost inextricable relationships with cities, and the streets, bars and brothels were their stomping ground. However, whilst the prostitute was driven by poverty, the *flâneur* was a privileged, wealthy man. Women were not free to use the city in the same way as men because of the moral and social constraints placed upon them (and some would argue that even in contemporary times, women continue to have restricted access to cities compared to men). The city was also positioned as a space of fear, chaos and uncertainty from which 'respectable' women should be protected. The link between women and cities became symbolized in the emergence of a series of binary oppositions which signified a split between respectable, worthy, clean, private, increasingly suburbanized women, on the one hand, and wanton, brazen, diseased urban prostitutes, on the other. These classifications of women as either respectable, and therefore absent from the city, or as key contributors to urban squalor are at two far ends of a spectrum and left for little in between. The modern city was a space of both fascination and disgust which many writers of the period, such as Dickens, Booth, Engels and Mayhew, sought to understand through the medium of writing, from fictional narrative through to social journalism. As Judith Walkowitz's (1980) work has shown, the prostitute emerges as a central figure in much of this writing. London was frequently depicted as a fog-filled, dark, powerful, seductive labyrinth – the prostitute always omnipresent. Reformers and journalists referred to prostitution using imperialistic language and spoke of the 'dark continents' of red-light districts; and, as Wilson (1996) argues, prostitution gathered its own literature of social investigation. The prostitute was perceived to be part of the 'moral miasma' of the Victorian 'cess pool' city of poverty, lawless-ness and disease. As Wilson notes, there was a fear that the immoral city could contaminate and spread disease even if one were just to breathe its air: 'According to the miasma theory of the spread of disease, you could catch an illness by breathing in the noxious smell of sewage' (1992: 39). Prostitution came to be seen as a central part of the miasma mainly because of the venereal disease (VD) epidemic of the era. There were many attempts to control VD through acts of par-liament. These were largely futile as the regulation was solely aimed at female prostitutes, who had to go for weekly checkups whilst their male clients did not. Prostitution was, as Wilson describes, 'a meta-phor for disorder and the overturning of the natural hierarchies and institutions of society. Rescue, reform and legislation were to rid the cities of this frightful evil' (1996: 60).

Modernity and the rise of a 'consumer society' did produce one significant innovation in women's use of the city in the form of new shopping spaces. The emergence of shopping arcades in the early nineteenth century and then of department stores by the 1850s allowed women new freedoms to use the city – albeit in fairly con-trolled ways. New consumption spaces also offered women new employment possibilities as shop workers. Window shopping and wandering through arcades and department stores were activities that women could comfortably engage in without transgressing the boundaries of their gender. Wilson argues that this is one area where women could indulge in *flâneur*-type activities: 'Although one could argue that shopping was for many women – perhaps the majority – a form of work rather than pleasure, at least for the leisured few it pro-vided the pleasures of looking, socializing and simply strolling – in the department store, a woman, too, could become a flâneur' (1996:

68). However, as Janet Wolff argues, '[O]f course, the literature of modernity . . . was not concerned with shopping' (1990: 58), and the connections between women and shopping were trivialized in our culture and neglected by academia until the 1980s. Moreover, although there were some possibilities for women to access urban life, they were clearly not free to wander city streets in the same way that men were – a point that we shall return to in more detail below.

Feminists have argued that there could never have been a female *flâneur*. As Wolff claims: 'There is no question of inventing the flâneuese; the essential point is that such a character was rendered impossible by the sexual divisions of the nineteenth century' (1990: 47). Unattended women were 'matter out of place' (Skeggs 1999). Drawing on the work of Laura Mulvey (1975) on the 'male gaze', Wolff goes on to observe that the *flâneur* is 'a man of pleasure, . . . a man who takes visual possession of the city, who has emerged in post-modern feminist discourse as the embodiment of the "male gaze". He represents men's visual and voyeuristic mastery over women' (1990: 6). Women were not in possession of the gaze but were only the object of it.

The difference between gender and use of the city was affected by class. Crudely, middle-class women were increasingly forced into the private realm whilst working-class women worked in factories, sweat shops or as street traders or prostitutes. Aside from its pivotal role as a site of industry and politics, the city was also seen as a space of chaos, complexity and vice from which 'respectable' women were to be protected. The spatial dimensions of this soon became very clear – as time moved on, the middle class increasingly moved to the newly developed suburbs whilst the city centre increasingly became the dwelling space of the poor. The growth of the railways allowed for the development of affluent commuter belts further and further away from the smog and squalor of the city. Whilst middle-class men used the work and leisure spaces of the city on a daily basis, middle-class women had very limited access to it. Wolff (1990) argues that middle-class women were 'more or less' consigned to the home. Wilson is critical of Wolff and feels her account is inaccurate because the period which she refers to (the late nineteenth century) was a period where women were beginning to become more active in the public sphere. Wilson, for example, points to the growing number of restaurants and tea rooms where women could socialize 'unattended by men'. Like shopping arcades and department stores, these commercial, quasi-public spaces offered women new access points and legitimated their reasons for being in the city.

When the male–female, public–private split was disrupted by the two world wars, during which women were required to work on farms or in munitions factories (for example), the ideologies of the 'naturalness' of the sexual division of labour were hugely undermined. Women were efficiently carrying out work previously exclusively undertaken by men. This paved the way for the huge transformations in terms of gender and work which gathered speed in the latter half of the twentieth century. Immediately after World War II, though, a massive campaign to re-domesticate women was waged. This was no easy task as not only had women proved they were capable of effectively carrying out men's work but many also enjoyed the experience, too. As Julie Wosk (2001) observes of the USA, a very large proportion of women wanted to keep their jobs after the war was over: 'A woman's bureau survey found that half of the women who had been housewives before the war wanted to continue working, and another contemporary survey found that women working in wartime wanted to keep their new employment: in 1944, 75–80 percent wanted to keep their jobs' (2001: 228).

As part of the propaganda war to get women back to the home, popular culture, particularly advertising, but also film and popular music, was mobilized in order to promote heavily idealized images of domestic femininity. New labour-saving domestic goods were being used to lure women back to domestic life and the imagery of the ideal housewife/mother dominated advertising and popular culture during the 1950s and 1960s. Here, then, we have a clear example of the links between gender, popular culture and space where popular culture has been used to reinforce and socially regulate notions of legitimate workspaces for women. As Imelda Whelehan notes: 'The years after the Second World War produced a retroactive ideological shift: a revivified "cult of the housewife" was effectively a consolidated attack on women's new-found freedom, devoted as it was to recreating and redefining the domestic spaces as women's space.' She goes on to write: '[M]aintaining the household was to be their proper destiny; indeed it became an identity in itself, to the exclusion of all others' (1996: 7).

This brief overview of some key debates about use of public and private space reveals that there are some powerful and significant gender dimensions at play. Whilst we can argue that many radical changes have occurred in terms of gender politics between the early city of modernity and the contemporary period, it is certainly not the case that men's and women's use of space is uniform and directly comparable.

We will now move to more recent examples of the gendered

relationships between gender, space and popular culture by focusing on two further case studies: youth subcultures and contemporary urban consumption spaces. We will use these case studies to consider more recent examples of gendered use of space.

Youth (Sub)Culture

In examining the subject of gender, popular culture and space, the example of youth subcultures is a highly productive case study to focus on. Firstly, youth subcultures are formations in which popular culture is actively produced, consumed and modified in highly symbolic and creative ways. As the work of Dick Hebdige (1979) has shown, youth subcultures are spaces of 'semiotic guerrilla warfare' where cultural products such as clothing, other bodily adornments and popular-cultural artefacts are used to make powerful statements about identity. Secondly, youth subcultures have a marked spatial dimension – they are highly visible entities, often involving 'gang-like' formations, and members usually have a striking visual appearance that deliberately and avowedly sets them apart from 'mainstream' society. With their emphasis on territoriality and street culture, youth subcultures are closely linked to space and place. They occupy a 'spectacular' presence in contemporary society – they are both the focus of moral panics and celebrated for their expressive resistance. Thirdly, they are entities in which gender roles are, in various ways, highly distinct – whether through the exaggeration of established gender roles or the subversion or transformation of them.

At a crucial time when gendered identities are being negotiated and defined (the teenage years), the gender dimensions of youth subcultures are multifarious. If we focus on the 1950s onwards, we can see youth subcultures as spaces that have oscillating and often contradictory relationships with mainstream rules about gender. Youth subcultures have variously operated as microcosms of patriarchal society in terms of gender relations or, alternatively, as liminal spaces in which traditional gender relations are transgressed. Likewise, some of the practices and performativity of gender which begin in the marginal space of the youth subculture can have an impact on mainstream society. The 'feminine' activities engaged in by some men in youth subcultures, such as the wearing of make-up and growing of long hair, have forced greater social fluidity in terms of gendered behaviour. As such they can be seen as hegemonic structures, and this is how the Birmingham Centre for Contemporary Cultural

Studies (hereafter the BCCCS) responded to them – as sites of struggle and resistance but whose practices can become incorporated into the mainstream.

It was Angela McRobbie and Sue Garber (1976) who first made the point that from both a research and participation angle, youth subcultures marginalized women. The BCCCS's celebrated work on youth subcultures – most notably Stuart Hall and Tony Jefferson's edited collection *Resistance through Rituals* (1998, first published in 1976) – was focused on almost exclusively on male academics writing about men in subcultures. Heavily influenced by recently translated Marxist texts emerging from Europe, notably those of Gramsci and Althusser, and the structuralist work of Roland Barthes (combined with Chicago School-influenced ethnographic methods), the BCCCS took a pioneering approach to the study of youth subcultures. Rather than positioning them as symbols of deviance and a social problem, the BCCCS looked at their creative, resistant and hegemonic aspects. However, in their descriptions of these various subcultures, women are rarely mentioned or interviewed. Quite simply they are denied a voice. McRobbie and Garber, whose essay appeared in the Hall and Jefferson collection, raise many important questions about this neglect. Were female members of youth subcultures as passive or invisible as these writings suggest? Did the male researchers overlook female experience whilst fetishizing male experience? If girls really were as absent or passive as is implied by this work, then why was this? McRobbie continued to pursue her critique of the women-blindness of research into youth subculture in her 1980 article 'Settling Accounts with Subcultures: A Feminist Critique', where she focuses on two landmark texts: Paul Willis's *Learning to Labour* (1977) and Dick Hebdige's *Subculture: The Meaning of Style* (1979), respectively. She highlights their neglect of gender/girls and wonders why, when they were so engaged with issues of class and ethnicity, they missed so many opportunities to interrogate the gender issues that they frequently begin to allude to.

By examining some key youth subcultures in chronological order, we can consider the extent to which they reveal significant changes in gender relations in society as a whole that have taken place over time.

In the youth subcultures of the 1950s and 1960s, males were at the centre whilst female members of youth subcultural groups had peripheral and passive roles. When people speak of 'teds', they are usually referring to the teddy boys – the first 'spectacular' postwar youth subculture – commonly represented by images of gangs of surly-looking males with big hair, big shoes and tight trousers.

Whilst there were teddy girls as well, their role within this subculture has been largely overlooked. Teddy girls were usually positioned as the girlfriend appendage of the teddy boy. The visual images from the time, the news stories, the moral panics, were squarely focused on the male teddy boy gangs. Pioneer of British Cultural Studies Richard Hoggart famously lambasted the teds (whom he referred to as 'the Juke Box Boys') for what he saw as their damaging and indiscriminate consumption of American popular culture in his influential text *The Uses of Literacy* (1958). In his vivid descriptions of the milk bar haunts of the teds, girls are peripheral and barely acknowledged – even though girls would have been present in these kinds of spaces. Everyone was fascinated by 'angry young men' but not women. Likewise the style gurus and role models of American popular culture so revered by the teds were male – Elvis, Eddie Cochran, Marlon Brando and the stars of Western films. These figures embodied forms of masculinity and male sexuality defined by rebelliousness, gangs and territorial battles:

> That state of mind which was 'America' for many British youngsters in the 1950s bore two unmistakable imprints: Hollywood film and popular music. . . . For many young men, the formalized gangster film types of the late 1940s and then the problematic male youth hero (Montgomery Clift, Marlon Brando, James Dean), fixed and condensed in a masculine style life as an imaginative gesture. (Chambers 1985: 32)

Whilst there were a handful of rebellious (fictional) female role models, such as the character of Rio McDonald, played by Jane Russell, in the film *The Outlaw* (1943), or that of Judy, played by Natalie Wood, in *Rebel without a Cause* (1955), for example, these were lone figures. Some recently unearthed photographs of teddy girls, by the film director Ken Russell taken in 1954, reveal teenage girls dressed in innovative and shocking clothing and with surly and rebellious facial expressions (Image 3). These photographs are rare documentary evidence that girls were more actively involved in ted culture than established accounts tell us. Whilst there is scant detail about the actions, biographies and opinions of teddy girls, documentary evidence such as these photographs suggest that girls were drawn to this lifestyle.

The teds first emerged in the East End of London in the early 1950s and they were a distinctly working-class youth subculture. They railed against the spatial disruptions of post-war town planning (according to Phil Cohen [1972]) and often reacted violently to tensions of class and ethnicity. The claiming of territory was important and this took

Image 3   In Your Dreams: 14-year-old Jean Rayner in the exploratory stage of teddyism. (©2006 TopFoto/Ken Russell Photo by Ken Russell, January 1955, from a series: 'The Last of the Teddy Girls')

on racial dimensions as the white teddy boys railed against the newly arrived migrant communities from former British colonies, as was the case with the notorious 'teddy boy riots' of the late 1950s.[3] The teddy boys could also be perceived as attempting to preserve an older form of masculinity because they felt alienated from new, more feminized, white-collar work. This generation experienced the absence of their fathers – most of whom had been fighting in World War II a decade

[3] There were two high-profile riots between teddy boy gangs and Jamaican youths, both in 1958. The first took place in the city of Nottingham and the second in the Notting Hill area of London.

earlier; some, of course, did not return. The war had also led to their
mothers working in traditional male jobs, so teds, and other young-
sters of this generation, had grown up with some huge social changes
in terms of gender. The post-war period produced uncertainty about
masculinity which the iconography of ted culture can be read as a
reaction to, through the emphasis on flick-knives, coshes, bootlace
ties, brothel creepers, quiffs – all avowedly masculine, aggressive and
threatening. The visual style of the teddy girls can be read as expression of hyper-femininity. The 'Dior look', the opulent big skirts, tiny
waists and plunging cleavages all link to accentuating the voluptu-
ousness of the female form (and very different to the straight lines of
female dress in the 1920s and 1930s). The 'excessive' use of fabric
and the emphasis on curves were also a reaction to the austerity of
ration-book culture in 1950s Britain. However, as the image of Jean
Rayner (p. 195) confirms, not all teddy girls conformed to the dress
code and habitus expected of them. Rayner is clearly displaying a look
that blurs elements of masculine and feminine 'teddy' style to create
something that is ahead of its time.

For girls, ted culture provided new spatial possibilities, but also a
number of constraints:

> Teddy-boy culture was an escape from the claustrophobia of the family,
> into the street and 'caff'. While many girls might adopt an appropriate
> way of dressing, complementary to the teds, they would be much less
> likely to spend the same amount of time hanging about on the streets.
> Girls had to be careful not to 'get into trouble' and excessive loiter-
> ing on street corners might be taken as a sexual invitation to the boys.
> (McRobbie and Garber 1976: 212)

As this quote suggests, the Victorian hang-ups about women 'without
a purpose' in public space still lingered and women hanging about
on the street remained heavily associated with being sexually available. The debates in the previous case study about men's power over
public space and the banishment of women to the domestic realm
clearly retained a resonance at this time.

The teds of the 1950s were open to the cultural imports coming
from the USA – notably rock and roll music – but closed to the new
cultural influences of the newly arrived West Indian migrants with
whom they engaged in racist conflict. The mods of the mid-sixties,
however, represent a youth subculture more open to new cultural
influences. This was a decade later, and a decade in which arguably more cultural change had occurred than at any other time in

history. Politically, women, gay people and ethnic minorities were fighting for their rights and social changes were starting to occur. The Victorian values that were still lingering in the 1950s were finally being replaced with a new mood of tolerance, even acceptance, of a wider variety of lifestyle choices. This might partly account for the openness of mod culture. Whilst it is still the male mod that is the primary source of attention, the lumpen-masculinity of the teddy boy has been replaced with a very new type of masculinity – not dissimilar to the so-called 'metrosexual' of the early twenty-first century, with some men expressing an open interest in fashion and grooming. The rocker, the natural descendant of the ted, was held in binary opposition to the mod in terms of style. At the centre of this opposition was a distinction between two types of masculinity. The leather-clad rockers rode throbbing big motorbikes; the mod drove the light, 'girlie' scooter. This extract from Paul Willis's study of (male) rockers in the 1960s clearly demonstrates this polarization of masculinity:

> Their appearance was aggressively masculine. The motor-cycle gear both looked tough, with its leather studs and denim, and by association with the motor-bike, took on some of the intimidating quality of the machine. . . . It is interesting to note that the outside group which was hated the most, the mods, were despised particularly for their feminine traits, and feminine ways of dressing. (Willis 1978: 20)

Mod boys were defined by their narcissistic habits and their active engagement with 'feminine' behaviour – which included an obsession with clothing, attention to detail, occasional wearing of make-up and a stylistic ethos of cleanliness and neatness. Often this was all wrapped up in an ex-army parka both to protect the immaculate outfit beneath and to reinforce a masculine subject position for the benefit of the rockers, who sought to question this. Did this less avowedly aggressive culture prove to be a more welcoming space for women? McRobbie and Garber argue that this is one explanation for higher levels of female participation in the mod subculture than in earlier youth subcultures:

> There were certainly thousands of 'mod' girls who made their appearance in the nightclubs, on the streets, at work and even on the fringes of the clashes between the mods and rockers during the various bank holiday weekends throughout the mid-1960s. . . . It might well be that the mod preoccupation with style and the emergence of the unisex look and the 'effeminate' mod man, gave girls a more legitimate place in the

subculture than had previously been the case. (McRobbie and Garber 1976: 213)

Looking at some documentary evidence from the time, footage of the audience on the *Ready, Steady, Go!* TV programme,[4] it is clear that there were significant numbers of female mods. There were also black mods – both male and female – and this is a multicultural subculture. In this period, dancing also becomes less connected with courtship, and individual, non-contact dancing led to both men and women dancing on their own. Women no longer needed to wait to be asked to dance by a man, or, worse, have to dance with a female companion in the absence of any offers from men. What is also clear is that, just as males within mod culture became more feminine in terms of their style, so too did the girls' style become more masculine or androgynous. Unlike the hyper-feminine look of the teddy girls and 1950s women's clothes generally – big skirts, tiny waist and voluptuous curves – the 1960s modette was far more boyish. The emphasis on curves falls out of fashion whilst shape-concealing ski pants and polo-necked jumpers and short haircuts become the style of the moment. But as Wilson notes, the mini-skirt, which emerged contemporaneously with the mods, is arguably the most sexualized clothing item in history:

> The clothing of the permissive society was often described as unisex, but in retrospect it doesn't look masculine or boyish. When girls – for all women were girls in those days – wore skirts that rose to the crotch and curtains of hair that descended to meet it, when they exposed nipples in see-through blouses and navels below crocheted tank tops that never met hipster pants, they were looking not like men or boys but like children . . . as personified by the newly famous models of the period, it was the decade of the rag doll, of the waif, of the pre-pubertal Twiggy. (1985: 148)

The role of fashion designers such as Mary Quant and Barbara Hulanicki (creator of the Biba fashion empire) meant that women had some control over the look and feel of female fashion in this period, and it is significant that women were beginning to be involved in cultural production. The 1960s was a decade which saw huge social change in terms of gender and sexuality. This was an era of

---

[4] As Iain Chambers notes: 'Nicknamed the "Mecca for Mods" *Ready, Steady, Go!* seemed the unique television programme, both then and since, to have had its finger on the pulse of an important part of contemporary teenage Britain' (1985: 76).

grass-roots protest from a number of quarters – the anti-war movement, the rise of feminism and civil rights. It was an era which saw a
new fascination with identity. However, when thinking about fashion
and the mid-1960s, an overwhelming image is that of the male
photographer capturing the image of the passive female model – as
captured in the Antonioni film *Blow-Up* (1966) (and later satirized in
Austin Powers films). This reminds us of the passivity of women and
their continued position 'to be looked at' (Mulvey 1975) and controlled by the male gaze.

What can be seen when comparing women's treatment within ted
culture to that of mod culture is that there are some significant shifts
in gender roles over a ten-year period. In summarizing key elements
of these changes, Michael Brake argues that

> [t]raditionally in the more dramatic forms of male-dominated subcul-
> tures, girls were in a structurally passive situation, reflecting their posi-
> tions outside. In the Ted subculture of the 1950s, girls were present
> during social activities but absent from the street corner culture. With
> Mods, girls were subordinate but mod 'cool' style allowed them to
> mingle in all girl groups or alone. With the bikers, they never pen-
> etrated the central masculine core, riding or owning a bike, but were
> always a pillion passenger. (1990: 172)

Despite some movements towards equality in women's treatment, it
is clear that a state of equality had yet to be realized. Whilst subcultures exist in a variety of spaces, it is their presence in public space
which has garnered the most attention, especially if that presence
has had a group or gang-like formation. These spectacular post-war
youth subcultures are notorious for their displays of masculinity
taking place in public spaces – notably the street. We have seen the
way in which girls were rendered absent or invisible from these spaces
and their roles left undocumented. A crucial piece of work to highlight in terms of this issue is McRobbie and Garber's identification
of bedroom culture and femininity (1976: 212). This recalls debates
raised in the first case study of this chapter, which introduced the
dichotomy between so-called 'public man' and 'private woman'.

The arrival of the punk subculture in the mid-1970s appears to be
a subculture which provided some (albeit limited) opportunities for
traditional gender roles to be subverted. The disregard of gender rules
by the immediate musical forerunners of punk, the New York Dolls,
Roxy Music and David Bowie, for example, saw a stylistic blending
of art school experimentation, bisexuality and 'gender bending' from
a male perspective. Punk also provided a space where women could

express themselves in 'unfeminine' ways and led to the emergence of some powerful feminist bands such as The Raincoats and, later, the riot grrrl movement (see M. Leonard 2007and Monem 2007). However, as we saw from earlier chapters, many commentators have been quick to point out that women were mainly subordinate within punk subculture and punk musical production. Lauraint Leblanc's research on female punks found a discourse of ambivalence from the women she interviewed. Leblanc observed the tensions and contradictions of gender and punk. In reflecting on an interview with a female punk, she comments:

> Like me, she felt troubled about the male-dominated gender dynamics in the punk subculture, a subculture that portrays itself as being egalitarian, and even feminist, but is actually far from being either. Yet like me, she had found that this same subculture gave her a place to be assertive and aggressive, to express herself in less 'feminine' ways than other girls. (Leblanc 1999: 6)

She goes on to note the paradoxical or contradictory relationship girls have to punk: '[G]ender is problematic for punk girls in a way that it is not for punk guys, because punk girls must accommodate female gender within subcultural identities that are deliberately coded as male' (Leblanc 1999: 8). To draw from Willis's use of the term 'homology', whilst the fit between a subculture and the male punk, ted, rocker, and so on, might be neat, there are a series of contradictory negotiations for women.

By the 1980s, youth subcultures become less 'spectacular'. In other words they lost their shock factor as the dress codes and lifestyles associated with subcultures became more integrated into mainstream culture. Commentators began to speak of postmodernity where previous subcultures were ransacked, thus bringing about the arrival of retro fashion and the sampling of old tunes in the newly emerging digital dance music scene. Subcultures became less easy to spot on the street and a youthful habitus was no longer the preserve of the teenager. As Robert Elms, journalist for influential youth style magazine *The Face*, declared in the British press in 1983: 'Nobody is a teenager any more because everyone is' (cited in Chambers 1987: 2). People were extending their youth; there were numerous niche fashion markets; previously subversive music was increasingly incorporated into advertising and soundtracks for mainstream television and film. Men and women had a wider repertoire of fashions, hairstyles and bodily adornments to select from. Late modern reflexive identity projects also incorporated the construction of individualized physical identities.

The rave and house cultures of the late 1980s and 1990s led to some further alterations to established gender roles. The centrality of the drug ecstasy had a powerful impact on courtship patterns. Under the influence of this allegedly libido-dulling drug, the sexual conquest element of club culture declined. Dancing in clubs, warehouse parties and raves was promoted as an egalitarian experience. Men were less aggressive and the dancing was on equal terms. Initially the new forms of dance culture saw the emergence of unisex fashions such as baggy t-shirts and jeans. However, in more recent years, women's dress and habitus have become far more sexualized within dance culture. There is also a notable absence of female DJs and club promoters. As we have argued elsewhere in this book, because the chain of institutions that youth subcultures are linked to – the music industry, the fashion industry, and so on – are still dominated by men, women are faced with limitations in terms of their participation and control of club culture.

The spaces of the city have become more influenced by subculture and youth culture. In many Western cities hedonistic behaviour is actively encouraged in some urban spaces through the promotion of the 'twenty-four-hour city' and 'night-time economy'. Policies to develop a European-style café culture have been developed in many cities and there has been a proliferation of bars and clubs and visible drinking spaces. We will now look at an example of new consumption spaces from a gender perspective.

Gender, Sex and the Contemporary City

From a spatial point of view, youth subcultures are transient and temporal. They are mobile in physical space and people move in and out of them over time. For this next case study we take the issue of gender and popular culture from the point of view of a more permanent stamp on the urban landscape: consumption spaces in the night-time economy. Looking at these spaces allows us to consider the relevance of the themes introduced earlier in this chapter. We have seen how in the nineteenth and twentieth centuries there were dominant linkages between women and private space and men and public space. We discussed the figure of the *flâneur*, one who is free to wander the streets for entertainment, as an essentially male figure. In examining youth subcultures, we saw that these provided some opportunities for women to appear on the street but also how invisible women often were in subcultures, how overlooked by researchers or consigned to the bedroom. The 'ideology of romance' also had spatial connotations as it essentially encouraged girls to aspire to get married and become housewives. McRobbie's analysis demonstrated how girls were never encouraged to think about the world of work and public life. Even in the latter part of the twentieth century, the male/public and female/private dichotomy continued to have currency.

Wolff spoke of the impossibility of the female *flâneur* (or *flâneuse*, as she might be called) in the city of modernity. We now need to consider whether she exists in the postmodern, post-industrial city and discuss a range of other questions connected with gender and the use of urban leisure spaces.

In terms of marginal groups and subcultures gaining more influence on mainstream culture, the emergence of gay leisure spaces in cities in recent decades is a case in point. The Marais area of Paris, De Waterkant in Cape Town and indeed entire cities, such as San Francisco and Brighton (UK), have become associated with gay culture. 'During the 1970s and the early 1980s, geographers and social scientists began to observe that gay men and lesbians were creating distinct social, political and cultural landscapes, then dubbed "gay ghettos" . . ., now more commonly referred to as "gay villages" ' (Casey 2004: 447). In recent decades the development of such areas has been closely linked to the regeneration and marketing of consumption spaces.

Let us look at an example of a gay space in Manchester, England. Manchester's Canal Street area, known as the 'Gay Village', is predominantly defined by male homosexuality, although some lesbian spaces coexist. The presence of an area such as this represents a dual, contradictory space in terms of its relationship to mainstream society and brings into play discussions about sexuality as well as gender. Does the colonization of a geographical space by a marginalized group represent the 'success' of neo-liberal social tolerance or is it a reaction to massive homophobic social intolerance? Is this a positive move of gay culture from the margins to the centre – the imposition of a gay habitus on urban space – or it is a ghetto created for gay people to escape from the prejudices of the heterosexual society? In terms of popular culture, Manchester's Gay Village is an interesting example to focus on. It is a space for cultural consumption and production of sexual identity which has also been refracted through the lens of popular culture because of its high-profile re-presentation in TV drama – the highly acclaimed *Queer as Folk*. The area is also renowned nationally, even internationally, because of its annual Mardi Gras parade. Initially used by the gay community because it was a marginal space, a 'dive' not considered valuable, its canal-side location emerged in urban regeneration terms as a prime site of cosmopolitan waterfront real estate. Although gay spaces existed in Manchester for over a century, the area wasn't widely known about until the 1990s, as Jon Binnie and Beverley Skeggs note:

> Known gay spaces have existed in Manchester since the early 1900s but the difference is that they were not consolidated by compact visibility. The 'Gay Village' became more visible to the heterosexual community during the 1990s with the development of an innovative modernist architecturally designed bar with 30-foot glass windows called Manto. The architectural design was a queer visual statement: 'We're here, we're queer – so get used to it.' (2006: 230)

The area's massive rise in terms of a public profile occurred at the same period as Manchester's pop and night-time economy blossomed. Its waterside location, abundance of regenerated, aesthetically beautiful nineteenth-century warehouses and its sophisticated pavement culture were soon keenly incorporated into city council and tourism promotion material. As Binnie and Skeggs note, the urban culture 'guru' Richard Florida (2004) regards gay culture as a valuable asset in defining urban 'creativity indexes', with 'a strong and vibrant gay community as an indicator of a place that is open to many different kinds of people': 'According to Florida, cities that embrace sexual difference also embrace ethnic and other cultural difference. This contentious and widely popularised claim suggests that gay culture occupies a pivotal role within the production and consumption of urban spaces as cosmopolitan' (Binnie and Skeggs 2006: 221).

As the area increasingly became well known as an exciting feature of Manchester's night-time economy, it rapidly altered from being a gay-only area to a popular stopping-off point on Manchester's bar and club circuit. This brought swathes of groups of heterosexual men and women, which contributed to some massive tensions over the use of this space. These various groups – defined first and foremost via their sexuality and gender – became involved in symbolic battles over space. The political battles fought to achieve gay rights should not be underestimated. For example, the Stonewall riots in New York – a clear case of the links between popular culture, gender and space – were centred on gay men's battles with the police in their fight for the right for men to dance with other men. The idea that the hard-won space of Manchester's Canal Street area, created out of necessity, should become colonized by the heterosexual community proved unpalatable to many in the gay community.

It was not only gay men and lesbians who were attracted to the area because it provided freedoms not offered in the straight night-time economy. Heterosexual women used the space of the Gay Village because of a perceived freedom from being harassed by heterosexual men in search of sexual encounters. As Skeggs (1999) argues, women feel free from the male gaze and the heterosexual market. However, this soon progressed into groups of women on hen nights with men on stag nights following after in quick succession. As Binnie notes:

> The 'key' to the 'success' of the gay village has been the production of a de-sexualized consumption space where an asexual non-threatening (especially to women) gay identity can be enacted. In this sense asexual gay identities and asexual 'mainstream' ones are converging. Gayness is used as a resource to attract women as consumers in the space, effeminate gay men are used to normalize the behaviour of heterosexual men. (2004: 166)

The presence of the hen night severely disrupts the intended concept of the space. A hen night is fully framed in the paradigm of the rituals of heterosexual marriage. Whilst there are cultural expectations that a stag might sow his wild oats, a hen is entitled to let her hair down, get drunk with her friends, but nothing more than that. A gay space provides a hen a space of controlled 'de-control'. That heterosexual women actively use this space invites the question as to whether women use such spaces because they can experience the feeling of being a *flâneur*. The fact that women are drawn to these places suggests that they do not feel there are opportunities for female *flâneurie* in other parts of the city.

Further power struggles came into play in the Gay Village, between gay men and lesbians, with some lesbian women feeling that they were heavily marginalized in the area. Indeed, the first lesbian bar, Vanilla, did not open until 1988, before which 'lesbian space in the village was restricted to one room above a male leather bar on Canal Street' (Binnie and Skeggs 2006: 230). In a possible explanation for the absence of fixed lesbian spaces, Gill Valentine notes Castells' argument that there are differences in the way men and women relate to space: '[M]en try to dominate and therefore achieve spatial superiority, whilst women have less territorial aspirations, attaching more importance to personal relationships and social networks' (1995: 96).

As with heterosexual spaces, men are the dominant force within gay spaces.

The conflicting uses of the Gay Village raise many issues and questions about power and use of space. It is clear that there are a number of contradictory tensions over use of space, which serves to remind us that use of space is deeply political – even in so-called cosmopolitan, tolerant and diverse cities. Let us unravel some key tensions. The emergence of gay spaces occurred because homophobia and criminalization of homosexual behaviour meant that gay people were forced to create their own spaces in order openly to perform their sexual identity. However, in the increasingly commodified city of consumption, gay spaces have become incorporated into the marketing of hedonistic, 'diverse', cosmopolitan spaces by mainstream city managers. This totally changes the nature and purpose of the space. With the case of Manchester's Gay Village, a small tract of land, comprised of a couple of streets, has been gentrified in much the same way as the SoHo of New York as described by Sharon Zukin (1982). In SoHo in the 1960s and 1970s, groups of avant-garde artists began to congregate in the low-rent warehouses and workshops of the largely defunct garment industry. An artistic bohemia developed, but, over time, affluent New Yorkers desired to live in the area because of its cool, artistic atmosphere. As more and more people flocked to SoHo, so, too, did property prices soar, which led to the displacement of the artists, who were no longer able to afford the rent. In much the same way, Manchester's Gay Village has attracted the interest of many outside the gay community, giving rise to a number of non-gay businesses opening up in the area, which has forced up property prices as well as leading to gay men and women increasingly becoming the subject of the heterosexual gaze. This has impacted on the way that gay people behave in their own space.

Mark Casey carried out research into lesbian experience of gay spaces in Newcastle's 'Pink Triangle'. As with Manchester, the gay village in Newcastle emerged as a site for heterosexual women on hen nights. Casey asks, '[B]ut where can lesbians go to escape heterosexual women's gaze, evaluation and threat?'(2004: 455). Casey's research found that the gangs of hen-nighters had a negative impact on lesbian space. Casey identified two problematic areas which led to the exclusion of lesbians in what was meant to be a 'lesbian-friendly space'. First of all, lesbians reported feeling excluded by friendships between gay men and straight women, for whom 'equal sexual desire by both groups for men may be perceived as a greater sharing experience' (2004: 453). Secondly the space had become ambiguous and there were negative reactions to lesbians making passes at straight women: '[I]f sexual identity cannot be read, mistakes over sexual identities may then be made' (2004: 457).

What we see in these studies of use of gay space by a variety of gay, lesbian and straight men and women are some deeply political issues in the type of space that has become increasingly commodified for the benefit of the leisure industry, urban managers and marketers. Far from suggesting tolerance of gay men and lesbians, this move implies that gay men and lesbian women are fetishized, gazed upon and marginalized in their own spaces. It also provokes the suggestion that women feel the need to use gay spaces because they feel restricted and vulnerable in heterosexual space.

Mainstream leisure spaces, whilst also incorporating elements from subcultures to create 'neo-bohemias', are likewise witnessing an increase of sexualized spaces. The spaces are based on masculine power and the masculine gaze. The last few years has seen a phenomenal rise of lap-dancing or pole-dancing clubs. In these spaces, women perform erotic dance acts for male paying customers and dancers take clients to private rooms to perform what are euphemistically described as 'private dances'. There have been extensive debates about the power structures of this relationship/transaction. In a report in the *Guardian* newspaper a lap-dancer described some of the reality of her work:

> You pay 'rent' to the club just to be there and if you can persuade someone to buy a dance, you get £20 – about 20% of which the club takes. Then there are the fines – £10 if you miss your turn to pole dance, if you're late, you're wearing the wrong shoes or you break the rules. There are so many ways to make money from you. You are constantly trying to make as much money as possible out of everybody, otherwise you are literally paying to be there. (Bell 2008)

Many argue that this is exploitative, degrading and a form of prostitution made respectable, brought into the mainstream, sold as light-hearted fun, purely to protect men's interests. There have been numerous campaigns to get lap-dancing clubs closed down. Cases of rape and sexual assault on women are reported to soar in the vicinity of a lap-dancing club. Others claim that lap-dancing is empowering for women and demonstrates a world of choice where women can express their sexuality in a regulated space. The research of Bernadette Barton found that whilst some women might enter the world of lap-dancing in a frame of empowerment, actual experience soon dulls this optimism:

> Depending on when you question a dancer about her feelings about her career – when she begins or later in her career – you are likely to get a different self-assessment of her power or oppression, as what dancers initially experience as pleasurable becomes increasingly fraught with problems. That power (or lack of it) is, however, neither as seamless nor as static as partisans in the sex wars portray it. (Barton 2002: 599)

It is certainly a popular contemporary discourse that the hyper-sexualization of girls and women can be read as symbol of progress, of emancipation, of freedom and equality. This new hyper-sexualized world is certainly not restricted to the privacy of the lap-dancing club. Contemporary landscapes and mediascapes are saturated with sexualized images and discourses and an underlying rhetoric that this is somehow good for women, even though men are rarely presented or offered for consumption in comparable ways. As McRobbie (2008) argues, there has been a dismantling and discrediting of feminism. To express reservation about the position of women in neo-liberal societies is positioned as prudish, or in the spirit of vulgar outmoded feminism. In her analysis of a wide range of contemporary media texts and discourses, Rosalind Gill identifies the rhetoric of post-feminism, which seeks to negate any criticism of the huge sexual inequalities that persist. She argues that there is a '[p]ernicious connection of this representational shift to neoliberal subjectivities in which sexual objectification can be (re-)presented not as something done to women by some men, but as the freely chosen wish of active, confident, assertive female subjects' (2007: 259). A discourse of individualism prevails which promotes the ideology that a wide variety of choices are available to everyone – agreeing to be sexualized is just part and parcel of a particular lifestyle choice. We live in a meritocratic society where fairness and justice prevail. Post-feminism, as Gill goes on to argue, involves an entanglement of feminist and anti-feminist ideas which are 'simultaneously taken for granted and repudiated' (2007: 269). We don't need feminism any more – the good bits of feminism have been assimilated into common-sense behaviour and the bad bits of feminism are condemned to ridicule. This seems to be a highly effective strategy for silencing anyone who dares to suggest that a phenomenon such as lap-dancing blatantly and unashamedly signifies unequal power relations between men and women.

Conclusion

In this chapter we have examined the relationships between gender and space. In particular we have been concerned with public space and consumption spaces in the modern through to late modern city – from the mid-nineteenth century through to the contemporary twenty-first century. Looking across such a wide time span allows us to make some conclusions about the changes and continuity in terms of men and women's use of the city.

The figure of the nineteenth-century city *flâneur* has been used by feminist writers as a vehicle for discussing the problem of women's unequal access to public space. At the heart of the debates about the *flâneur* is the issue of being able to be in the city without a purpose, just for fun. In the nineteenth-century city this was not a possibility that was open to women. The arrival of new consumption spaces such as shopping arcades and department stores offered women a glimpse of the freedoms available to men. In these quasi-public consumption spaces, affluent women were able to be in cities for non-work-related reasons. However, women were not free to roam the streets, public squares and bars in comparable ways to men. Women were the object of the male gaze but had little opportunity to be gazers themselves.

If we move forward almost two hundred years, what possibility is there for the female *flâneur* (or *flâneuse*) now? On the face of it, it is a common assumption that in Westernized cities, women have the freedom to walk in the city without purpose, for pleasure. However, on scrutiny, it is clear that there are still significant differences in men and women's use of urban space. A group of scholars recently carried out some research on the *flâneur* and *flâneuse* of the twenty-first century in four Dutch cities. The researchers captured the use of these cities at different times of the day and night. What their research findings revealed was that there were significant differences in terms of men's and women's use of urban space once the shops had closed: 'Women are using the street as corridors and not as a destination itself. When women are using the square in the evening or at night, other women or men usually accompany them. The flâneuse is limited in her freedom, because she feels unsafe after shops' closing time' (Nguyen and van Nes 2009: 6). These findings are echoed in similar research on cities across the globe. There are still huge problems about the safety of women in public space, especially at night and after commercial centres and retail spaces have closed for the day.

We saw how new consumption spaces in cities bring with them

a complexity of contradictions in terms of gender and sexuality. Issues of power and ownership of space remain central, and certain groups, particularly those who fall outside Raewyn Connell and James Messerschmidt's (2005) category of 'hegemonic masculinity', are frequently marginalized and excluded from urban consumption zones. Even when alternative spaces are developed, the power struggles remain important. This reminds us that public space, urban space, is never 'neutral' but laden with meaning. The ability to consume or produce popular culture in the city is variable and contingent on gendered and sexual identities.

In our survey of gender and youth subcultures, we saw ways in which youth subcultures did offer some opportunities for girls to break free from traditional gender expectations, but also how many youth subcultures emerged as microcosms of patriarchal society with girls occupying passive and low-status subject positions. The group formations provided by youth subcultures did, however, offer girls some access to street-based cultures, and new experimental fashion and bodily adornments provided a wider range of femininities to choose from, or even create.

In this chapter we have surveyed a range of spaces of popular culture with issues of gender at the forefront of our minds. Access to and power within space are strongly determined by gender. Whilst women are no longer absent from the city (as they were in the nineteenth century), they are not yet free to exist in the city in the same ways as men.

8

Conclusion

Prisoners of Gender?

In this book we have examined the dynamics of gender and popular culture from numerous angles, including how gender is produced by popular culture but also who produces popular culture. We have looked at how men and women are represented in culture, analysed gender-differentiated consumption practices and reflected on gender and popular culture in space and place. These analyses have spanned numerous historical periods, from early modernity through to the twenty-first century. This has allowed us not only to make comparisons across time, but also to fully understand contemporary issues around gender and popular culture, which are rooted in complex histories. Whilst we have provided some broad overviews, we have also focused in on rich case studies. In this way we were able to map some dominant and recurring patterns and test them on detailed examples, some of which are based on our empirical research.

In the early city of modernity, women could not 'hang around' in cities without causing a stir, without the implication of some sort of moral wrongdoing. In the twenty-first century, women are no longer consigned to the domestic sphere; in modern cities, women are able to shop, socialize and, in some areas, wander. Popular media such as *Sex and the City* (*SATC*) represent women doing just that. In *SATC*, women are portrayed as powerful, independent individuals. These women have important jobs, they own property, they are educated, they can consume the city and consume in the city. They engage in sexual relationships where they are active agents rather than passively waiting to be chosen. This and other pervasive media texts tell us that equality has been achieved; we are all individuals now. We have choice; we have agency and power.

Yet we have clearly found that women are not free to use public space in the same way as men. Heterosexual women's use of gay spaces suggests that women experience levels of discomfort in 'mainstream' urban leisure spaces. They feel restricted, vulnerable or conspicuous. Although we are encouraged to believe that new consumption-based lifestyles are available to all, we have seen how women's binge drinking is castigated as deviant and 'unfeminine'. In some people's eyes, this sort of behaviour invites sexual abuse. Is this why women like hanging out in gay spaces? Clearly there are large, often unspoken clouds of gender rules lingering in the atmosphere which restrict women's use of space.

In terms of cultural production, we have found that, far from a meritocratic world where individuals are masters of their own identity and biography and free to experiment in any enclave of work, powerful cultural myths pervade the deep recesses of society's psyche. These myths transmit ideologies which promote the idea that exceptional creative talent, creative genius, is a masculine force. There are powerful ideologies which suggest that technology is a masculine realm which women's more 'creative' brains are not suited to grasping fully. Women are frequently stereotyped as being creative and emotional – and the two concepts are often linked – yet somehow they are not creative geniuses; they have the 'wrong sort' of creativity. Interestingly, in the context of this book, three of the four protagonists in *SATC* work in the cultural industries: Carrie is a writer, Charlotte an art dealer and Samantha runs her own public relations company. In the real world, women in these roles are still exceptional cases. Furthermore, it is only Carrie who is actually a frontline cultural producer. There is conclusive evidence that women are severely underrepresented in terms of frontline cultural production. They are not involved in producing the creative content that plays such a central role in defining identity. Women are not promoted as having the attributes of the 'ideal' cultural industries worker (Tams 2002).

There are powerful interlinking chains of production, mediation and consumption. We have argued that at every level these are saturated with ideas about how men and women should behave and what they have the right to do. Each has a knock-on effect on the other: because men are in charge of popular culture, the culture that is produced, distributed and consumed reflects the interest of a male powerbase. The dominance of men as cultural producers has an impact on how gender is represented and valued. Whilst there have been some disruptions, the nature of the gaze it is still mainly defined in terms of hegemonic masculinity.

As many theorists discussed in this book have observed, there is an ongoing dismantling and discrediting of feminism which offers dissenters no space for complaint. This sabotaging of feminism is very subtle but ubiquitous. It is suggested that feminism is an outmoded, comical ideology which has become redundant because we now have gender equality. It has been made to appear so ridiculous and 'angry' that young people struggle to identify with it. We still live in a gender-unequal world, but now those who experience discrimination on gender grounds have no forum to complain in. There is a pervasive discourse of freedom. Women are free to become lap-dancers. The male gaze no longer has to be mediated by celluloid. In neo-liberal society, men can pay to gaze upon a real highly sexualized woman.

Pure choice is an illusion which is shored up and maintained by popular culture. Because popular culture is mainly seen to be fun and light-hearted, the seriousness of the underlying misogyny and gender regimes is diluted. As Lisa McLaughlin and Cynthia Carter observe:

> [T]he presence of more women in the newsroom or the boardroom or behind the camera amounts to small change if women simply are expected to conform to masculinist environments that remain off-limits for transformation. Feminist progress may be measured by the degree to which we have moved beyond 'separate spheres', but gender continues to constitute a structuring presence within existing social spaces. (2004: 235)

Masculinity and Femininity: Continuity and Change

In modern societies, the 1960s ushered in major socio-cultural breaks from tradition and since then there have been significant changes in gender relations and conditions. Yet it is also remarkable how much continuity we can trace throughout the same period. This pattern of continuity and change has been best exemplified in the book by the new femininity which today allows women to enjoy a wide range of behaviours and attitudes previously thought unfitting, such as having casual sex or enjoying leisure time going shopping, drinking and clubbing. However, the emergence of this new, freer femininity has coincided with the return of conventional, conservative notions of femininity which heavily criticize women who engage in any of these 'unfeminine' behaviours. Men never face quite the same level of scrutiny and critique as women; even in 2011 there are different norms and expectations governing men's and women's behaviours. It appears that femininity has been diversified but that conventional notions of what it is to be feminine, helped along by post-feminism, continue powerfully to assert themselves as the most superior and appropriate type of femininity. This process highlights that popular culture is not one monolithic whole but a collection of diverse institutions, texts and producers. Media mostly addressed to and consumed by women, such as women's and girls' magazines, seem to embrace the new femininity while conservative media with mixed audiences, such as the *Daily Mail*, are vigorously opposed.

Masculinity has also undergone enormous changes since the 1960s, diversifying into several types and discourses. The figures of the new man and the new lad exemplify the contradictory trends which have marked these changes. On the one hand, masculinity has been brought closer to femininity. For example, physical appearance is now considered important for men, too, and the idea of a rounded individual requires men to possess traditionally 'feminine' characteristics such as being caring or able to express emotions. On the other hand, there has been a return to an old-school type of masculinity embodied by the new lad. This type of masculinity disavows all things feminine as well as the changes in masculinity ushered in by the new man, which are seen as 'feminizing' men. Instead, it asserts a return to a 'natural' masculinity centred on the objectification of women, male bonding and a macho conception of male sexuality as insatiable. This trend very much maps onto post-feminist claims of returning women to a 'natural' femininity.

Struggles over the meanings of masculinity and femininity therefore seem to revolve around 'nature'. Movements of social change from the 1960s to the 1980s, such as feminism or the new man culture, have been denounced by counter-movements since the 1990s, notably new lad culture and post-feminism, as forcing 'unnatural' behaviours and attitudes onto men and women. This critique is discursively effective because the concept of nature is one of the most powerful ideologies. If something is presented as natural, it appears as an objective and unchangeable 'fact' and is therefore rendered beyond critique (Fairclough 1989). In the case of gender debates, claims about 'naturalness' are claims about gender difference; men and women are conceptualized as fundamentally and essentially different species, whose difference is grounded in biology rather than social conditions. We hope that this book has provided a comprehensive critique of this view. Looking at changes in femininity and masculinity since the 1960s, we have to conclude that it is too easy to recount social change as a movement towards greater gender equality and convergence of masculinity and femininity. There have certainly been elements of this, but they have been coupled with a renewed emphasis on gender difference in the last two decades.

The Importance of Culture

In contemporary modern societies, gender equality has been achieved in many respects. Equal opportunities and anti-discrimination legislation ensure, at least theoretically, that women have the same rights and opportunities as men, both at home and in the workplace. Moreover, there have been considerable cultural lifestyle changes which have led to more women than ever being in employment and men being more involved in the upbringing of children. In the context of these considerable social changes, popular culture emerges as one of the key sites for the (re)production of gender norms, identities and relations. We have traced throughout this book how notions of appropriate masculinity and femininity, based on the idea of essential gender difference, continue to be reinforced throughout popular culture. Culture is arguably a more subtle sphere for the construction of gender norms and relations than, say, the law or social policy because it is less tangible and not commonly thought of as a site of power. It is no longer acceptable for the law to enshrine different treatment of men and women, but popular cultural texts continuously get away with constructing women as inferior, reducing them to their physical appearance, trivializing their tastes, denying them rights that men take for granted and holding them responsible for men's behaviour. Of course we have seen that consumers can critically engage with such representations and do not necessarily buy into them. But in the new media age, popular culture is more pervasive than ever and discourses constructing gender difference are cumulative. The symbolic nature of popular culture leads many to think of it as not that important when it comes to gender, but this lack of concern and awareness is exactly what makes culture such a powerful site for the (re)production of gender norms, identities and relations, especially at a time when gender equality is, on the surface, a widely accepted ideal.

References

Abercrombie, N., Turner, B.S. and Hill, S. (1980) *The Dominant Ideology Thesis*. London: Allen & Unwin.

Abercrombie, N., Turner, B.S. and Hill, S. (1990) *Dominant Ideologies*. London: Routledge.

Abrams, M. (1959) *The Teenage Consumer*. London: London Press Exchange.

Acker, J. (1990) 'Hierarchies, jobs, bodies: a theory of gendered organizations', *Gender and Society*, 4 (2), 139–58.

Acker, J. (1992) 'Gendering organizational theory', in A.J. Mills and P. Tancred (eds) *Gendering Organizational Analysis*. Newbury Park, CA: Sage.

Adkins, L. (1999) 'Community and economy: a retraditionalization of gender?', *Theory, Culture and Society*, 16 (1), 119–39.

Adorno, T. and Horkheimer, M. (1993) 'The culture industry: enlightenment as mass deception', in S. During (ed.) *The Cultural Studies Reader*. London: Routledge.

Anderson, B. (1983) *Imagined Communities: Reflections on the Origin and Spread of Nationalism*. London: Verso.

Ang, I. and Hermes, J. (1996) 'Gender and/in media consumption', in J. Curran and M. Gurevitch (eds) *Mass Media and Society*, 2nd edn. London: Arnold.

Atkinson, C. (1999) 'Media: new lad takes on the new world', *Independent*, 23 February, available online at *http://www.independent.co.uk/arts-entertainment/media-new-lad-takes-on-the-new-world-1072676.html*, accessed 10 July 2011.

Attwood, F. (2005) '"Tits and ass and porn and fighting": male heterosexuality in magazines for men', *International Journal of Cultural Studies*, 8 (1), 83–100.

Ballaster, R., Beetham, M., Frazer, E. and Hebron, S. (1991) *Women's Worlds: Ideology, Femininity and the Woman's Magzine*. Basingstoke: Palgrave Macmillan.

Banks, M. (2007) *The Politics of Cultural Work*. Basingstoke: Palgrave Macmillan.

Banks, M. and Milestone, K. (2011) 'Individualization, gender and cultural work', *Gender, Work and Organization*, 18 (1), 73–89.

Barbrook, R. (1998) 'The hi-tech gift economy', *First Monday*, 3 (12), available online at *http://firstmonday.org/htbin/cgiwrap/bin/ojs/index.php/fm/article/view/631/552*, accessed 1 July 2011.

Bartky, S.L. (1990) *Femininity and Domination: Studies in the Phenomenology of Oppression*. London: Routledge.

Barton, B. (2002) 'Dancing on the Möbius strip: challenging the sex war paradigm', *Gender & Society*, 16 (5), 585–602.

Battersby, C. (1989) *Gender and Genius: Towards a Feminist Aesthetic*. London: Women's Press.

Baudrillard, J. (1988) *The Ecstasy of Communication*. New York: Semiotext(e).

Bauman, Z. (2000) *Liquid Modernity*. Cambridge: Polity.

Bayton, M. (1997) 'Women and the electric guitar', in S. Whiteley (ed.) *Sexing the Groove: Popular Music and Gender*. London: Routledge.

Bayton, M. (1998) *Frock Rock: Women Performing Popular Music*. Oxford: Oxford University Press.

BBC (2011) 'Ken Clarke clarifies "serious rape" remarks", 18 May, available online at *http://www.bbc.co.uk/news/uk-13436429*, accessed 1 July 2011.

Beck, U. (1992) *Risk Society: Towards a New Modernity*. London: Sage.

Bell, R. (2008) 'I was seen as an object, not a person', *Guardian*, 19 March, available online at *http://www.guardian.co.uk/world/2008/mar/19/gender.uk*, accessed 10 June 2011.

Benedict, H. (1992) *Virgin or Vamp? How the Press Covers Sex Crimes*. Oxford: Oxford University Press.

Benwell, B. (2003) 'Ambiguous masculinities: heroism and anti-heroism in the men's lifestyle magazines', in B. Benwell (ed.) *Masculinity and Men's Lifestyle Magazines*. Oxford: Blackwell.

Benwell, B. (2004) 'Ironic discourse: evasive masculinity in men's lifestyle magazines', *Men and Masculinities*, 7 (1), 3–21.

Berger, J. (1972) *Ways of Seeing* London: BBC Publications.

Berrington, E. and Jones, H. (2001) 'Reality vs myth: constructions of women's insecurity', *Feminist Media Studies*, 2 (3), 307–23.

Beynon, J. (2002) *Masculinities and Culture*. Buckingham: Open University Press.

Binnie J. (2004) 'Quartering sexualities: gay villages and sexual citizenship', in D. Bell and M. Jayne (eds) *City of Quarters*. Aldershot: Ashgate.

Binnie, J. and Skeggs, B. (2006) 'Cosmopolitan knowledge and the production and consumption of sexualised space: Manchester's gay village', in J. Binnie, J. Holloway, S. Millington and C. Young (eds) *Cosmopolitan Urbanism*. London: Routledge.

Biskind, P. (1998) *Easy Riders, Raging Bulls: How the Sex-Drugs-and-Rock 'n' Roll Generation Changed Hollywood*. London: Bloomsbury.

Bosman, J. (2005) 'Stuck at the edges of the ad game', *New York Times*, 22 November.

Bourdieu, P. (1984) *Distinction: A Social Critique of the Judgement of Taste*. London: Routledge.

Bovone, L. (2005) 'Fashionable quarters in the postindustrial city: the Tichinese of Milan', *City and Community*, 4 (4), 359–80.

Bradby, B. (1993) 'Sampling sexuality: gender, technology and the body in dance music', *Popular Music*, 12 (2), 155–76.

Bradby, B. and Laing, D. (2001) 'Introduction to gender and sexuality special issue', *Popular Music*, 20 (3), 295–300.

Brake, M. (1990) *Comparative Youth Culture: The Sociology of Youth Culture and Youth Subcultures in Britain and America*. London: Routledge.

Breen, M.J. (2007) 'Mass media and new media technologies', in E. Devereux (ed.) *Media Studies: Key Issues and Debates*. London: Sage.

Brickell, C. (2005) 'Masculinities, performativity, and subversion: a sociological appraisal', *Men and Masculinities*, 8 (1), 24–43.

Broyles, S. and Grow, J. (2008) 'Creative women in advertising agencies: why so few "babes in boyland"?', *Journal of Consumer Marketing*, 25 (1), 4–6.

Bruckman, A. (1993) 'Gender swapping on the internet', presented at The Internet Society, San Francisco, available online at *http://www.cc.gatech.edu/~asb/papers/gender-swapping.txt*, accessed 11 June 2011.

Brunsdon, C. (1981) '*Crossroads*: notes on soap opera', *Screen*, 22 (4), 32–47.

Brunsdon, C. and Morley, D. (1978) *Everyday Television: Nationwide*. London: British Film Institute.

Butler, J. (1990) *Gender Trouble*. London: Routledge.

Caldwell, J. (2008) *Production Culture: Industrial Reflexivity and Critical Practice in Film and Television*. Durham, NC: Duke University Press.

Carr, D. (2007) 'Contexts, pleasures and preferences: girls playing computer games', in S. Weber and S. Dixon (eds) *Growing up Online: Young People and Digital Technologies*. Basingstoke and New York: Palgrave Macmillan.

Casey, M. (2004) 'De-dyking queer space(s): heterosexual female visibility in gay and lesbian spaces', *Sexualities*, 7 (4), 446–61.

Cassell, J. and Jenkins, H. (1998) 'Chess for girls? Feminism and computer games', in J. Cassell and H. Jenkins (eds) *From Barbie to Mortal Kombat: Gender and Computer Games*. London: MIT Press.

Castells, M. (1996) *The Rise of Network Society*. Oxford: Blackwell.

Chambers, I. (1985) *Urban Rhythms: Pop Music and Popular Culture*. Basingstoke: Macmillan.

Chambers, I. (1987) 'Maps for the metropolis: a possible guide to the future', *Cultural Studies*, 1 (1), 1–21.

Chapman, R. (1988) 'The great pretender: variations on the new man theme', in R. Chapman and J. Rutherford (eds) *Male Order: Unwrapping Masculinity*. London: Lawrence & Wishart.

Charles, N. (2002) *Gender in Modern Britain*. Oxford: Oxford University Press.

218 References

Christopherson, S. (2008) 'Beyond the self-expressive creative worker: an industry perspective on entertainment media', *Theory, Culture & Society*, 25 (7/8), 73–95.

Citron, M. (1993) *Gender and the Musical Canon*. Cambridge: Cambridge University Press.

Cohan, S. (2007) 'Queer eye for the straight guise: camp, postfeminism, and the fab five's makeovers of masculinity', in Y. Tasker and D. Negra (eds) *Interrogating Postfeminism*. Durham, NC: Duke University Press.

Cohen, P. (1972) *Sub-Cultural Conflict and Working-Class Community*. Working Papers in Cultural Studies, no.2. Birmingham: University of Birmingham.

Cohen, R. (2008) *Global Diasporas: An Introduction*, 2nd edn. London: Routledge.

Cohen, S. (1997) 'Men making a scene: rock music and the production of gender', in S. Whiteley (ed.) *Sexing the Groove: Popular Music and Gender*. London: Routledge.

Cohen, S. (2001) 'Pop music, gender and sexuality', in S. Frith, W. Straw and J. Street (eds) *The Cambridge Companion to Rock and Pop*. Cambridge: Cambridge University Press.

Colebrook, C. (2004) *Gender*. Basingstoke: Palgrave.

Connell, R.W. (1987) *Gender and Power*. Cambridge: Polity.

Connell, R.W. (2004) 'The social organization of masculinity', in S.M. Whitehead and F.J. Barrett (eds) *The Masculinities Reader: Key Themes and New Directions*. Cambridge: Polity.

Connell, R.W. (2005) *Masculinities*, vol. 1. Cambridge: Polity.

Connell, R.W. and Messerschmidt, J. (2005) 'Hegemonic masculinity: rethinking the concept', *Gender & Society*, 19 (6), 829–59.

Cooke, L. (2001) 'The police series', in G. Creeber (ed.) *The Television Genre Book*. London: British Film Institute Publishing.

Coote, A. and Campbell, B. (1982) *Sweet Freedom: The Struggle for Women's Liberation*. Oxford: Blackwell.

Creativity (2006) 'The *Creativity* 50: the most influential creative people of the last two decades', *Creativity*, 14, 38–52.

Croteau, D. and Hoynes, W. (2003) *Media/Society: Industries, Images and Audiences*, 3rd edn. London: Pine Forge.

Cuneo, A.Z. and Petrecca, L. (1997) 'Women target boys club of ad creatives', *Advertising Age*, 68 (45), 24.

Daly, K. and Chasteen, A.L. (1997) 'Crime news, crime fear, and women's everyday life', in M.A. Fineman and M.T. McCluskey (eds) *Feminism, Media and the Law*. Oxford: Oxford University Press.

Davidoff, L. and Hall, C. (1987) *Family Fortunes: Men and Women of the English Middle Class 1780–1850*. London: Hutchinson.

Davies, B. (2002) 'Becoming male or female', in S. Jackson and S. Scott (eds) *Gender: A Sociological Reader*. London: Routledge.

Day, K., Gough, B. and McFadden, M. (2004) 'Warning! Alcohol can seriously damage your feminine health', *Feminist Media Studies*, 4 (2), 165–83.

de Beauvoir, S. (1972) *The Second Sex*. Harmondsworth: Penguin.

Dean, M. (1999) *Governmentality: Power and Rule in Modern Society*. London: Sage.

Deuze, M. (2007) *Media Work*. Cambridge: Polity.

Donath, J.S. (1999) 'Identity and deception in the virtual community', in M.A. Smith and P. Kollock (eds) *Communities in Cyberspace*. London: Routledge.

Doughty, S. (2006) 'Juries "reject rape claims if the woman was drunk"', *Daily Mail*, 7 December, p. 24.

Douglas, S. and Michaels, M.W. (2004) *The Mommy Myth: The Idealization of Motherhood and How It Has Undermined Women*. New York: Free Press.

Dudley Edwards, R. (2006) 'The rape of common sense?', *Daily Mail*, 8 March, p. 14.

Eagleton, T. (2000) *The Idea of Culture*. Oxford: Blackwell.

Easthope, A. (1992) *What's a Man Gotta Do: The Masculine Myth in Popular Culture*. London: Routledge.

Edwards, T. (1997) *Men in the Mirror: Men's Fashions, Masculinity and Consumer Society*. London: Cassell.

Edwards, T. (2003) 'Sex, booze and fags: masculinity, style and men's magazines', in B. Benwell (ed.) *Masculinity and Men's Lifestyle Magazines*. Oxford: Blackwell.

Estrich, S. (1987) *Real Rape*. Cambridge, MA: Harvard University Press.

Fairclough, N. (1989) *Language and Power*. London: Longman.

Faludi, S. (1991) *Backlash: The Undeclared War against Women*. London: Chatto & Windus.

Feasey, R. (2008) *Masculinity and Popular Television*. Edinburgh: Edinburgh University Press.

Featherstone, M. (2007) *Consumer Culture and Postmodernism*, 2nd edn. London: Sage.

Finch, E. and Munro, V.E. (2005) 'Juror stereotypes and blame attribution in rape cases involving intoxicants', *British Journal of Criminology*, 45 (1), 25–38.

Firminger, K.B. (2006) 'Is he boyfriend material? Representations of males in teenage girls' magazines', *Men and Masculinities*, 8 (3), 298–308.

Fiske, J. (1989a) *Understanding Popular Culture*. London: Unwin Hyman.

Fiske, J. (1989b) *Television Culture*. London: Routledge.

Florida, R. (2002) *The Rise of the Creative Class*. New York: Basic Books.

Florida, R. (2004) 'Revenge of the squelchers', available online at *http://creativeclass.com/rfcgdb/articles/Revenge%20of%20the%20Squelchers.pdf*, accessed 10 June 2011.

Friedan, B. (1963) *The Feminine Mystique*. London: Gollancz.

Frith, S. and Horne, H. (1987) *Art into Pop*. London: Methuen.

Frith, S. and McRobbie, A. (1990) 'Rock and sexuality', in S. Frith and A. Goodwin (eds) *On Record: Rock, Pop and the Written Word*. London: Routledge.

Furedi, F. (2001) *Paranoid Parenting: Abandon your Anxieties and Be a Good Parent*. London: Allen Lane.

Gaar, G. (1993) *She's a Rebel: The History of Women in Rock and Roll*. London: Blandford.

Gamman, L. and Marshment, M. (1988) *The Female Gaze: Women as Viewers of Popular Culture*. London: The Women's Press.

Garratt, S. (1990) 'Teenage dreams', in S. Frith and A. Goodwin (eds) *On Record, Rock, Pop and the Written Word*. London: Routledge.

Gates, P. (2006) *Detecting Men: Masculinity and the Hollywood Detective Film*. Albany: State University of New York Press.

Gauntlett, D. (1997) 'Ten things wrong with the "effects" model', in R. Dickinson, R. Harindranath and O. Linne (eds) *Approaches to Audiences: A Reader*. London: Arnold.

Geraghty, C. (1991) *Women and Soap Opera: A Study of Prime Time Soaps*. Cambridge: Polity.

Giddens, A. (1991) *Modernity and Self-Identity*. Cambridge: Polity.

Giedion, S. (2008) *Space, Time and Architecture: The Growth of a New Tradition*, 5th edn. Cambridge, MA: Harvard University Press.

Gill, R. (2002) 'Cool, creative and egalitarian? Exploring gender in project-based new media work', *Information and Communication Studies*, 5 (1), 70–89.

Gill, R. (2003) 'Power and the production of subjects: the genealogy of the new man and the new lad', in B. Benwell (ed.) *Masculinity and Men's Lifestyle Magazines*. Oxford: Blackwell.

Gill, R. (2007) *Gender and the Media*. Cambridge: Polity.

Gill, R. and Pratt, A. (2008) 'In the social factory? Immaterial labour, precariousness and cultural work', *Theory, Culture & Society*, 25 (7/8), 1–30.

Gill, R., Henwood, K. and McLean, C. (2000) 'The tyranny of the "six-pack"? Understanding men's responses to representations of the male body in popular culture', in C. Squire (ed.) *Culture in Psychology*. London: Routledge.

Gledhill, C. (1997) 'Genre and gender: the case of soap opera', in S. Hall (ed.) *Representation: Cultural Representations and Signifying Practices*. London: Sage.

Goffman, E. (1959) *The Presentation of Self in Everyday Life*. Harmondsworth: Penguin Books.

Gordon, C. (1991) 'Governmental rationality: an introduction', in G. Burchell, C. Gordon and P. Miller (eds) *The Foucault Effect: Studies in Governmentality*. Hemel Hempstead: Harvester Wheatsheaf.

Grant, G. (2006) 'Drink claims record number of women', *Daily Mail*, 29 July, 22.

Gray, A. (1992) *Video Playtime: The Gendering of a Leisure Technology*. London: Routledge.

Greed, C. (1994) *Women and Planning: Creating Gendered Realities*. London: Routledge.

Greenwood, D. and Isbell, L.M. (2002) 'Ambivalent sexism and the dumb blonde: men's and women's reactions to sexist jokes', *Psychology of Women Quarterly*, 26 (4), 341–50.

Gregory, M. (2009) 'Inside the locker room: male homosociability in the advertising industry', *Gender, Work and Organization*, 16 (3), 323–47.

Grosz, E. (1994) *Volatile Bodies: Towards a Corporeal Feminism*. Bloomington: Indiana University Press.

Habermas, J. (1989) *The Structural Transformation of the Public Sphere*. Cambridge: Polity.

Hall, S. (1980) 'Encoding/decoding', in S. Hall, D. Hobson, A. Lowe and P. Willis (eds) *Culture, Media, Language: Working Papers in Cultural Studies, 1972–1979*. London: Hutchinson.

Hall, S. (1982) 'The rediscovery of ideology: return of the repressed in media studies', in M. Gurevitch (ed.) *Culture, Society and the Media*. London: Methuen.

Hall, S. (1997a) 'Introduction', in S. Hall (ed.) *Representation: Cultural Representations and Signifying Practices*. London: Sage.

Hall, S. (1997b) 'The work of representation', in S. Hall (ed.) *Representation: Cultural Representations and Signifying Practices*. London: Sage.

Hall, S. (1997c) 'The spectacle of the Other', in S. Hall (ed.) *Representation: Cultural Representations and Signifying Practices*. London: Sage.

Hall, S. (2001) 'Foucault: power, knowledge and discourse', in M. Wetherell, S. Taylor and S. Yates (eds) *Discourse Theory and Practice: A Reader*. London: Sage.

Hall, S. and Jefferson, T. (1998) *Resistance through Rituals: Youth Subcultures in Post-War Britain*, 2nd edn. London: Routledge.

Halloran, J. (1970) *The Effects of Television*. London: Panther Books.

Haraway, D. (1991) *Simians, Cyborgs and Women: The Reinvention of Nature*. London: Routledge.

Harris, P. (2005) 'Just another girls' night out', *Daily Mail*, 18 October, 10.

Hartley, J. (2005) *The Creative Industries*. Oxford: Blackwell.

Harvey, D. (1989) *The Condition of Postmodernity*. Oxford: Blackwell.

Hatoum, I.J. and Belle, D. (2004) 'Mags and abs: media consumption and bodily concerns in men', *Sex Roles*, 51 (7/8), 397–407.

Haug, F. (1983) *Female Sexualization*. London: Verso.

Hebdige, D. (1979) *Subculture: The Meaning of Style*. London: Methuen.

Heidensohn, F. (1985) *Women and Crime*. Basingstoke: Macmillan.

Henwood, F., Miller, N., Senker, P. and Wyatt, S. (2000) *Technology and In/equality: Questioning the Information Society*. London: Routledge.

Hermes, J. (1995) *Reading Women's Magazines.* Cambridge: Polity.

Herring, S. (1996) 'Posting in a different voice: gender and ethics in computer-mediated communication', in C. Ess (ed.) *Philosophical Perspectives on Computer-Mediated Communication.* Albany: State University of New York Press.

Hesmondhalgh, D. (2007) *The Cultural Industries.* London: Sage.

Hey, V. (1986) *Patriarchy and Pub Culture.* London: Tavistock.

Hobson, D. (1991) 'Soap operas at work', in E. Seiter, H. Borchers, G. Kreutzner and E.M. Warth (eds) *Remote Control: Television, Audiences and Cultural Power.* London: Routledge.

Hoggart, R. (1958) *The Uses of Literacy: Aspects of Working-Class Life with Special Reference to Publications and Entertainments.* Harmondsworth: Penguin.

Holland, P. (2004) 'The politics of the smile: "soft news" and the sexualisation of the popular press', in C. Carter and L. Steiner (eds) *Critical Readings: Media and Gender.* Maidenhead: Open University Press.

Hollows, J. (2003) 'Oliver's twist: leisure, labour and domestic masculinity in *The Naked Chef*, *International Journal of Cultural Studies*, 6 (2), 229–48.

Hollway, W. (1996) 'Gender difference and the production of subjectivity', in S. Jackson and S. Scott (eds) *Feminism and Sexuality: A Reader.* Edinburgh: Edinburgh University Press.

Hunt, D. (2007) *Whose Stories Are We Telling? The 2007 Hollywood Writers Report.* Los Angeles: Writers Guild of America West.

Jackson, P., Stevenson, N. and Brooks, K. (2001) *Making Sense of Men's Magazines.* Cambridge: Polity.

Jacobs, James (2001) 'Hospital drama', in Creeber, G. (ed.) *The Television Genre Book.* London: British Film Institute Publishing.

Jacobs, Jane (1961) *The Death and Life of Great American Cities.* New York: Vintage Books.

Jenkins, H. (2006) 'Introduction: confessions of an aca/fan', in H. Jenkins (ed.) *Fans, Bloggers, and Gamers: Exploring Participatory Culture.* New York: New York University Press.

Jessop, B. (1990) 'Regulation theories in retrospect', *Economy and Society*, 19 (2), 153–216.

Kafai, Y.B., Heeter, C., Denner, J. and Sun, J.Y. (2008) 'Preface: pink, purple, casual or mainstream games: moving beyond the gender divide', in Y.B. Kafai, C. Heeter, J. Denner and J.Y. Sun (eds) *Beyond Barbie and Mortal Kombat: New Perspectives on Gender and Gaming.* London: MIT Press.

Kearney, M.C. (2006) *Girls Make Media.* New York: Routledge.

Kehily, M.J. (1999) 'More sugar? Teenage magazines, gender displays and sexual learning', *European Journal of Cultural Studies*, 2 (1), 65–89.

Kennedy, H. (2009) 'Going the extra mile: emotional and commercial imperatives in new media work', *Convergence*, 15 (2), 177–96.

Kibby, M. and Costello, B. (1999) 'Displaying the phallus: masculinity and the performance of sexuality on the internet', *Men and Masculinities*, 1 (4), 352–64.

Kilbourne, J. (2003) '"The more you subtract, the more you add": cutting girls down to size', in G. Dines and J.M. Humez (eds) *Gender, Race and Class: A Text-Reader*. London: Sage.

Kimmel, M.S. (2006) *Manhood in America: A Cultural History*, 2nd edn. Oxford: Oxford University Press.

Kitzinger, J. (1998) 'Resisting the message: the extent and limits of media influence', in D. Miller, J. Kitzinger, K. Williams and P. Beharrell (eds) *The Circuit of Mass Communication: Media Strategies, Representation and Audience Reception in the AIDS Crisis*. London: Sage.

Kitzinger, J. (1999) 'A sociology of media power: key issues in audience reception research', in G. Philo (ed.) *Message Received: Glasgow Media Group Research 1993–1998*. Harlow: Longman.

Klein, D. (2000) *Women in Advertising – 10 Years On*. Commissioned by the Institute of Practitioners in Advertising, UK.

Kramer, K.M. (1994) 'Rule by myth: the social and legal dynamics governing alcohol-related acquaintance rapes', *Stanford Law Review*, 47 (1), 115–60.

Laing, D. (1985) *One Chord Wonders*. Milton Keynes: Open University Press.

Lash, S. and Lury, C. (2007) *Global Culture Industry*. Cambridge: Polity.

Lawler, S. (2000) *Mothering the Self: Mothers, Daughters, Subjects*. London: Routledge.

Leblanc, L. (1999) *Pretty in Punk: Girl's Gender Resistance in a Boy's Subculture*. New Brunswick, NJ: Rutgers University Press.

Lees, S. (1995) 'Media reporting of rape: the 1993 British "date rape" controversy', in D. Kidd-Hewitt and R. Osborne (eds) *Crime and the Media*. London: Pluto.

Lees, S. (1996) *Carnal Knowledge: Rape on Trial*. London: The Women's Press.

Lefebvre, H. (1991) *The Production of Space*. Oxford: Blackwell.

Leonard, M. (1997) '"Rebel girl, you are queen of my world": feminism, "subculture", and grrrl power', in S. Whiteley (ed.) *Sexing the Groove: Popular Music and Gender*. London: Routledge.

Leonard, M. (2007) *Gender in the Music Industry: Rock, Discourse and Girl Power*. Aldershot: Ashgate.

Leonard, S. (2007) '"I hate my job, I hate everyone here": adultery, boredom and the "working girl" in twenty-first century American cinema', in Y. Tasker and D. Negra (eds) *Interrogating Postfeminism*. Durham, NC, and London: Duke University Press.

Lind, A. and Brzuzy, S. (2008) *Battleground, Women, Gender*. Westport, CT: Greenwood Press.

Lindner, K. (2004) 'Images of women in general interest and fashion maga-
    zine advertisements from 1955 to 2002', *Sex Roles*, 51 (7/8), 409–21.
Livingstone, S. (1996) 'On the continuing problem of media effects', in
    J. Curran and M. Gurevitch (eds) *Mass Media and Society*, 2nd edn.
    London: Arnold.
Lloyd, F. (1993) *Deconstructing Madonna*. London: Batsford Books.
Lloyd, R. (2006) *Neo-Bohemia: Art and Commerce in the Post-Industrial City*.
    New York: Routledge.
Lovett, J. and Kelly, L. (2009) *Different Systems, Similar Outcomes? Tracking
    Attrition in Reported Rape Cases across Europe*. London: Child and Woman
    Abuse Studies Unit, London Metropolitan University. Funded by the
    European Commission.
Lupton, D. (1999) 'Risk and the ontology of pregnant embodiment', in
    D. Lupton (ed.) *Risk and Sociocultural Theory: New Directions and
    Perspectives*. Cambridge: Cambridge University Press.
Lury, C. (1993) *Cultural Rights: Technology, Legality and Personality*. London:
    Routledge.
Lyons, A.C., Dalton, S.I. and Hoy, A. (2006) '"Hardcore drinking": por-
    trayals of alcohol consumption in young women's and men's magazines',
    Journal of Health Psychology, 11 (2), 223–32.
Lyotard, J.-F. (1986) *The Post-Modern Condition: A Report on Knowledge*.
    Manchester: Manchester University Press
Macdonald, M. (2003) *Exploring Media Discourse*. London: Hodder Arnold.
McDowell, L. (1999) *Gender, Identity and Place: Understanding Feminist
    Geographies*. Minneapolis: University of Minnesota Press.
MacKinnon, K. (2003) *Representing Men: Maleness and Masculinity in the
    Media*. London: Arnold.
McLaughlin, L. and Carter, C. (2004) 'Complicating gendered spaces',
    Feminist Media Studies, 4 (3), 235–8.
McRobbie, A. (1977) '*Jackie*: an ideology of adolescent femininity', BCCCS
    Stencilled Paper, University of Birmingham.
McRobbie, A. (1980) 'Settling accounts with subcultures: a feminist cri-
    tique', *Screen Education*, 34, 37–49.
McRobbie, A. (1988) 'Second-hand dresses and the role of the ragmarket',
    in A. McRobbie (ed.) *Zoot Suits and Suits and Second Hand Dresses*.
    Boston: Unwin Hyman.
McRobbie, A. (1990) *Feminism and Youth Culture*. Basingstoke: Macmillan.
McRobbie, A. (1994) *Postmodernism and Popular Culture*. London: Routledge.
McRobbie, A. (1997) '*More!* New sexualities in girls' and women's maga-
    zines', in A. McRobbie (ed.) *Back to Reality? Social Experience and Cultural
    Studies*. Manchester: Manchester University Press.
McRobbie, A. (1998) *British Fashion Design: Rag Trade or Image Industry?*
    London: Routledge.
McRobbie, A. (2000) *Feminism and Youth Culture*, 2nd edn. New York:
    Routledge.

References

References 225

McRobbie, A. (2002) 'Clubs to companies: notes on the decline of political culture in speeded up creative worlds', *Cultural Studies*, 16 (4), 516–31.

McRobbie, A. (2008) *The Aftermath of Feminism*. London: Sage.

McRobbie, A. and Garber, J. (1976) 'Girls and subcultures', in S. Hall and T. Jefferson (eds) *Resistance through Rituals: Youth Subcultures in Post-War Britain*. London: Hutchinson.

Madge, C. and Weinberger, B. (1973) *Art Students Observed*. London: Faber and Faber.

Mansvelt, J. (2005) *Geographies of Consumption*. London: Sage.

Marshall, B. and Witz, A. (2004). *Engendering Social Theory*. Maidenhead: Open University Press.

Massey, D. (1994) *Space, Place and Gender*. Cambridge: Polity.

Mayhew, E. (2005) 'Musical production and the politics of desire: positioning the producer: gender divisions in creative labour and value', in S. Whitely, A. Bennett and S. Hawkins (eds) *Music, Space and Place*. Aldershot: Ashgate.

Measham, F. and Brain, K. (2005) '"Binge" drinking, British alcohol policy and the new culture of intoxication', *Crime Media Culture*, 1 (3), 262–83.

Metz, W. (2007) *Bewitched: TV Milestones*. Detroit: Wayne State University Press.

Meyer, A. (2007) *The Child at Risk: Paedophiles, Media Responses and Public Opinion*. Manchester: Manchester University Press.

Meyer, A. (2010) '"Too drunk to say no": binge drinking, rape and the *Daily Mail*', *Feminist Media Studies*, 10 (1), 19–34.

Meyers, C.B. (2009) 'From sponsorship to spots: advertising and the development of electronic media', in J. Holt and A. Perren (eds) *Media Industries: History, Theory and Method*. Oxford: Wiley-Blackwell.

Milestone, K. (2002) 'Creating and defending pop cultural spaces in the contemporary city', in T. Johanson and O. Sernhede (eds) *Lifestyle, Desire and Politics*. Gothenburg: Daidalos.

Mills, S. (2003) *Michel Foucault*. London: Routledge.

Modleski, T. (1982) *Loving with a Vengeance: Mass-Produced Fantasies for Women*. Hamden, CT: Archon Books.

Monem, N. (2007) *Riot Grrrl: Revolution Girl Style Now!* London: Black Dog.

Mooney, A. (2008) 'Boys will be boys: men's magazines and the normalization of pornography', *Feminist Media Studies*, 8 (3), 247–65.

Moore, S. (1988) 'Here's looking at you kid!', in L. Gamman and M. Marshment (eds) *The Female Gaze: Women as Viewers of Popular Culture*. London: The Women's Press.

Morley, D. (1986) *Family Television: Cultural Power and Domestic Leisure*. London: Comedia.

Morley, D. (1991) 'Changing paradigms in audience studies', in E. Seiter, H. Borchers, G. Kreutzner and E.M. Warth (eds) *Remote Control: Television, Audiences and Cultural Power*. London: Routledge.

Morley, D. (1992) *Television Audiences and Cultural Studies*. London: Routledge.

Mort, F. (1996) *Cultures of Consumption: Masculinities and Social Space in Late Twentieth-Century Britain*. London: Routledge.

Mulvey, L (1975) 'Visual pleasure and narrative cinema', *Screen*, 16 (3), 6–18.

Mulvey, L. (2009) *Visual and Other Pleasures*, 2nd edn. Basingstoke: Palgrave Macmillan.

Nayak, A. and Kehily, M.J. (2008) *Gender, Youth and Culture: Young Masculinities and Femininities*. Basingstoke: Palgrave Macmillan.

Negra, D. (2009) *What a Girl Wants? Fantasizing the Reclamation of Self in Postfeminism*. London: Routledge.

Nguyen, T.M. and van Nes, A. (2009) 'Gender differences in the urban environment: the flâneur and flâneuse of the 21st century', in D. Koch, L. Marcus and J. Steen (eds) Proceedings of the 7th International Space Syntax Symposium, available online at *http://www.sss7.org/Proceed ings/08%20Spatial%20Configuration%20and%20Social%20Structures/S122 _vanNes_Nguyen.pdf*, accessed 13 June 2011.

Nixon, S. (1996) *Hard Looks: Masculinities, Spectatorship and Contemporary Consumption*. London: UCL Press.

Nixon, S. (1997) 'Exhibiting masculinity', in S. Hall (ed.) *Representation: Cultural Representations and Signifying Practices*. London: Sage.

Nixon, S. (2003) *Advertising Cultures*. London: Sage.

O'Brien, J. (1999) 'Writing in the body: gender (re)production in online interaction', in M.A. Smith and P. Kollock (eds) *Communities in Cyberspace*. London: Routledge.

O'Connor, J. (2000) 'The definition of the cultural industries', *The European Journal of Arts Education*, 2 (3), 15–27.

O'Connor, J. (2007) *The Cultural and Creative Industries: A Review of the Literature*. Report for Creative Partnerships, Arts Council of England.

Osgerby, B. (2003) 'A pedigree of the consuming male: masculinity, consumption and the American "leisure class"', in B. Benwell (ed.) *Masculinity and Men's Lifestyle Magazines*. Oxford: Blackwell.

Owen, J. and Milestone, K. (2005) 'Gender and new media companies', paper presented at the CRESC conference Culture and Social Change: Disciplinary Exchanges.

Parker, R. and Pollock, G. (1981) *Old Mistresses: Women, Art and Ideology*. London: Routledge & Kegan Paul.

Pelletier, C. (2008) 'Gaming in context: how young people construct their gendered identities in playing and making games', in Y.B. Kafai, C. Heeter, J. Denner and J.Y. Sun (eds) *Beyond Barbie and Mortal Kombat: New Perspectives on Gender and Gaming*. London: MIT Press.

Perkins, T. (1997) 'Rethinking stereotypes', in T. O'Sullivan and Y. Jewkes (eds) *The Media Studies Reader*. London: Arnold.

Perrons, D. (2003) 'The new economy and the work–life balance: a case study of new media in Brighton and Hove', *Gender, Work and Organization*, 10 (1), 65–93.

Pickering, M. (2001) *Stereotyping: The Politics of Representation*. Basingstoke: Palgrave Macmillan.

Pini, M. (2001) *Club Culture and Female Subjectivity: The Move from Home to House*. Basingstoke: Palgrave Macmillan.

Platell, A. (2006) 'Why I as a woman say these new rape laws insult my sex and are unfair to men', *Daily Mail*, 17 October, 13.

Powdermaker, H. (1951) *Hollywood: The Dream Factory*. London Secker and Warburg.

Radway, J. (1984) *Reading the Romance: Women, Patriarchy and Popular Literature*. New York: Verso.

Reddington, H. (2007) *The Lost Women of Rock Music: Female Musicians of the Punk Era*. Aldershot: Ashgate.

Rees, T. (1998) *Mainstreaming Equality in the European Union*. London: Routledge.

Rees, T. (2006) 'Promoting equality in the private and public sectors', in D. Perrons (ed.) *Gender Division and Working Time in the New Economy: Public Policy and Changing Patterns of Work in Europe and North America*. Cheltenham: Edward Elgar.

Richards, N. and Milestone, K. (2000) 'What difference does it make? Women's pop cultural production in Manchester', *Sociological Research Online*, 5 (1), available online at *http://www.socresonline.org.uk/5/1/richards.html*, accessed 4 July 2011.

Ritzer, G. (1998) *The McDonaldization Thesis: Extensions and Explorations*. London: Sage.

Roberts, M. (2007) 'The fashion police: governing the self in *What Not to Wear*', in Y. Tasker and D. Negra (eds) *Interrogating Postfeminism*. Durham, NC, and London: Duke University Press.

Rodino, M. (1997) 'Breaking out of binaries: reconceptualizing gender and its relationship to language in computer-mediated communication', *Journal of Computer-Mediated Communication*, 3 (3), available online at *http://www3.interscience.wiley.com/cgi-bin/fulltext/120837733/HTML START*, accessed 13 June 2011.

Rose, N. (1989) *Governing the Soul: The Shaping of the Private Self*. London: Routledge.

Savage, J. (1991) *England's Dreaming: Anarchy, Sex Pistols, Punk Rock and Beyond*. London: Faber.

Schatz, T. (2009) 'Film industry studies and Hollywood history', in J. Holt and A. Perren (eds) *Media Industries: History, Theory and Method*. Oxford: Wiley-Blackwell.

Seiter, E. (1999) *Television and New Media Audiences*. Oxford: Clarendon Press.

Seiter, E., Borchers, H., Kreutzner, G. and Warth, E.M. (1991) '"Don't treat us like we're so stupid and naïve": towards an ethnography of soap opera viewers', in E. Seiter, H. Borchers, G. Kreutzner and E.M. Warth (eds) *Remote Control: Television, Audiences and Cultural Power*. London: Routledge.

Sex in the Noughties: Nuts vs Zoo (2007), Channel 4, broadcast 4 December.

Shields, R. (1990) *Places on the Margins*. London: Routledge.

Shonfield, K. (2000) *Walls Have Feelings: Architecture, Film and the City*. London: Routledge.

Simonds, W. (1992) *Women and Self-Help Culture: Reading between the Lines*. New Brunswick, NJ: Rutgers University Press.

Skeggs, B. (1997) *Formations of Class and Gender: Becoming Respectable*. London: Sage.

Skeggs, B. (1999) 'Matter out of place: visibility and sexualities in leisure spaces', *Leisure Studies*, 18 (3), 213–32.

Skeggs, B. (2001) 'The toilet paper: femininity, class and mis-recognition', *Women's Studies International Forum*, 24 (3/4), 295–307.

Skeggs, B. (2004) *Class, Self, Culture*. London: Routledge.

Skeggs, B. (2009) 'The moral economy of person production: the class relations of self-performance on "reality" television', *The Sociological Review*, 57 (4), 626–44.

Skeggs, B. and Wood, H. (2008) 'The labour of transformation and circuits of value "around" reality television', *Continuum: Journal of Media and Cultural Studies*, 22 (4), 559–72.

Smith, C. (1998) *Creative Britain*. London: Faber and Faber.

Spender, D. (1995) *Nattering on the Net: Women, Power and Cyberspace*. Melbourne: Spinifex.

Spicer, A. (2003) *Typical Men: The Representation of Masculinity in Popular British Cinema*. London: I.B. Tauris.

Spicer, A. (2004) 'The reluctance to commit: Hugh Grant and the new British romantic comedy', in P. Powrie, A. Davies and B. Babington (eds) *The Trouble with Men: Masculinities in European and Hollywood Cinema*. London: Wallflower Press.

Storey, J. (1993) *An Introduction to Cultural Theory and Popular Culture*. Hemel Hempstead: Harvester Wheatsheaf.

Straw, W. (1991) 'Systems of articulation, logics of change: communities and scenes in popular music', *Cultural Studies*, 5 (3), 368–88.

Straw, W. (1997) 'Sizing up record collections: gender and connoisseurship in rock music culture', in S. Whiteley (ed.) *Sexing the Groove: Popular Music and Gender*. London: Routledge.

Strinati, D. (2004) *An Introduction to Theories of Popular Culture*. London: Routledge.

Talbot, M. (2007) *Media Discourse: Representation and Interaction*. Edinburgh: Edinburgh University Press.

Tams, E. (2002) 'Creating divisions: creativity, entrepreneurship and gendered inequality', *City*, 6 (3), 393–402.

Taylor, L. (2005) 'All for him: articles about sex in American lad magazines', *Sex Roles*, 52 (3/4), 153–63.

Taylor, N. and Courtenay-Smith, N. (2006) 'Death of femininity', *Daily Mail*, 27 December, 36.

Tebbel, C. (2000) *Body Snatchers: How the Media Shapes Women*. Sidney: Finch.

Thornham, S. (2007) *Women, Feminism and Media*. Edinburgh: Edinburgh University Press.

Thornton, S. (1995) *Club Cultures: Music, Media and Subcultural Capital*. Cambridge: Polity.

Tincknell, E., Chambers, D., Van Loon, J. and Hudson, N. (2003) 'Begging for it: "new femininities", social agency, and moral discourse in contemporary teenage and men's magazines', *Feminist Media Studies*, 3 (1), 47–63.

Turkle, S. (1995) *Life on the Screen: Identity in the Age of the Internet*. New York: Simon & Schuster.

Urry, J. (1995) *Consuming Places*. London: Routledge.

Valentine, G. (1995) 'Out and about: geographies of lesbian landscapes', *International Journal of Urban and Regional Research*, 19 (1), 96–111.

Valentine, G. and McKendrick, J. (1997) 'Children's outdoor play: exploring parental concerns about children's safety and the changing nature of childhood', *Geoforum*, 28 (2), 219–35.

Van Doorn, N., Wyatt, S. and Van Zoonen, L. (2008) 'Revisiting textual performances of gender and sexuality on the internet', *Feminist Media Studies*, 8 (4), 357–74.

Veblen, T. (1912) *The Theory of the Leisure Class*. New York: Macmillan.

Wajcman, J. (1991) *Feminism Confronts Technology*. Cambridge: Polity.

Walby, S. (1990) *Theorizing Patriarchy*. Oxford: Blackwell.

Walby, S. and Allen, J. (2004) *Domestic Violence, Sexual Assault and Stalking: Findings from the British Crime Survey*. London: Home Office. Available online at *http://www.broken-rainbow.org.uk/research/Dv%20crime%20survey.pdf*, accessed 13 June 2011.

Walkerdine, V. (2006) 'Playing the game: young girls performing femininity in video game play', *Feminist Media Studies*, 6 (4), 519–37.

Walkowitz, J.R. (1980) *Prostitution and Victorian Society: Women, Class and the State*. Cambridge: Cambridge University Press.

Walser, R. (1993) *Running with the Devil: Power, Gender and Madness in Heavy Metal Music*. Middleton, CT: Wesleyan University Press.

Warwick, J. (2004) 'He's got the power: the politics of production in girl group music', in S. Whitely, A. Bennett and S. Hawkins (eds) *Music, Space and Place*. Aldershot: Ashgate.

Wearing, S. (2007) 'Subjects of rejuvenation: aging in postfeminist culture', in Y. Tasker and D. Negra (eds) *Interrogating Postfeminism*. Durham, NC, and London: Duke University Press.

Webb, J. (2009) *Understanding Representation*. London: Sage.

West, C. and Zimmerman, D.H. (1987) 'Doing gender', *Gender & Society*, 1 (2), 125–51.

Whelehan, I. (1996) *Modern Feminist Thought: From the Second Wave to 'Post-Feminism'*. Edinburgh: Edinburgh University Press.

Whelehan, I. (2000) *Overloaded: Popular Culture and the Future of Feminism*. London: The Women's Press.

Williams, R. (1958) *Culture and Society, 1780–1950*. London: Chatto and Windus.

Williams, R. (1983) *Keywords*. London: Fontana.

Williamson, J. (1978) *Decoding Advertisements: Ideology and Meaning in Advertising*. London: Marion Boyars.

Willis, P. (1977) *Learning to Labour: How Working Class Kids Get Working Class Jobs*. Farnborough: Saxon House.

Willis, P. (1978) *Profane Culture*. London: Routledge & Kegan Paul.

Willis, P., with Jones, S., Canaan, J. and Hurd, G. (1990) *Common Culture: Symbolic Work at Play in the Everyday Cultures of the Young*. Milton Keynes: Open University Press.

Wilson, E. (1985) *Adorned in Dreams: Fashion and Modernity*. London: Virago.

Wilson, E. (1992) *The Sphinx in the City: Urban Life, the Control of Disorder and Women*. London: Virago.

Wilson, E. (1996) 'The invisible *flâneur*', in S. Watson and K. Gibson (eds) *Postmodern Cities and Spaces*. Oxford: Blackwell.

Wolff, J. (1990) *Feminine Sentences: Essays on Women and Culture*. Cambridge: Polity.

Women's Unit (2000) *More Choice for Women in the New Economy: The Facts*. London: Cabinet Office.

Wood, H. (2005) 'Texting the subject: women, television, and modern self-reflexivity', *The Communication Review*, 8 (2), 115–35.

Wood, H. (2006) 'The mediated conversational floor: an interactive approach to audience reception analysis', *Media, Culture & Society*, 29 (1), 75–103.

Wosk, J. (2001) *Women and the Machine: Representations from the Spinning Wheel to the Electronic Age*. London: Johns Hopkins University Press.

Wright, K. (2001) 'The gaming industry and the female market', was at *http://www.womengamers.com/articles/market/html*, accessed 22 January 2006, no longer available online.

Wynne, D. and O'Connor, J. (1996) *From the Margins to the Centre: Cultural Production and Consumption in the Post-Industrial City*. Aldershot: Ashgate.

Yee, N. (2008) 'Maps of digital desires: exploring the topography of gender and play in online games', in Y.B. Kafai, C. Heeter, J. Denner and J.Y. Sun (eds) *Beyond Barbie and Mortal Kombat: New Perspectives on Gender and Gaming*. London: MIT Press.

Young, R. (1995) *Colonial Desire: Hybridity in Theory, Culture and Race*. London: Routledge.

Zelizer, V.A. (1994) *Pricing the Priceless Child: The Changing Social Value of Children*. Princeton:, Princeton University Press.
Zukin, S. (1982) *Loft Living: Culture and Capital in Urban Change*. Baltimore: Johns Hopkins University Press.

Index

work (and women) (*cont.*)
  in films/dramas 101–3
  minimizing of professional roles by
    popular culture 101–3
  in television 103–4
  in women's magazines
    100–1
World of Warcraft 176
Wosk, Julie 191
Wynne, Derek 65

Yee, Nick 176
youth, obsession with 97–8

youth subcultures 192–201, 201–2,
    209
  and BCCCS 192–3
  feminine activities engaged in by
    men 192–3
  marginalization of women 193
  mods and rockers 196–8, 199
  and punk 199–200
  and space 185
  teddy boys/teddy girls 193–5, *195*

Zimmerman, Don 13
Zoo 125–6, 127, 129, 133